SAXON
ALGEBRA 1

Student Edition

SAXON™

An Imprint of HMH
Supplemental Publishers Inc.

www.SaxonPublishers.com
1-800-531-5015

ISBN 13:   978-1-6027-7301-1
ISBN 10:   1-6027-7301-7

2 3 4 5 6 7 8 073 15 14 13 12 11 10 09 08

Table of Contents

DISTRIBUTED STRANDS

- Algebra Foundations
- Functions and Relations
- Equations
- Linear Equations and Functions
- Polynomials
- Rational Expressions and Functions
- Inequalities
- Systems of Equations and Inequalities
- Radical Expressions and Functions
- Quadratic Equations and Functions
- Absolute-Value Equations and Inequalities
- Probability and Data Analysis

Section 2: Lessons 11-20, Investigation 2

Section 3: Lessons 21-30, Investigation 3

DISTRIBUTED STRANDS

Algebra Foundations		Inequalities
Functions and Relations		Systems of Equations and Inequalities
Equations		Radical Expressions and Functions
Linear Equations and Functions		Quadratic Equations and Functions
Polynomials		Absolute-Value Equations and Inequalities
Rational Expressions		Probability and Data Analysis

Section 4: Lessons 31-40, Investigation 4

Section 5: Lessons 41-50, Investigation 5

DISTRIBUTED STRANDS

- Algebra Foundations
- Functions and Relations
- Equations
- Linear Equations and Functions
- Polynomials
- Rational Expressions

- Inequalities
- Systems of Equations and Inequalities
- Radical Expressions and Functions
- Quadratic Equations and Functions
- Absolute-Value Equations and Inequalities
- Probability and Data Analysis

Section 6: Lessons 51-60, Investigation 6

Section 7: Lessons 61-70, Investigation 7

DISTRIBUTED STRANDS

- Algebra Foundations
- Functions and Relations
- Equations
- Linear Equations and Functions
- Polynomials
- Rational Expressions
- Inequalities
- Systems of Equations and Inequalities
- Radical Expressions and Functions
- Quadratic Equations and Functions
- Absolute-Value Equations and Inequalities
- Probability and Data Analysis

Section 8: Lessons 71-80, Investigation 8

Section 9: Lessons 81-90, Investigation 9

DISTRIBUTED STRANDS

- Algebra Foundations
- Functions and Relations
- Equations
- Linear Equations and Functions
- Polynomials
- Rational Expressions

- Inequalities
- Systems of Equations and Inequalities
- Radical Expressions and Functions
- Quadratic Equations and Functions
- Absolute-Value Equations and Inequalities
- Probability and Data Analysis

Section 10: Lessons 91-100, Investigation 10

Section 11: Lessons 101-110, Investigation 11

DISTRIBUTED STRANDS

Algebra Foundations

Functions and Relations

Equations

Linear Equations and Functions

Polynomials

Rational Expressions

Inequalities

Systems of Equations and Inequalities

Radical Expressions and Functions

Quadratic Equations and Functions

Absolute-Value Equations and Inequalities

Probability and Data Analysis

Section 12: Lessons 111-120, Investigation 12

Classifying Real Numbers

Warm Up

1. Vocabulary A _____ (*Venn diagram, line plot*) shows the relationship
$(SB\ 30)$ between sets.

Start off each lesson by practicing prerequisite skills and math vocabulary that will make you more successful with today's new concept.

Write each fraction as a decimal.

2. $\dfrac{2}{9}$
$(SB\ 5)$

3. $4\dfrac{3}{8}$
$(SB\ 5)$

Write each decimal as a fraction in simplest form.

4. 0.6
$(SB\ 6)$

5. 5.75
$(SB\ 6)$

New Concepts

A **set** is a collection of objects. Each object in the set is called an element. A set is written by enclosing the elements within braces. There are three types of sets. A set with no elements is called the null or **empty set.** A set with a finite number of elements is a **finite set.** An **infinite set** has an infinite number of elements.

$\{12, 24, 36\}$	$\{1, 3, 5,...\}$	$\{\ \}$ or $\varnothing$
finite set	infinite set	null or empty set

The subsets of real numbers are infinite sets.

Reading Math

The three dots inside the braces are called an ellipsis. An ellipsis shows that the numbers in the set continue on without end.

Subsets of Real Numbers	
Natural Numbers	The numbers used to count objects or things. $\{1, 2, 3, 4,...\}$
Whole Numbers	The set of natural numbers and zero. $\{0, 1, 2, 3, 4,...\}$
Integers	The set of whole numbers and the opposites of the natural numbers. $\{..., -4, -3, -2, -1, 0, 1, 2, 3, 4,...\}$
Rational Numbers	Numbers that can be written in the form $\frac{a}{b}$, where a and b are integers and $b \neq 0$. In decimal form, rational numbers either terminate or repeat. Examples: $\frac{1}{2}, 0.\overline{3}, -\frac{2}{3}, 0.125$
Irrational Numbers	Numbers that cannot be written as the quotient of two integers. In decimal form, irrational numbers neither terminate nor repeat. Examples: $\sqrt[3]{5}, \sqrt{2}, -\sqrt{2}, 3\sqrt{3}, \pi, 3\pi$
Real Numbers	The set including all rational and irrational numbers.

Online Connection
www.SaxonMathResources.com

The Venn diagram below shows how the sets of numbers are related.

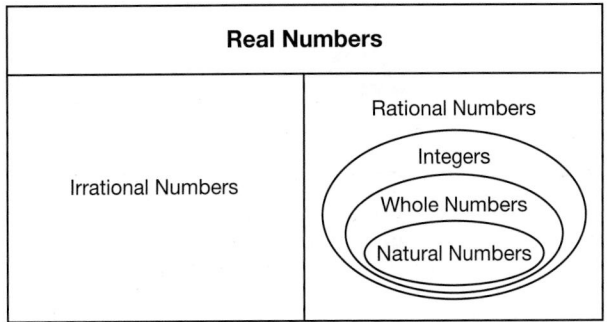

Example 1   Identifying Sets

For each number, identify the subsets of real numbers to which it belongs.

a. $\dfrac{1}{2}$

SOLUTION

{rational numbers, real numbers}

b. 5

SOLUTION

{natural numbers, whole numbers, integers, rational numbers, real numbers}

c. $3\sqrt{2}$

SOLUTION

{irrational numbers, real numbers}

Example 2   Identifying Sets for Real-World Situations

Identify the set of numbers that best describes each situation. Explain your choice.

a. the value of the bills in a person's wallet

SOLUTION The set of whole numbers best describes the situation. The wallet may contain no bills or any number of bills.

b. the balance of a checking account

SOLUTION The set of rational numbers best describes the situation. The balance could be positive or negative and may contain decimal amounts.

c. the circumference of a circular table when the diameter is a rational number

SOLUTION The set of irrational numbers describes the situation. Since circumference is equal to the diameter multiplied by pi, it will be an irrational number.

The **intersection of sets** A and B, $A \cap B$, is the set of elements that are in A and B. The **union** of A and B, $A \cup B$, is the set of all elements that are in A or B.

Example 3 Finding Intersections and Unions of Sets

Find $A \cap B$ and $A \cup B$.

a. $A = \{2, 4, 6, 8, 10, 12\}$; $B = \{3, 6, 9, 12\}$

SOLUTION

$A \cap B = \{6, 12\}$; $A \cup B = \{2, 3, 4, 6, 8, 9, 10, 12\}$

b. $A = \{11, 13, 15, 17\}$; $B = \{12, 14, 16, 18\}$

SOLUTION

$A \cap B = \{ \}$ or $\varnothing$; $A \cup B = \{11, 12, 13, 14, 15, 16, 17, 18\}$

In some lessons, **Explorations** allow you to go into more depth with the mathematics by investigating math concepts with manipulatives, through patterns, and in a variety of other ways.

A set of numbers has **closure,** or is closed, under a given operation if the outcome of the operation on any two members of the set is also a member of the set. For example, the sum of any two natural numbers is also a natural number. Therefore, the set of natural numbers is closed under addition.

One example is all that is needed to prove that a statement is false. An example that proves a statement false is called a **counterexample.**

Example 4 Identifying a Closed Set Under a Given Operation

Determine whether each statement is true or false. Give a counterexample for false statements.

a. The set of whole numbers is closed under addition.

SOLUTION

Verify the statement by adding two whole numbers.

$$2 + 3 = 5$$
$$9 + 11 = 20$$
$$100 + 1000 = 1100$$

The sum is always a whole number.

The statement is true.

b. The set of whole number is closed under subtraction.

SOLUTION

Verify the statement by subtracting two whole numbers.

$$6 - 4 = 2$$
$$100 - 90 = 10$$
$$4 - 6 = -2$$

$4 - 6$ is a counterexample. The difference is not a whole number.

The statement is false.

For each number, identify the subsets of real numbers to which it belongs.
(Ex 1)

a. -73 b. $\dfrac{5}{9}$ c. 18π

Identify the set of numbers that best describes each situation. Explain your choice.
(Ex 2)

d. the number of people on a bus

e. the area of a circular platform

f. the value of coins in a purse

Find $C \cap D$ and $C \cup D$.
(Ex 3)

g. $C = \{4, 8, 12, 16, 20\}; D = \{5, 10, 15, 20\}$

h. $C = \{6, 12, 18, 24\}; D = \{7, 14, 21, 28\}$

Verify Determine whether each statement is true or false. Provide a counterexample for false statements.
(Ex 4)

i. The set of whole numbers is closed under multiplication.

j. The set of natural numbers is closed under division.

1. Multiply 26.1×6.15.
(SB 2)

2. Add $\dfrac{4}{7} + \dfrac{1}{8} + \dfrac{1}{2}$.
(SB 3)

3. Divide $954 \div 0.9$.
(SB 2)

4. Add $\dfrac{3}{5} + \dfrac{1}{8} + \dfrac{1}{8}$.
(SB 3)

5. Write $\dfrac{3}{8}$ as a decimal.
(SB 5)

6. Write $0.66\overline{6}$ as a fraction.
(SB 6)

7. Add $2\dfrac{1}{2} + 3\dfrac{1}{5}$.
(SB 3)

8. Name a fraction equivalent to $\dfrac{2}{5}$.
(SB 7)

9. Error Analysis Two students determine the prime factorization of 72. Which student is correct? Explain the error.
(SB 12)

Student A	Student B
72	72
$= 9 \cdot 8$	$= 9 \cdot 8$
$= 9 \cdot 4 \cdot 2$	$= 9 \cdot 4 \cdot 2$
$= 9 \cdot 2 \cdot 2 \cdot 2$	$= 3 \cdot 3 \cdot 2 \cdot 2 \cdot 2$

10. Find the prime factorization of 144.
(SB 12)

11. Write 0.15 as a percent. If necessary, round to the nearest tenth.
(SB 5)

12. Write 7.2 as a percent. If necessary, round to the nearest tenth.
(SB 5)

The **Lesson Practice** lets you check to see if you understand today's new concept.

The italic numbers refer to the Example in this lesson in which the major concept of that particular problem is introduced. You can refer to the lesson examples if you need additional help.

The *italic numbers* refer to the lesson(s) in which the major concept of that particular problem is introduced. You can refer to the examples or practice in that lesson, if you need additional help.

*13. Use braces and digits to designate the set of natural numbers.
(1)

*14. The set {0, 1, 2, 3,…} represents what set of numbers?
(1)

*15. Represent the following numbers as being members of set *K*: 2, 4, 2, 0, 6, 0, 10, 8.
(1)

*16. **Multiple Choice** Which of the following numbers is an irrational number?
(1)

    A 15   **B** $\sqrt{15}$ **C** 15.15151515…   **D** $-\dfrac{15}{3}$

*17. **Measurement** The surface area of a cube is defined as $6s^2$, where *s* is the length of
(1) the side of the cube. If *s* is an integer, then would the surface area of a cube be a rational or irrational number?

18. **Verify** True or False: A right triangle can have an obtuse angle. Explain your
(SB 1) answer.

19. (**Anatomy**) A baby's head is approximately one fourth of its total body length. If the
(SB 3) baby's body measures 19 inches, what does the baby's head measure?

20. True or False: An acute triangle has 3 acute angles. Explain your answer.
(SB 13)

21. True or False: A trapezoid has two pairs of parallel sides. Explain your answer.
(SB 14)

*22. (**Track Practice**) Tyrone ran 7 laps on the quarter-mile track during practice. Which
(1) subset of real numbers would include the distance Tyrone ran at practice?

23. True or False: A parallelogram has two pairs of parallel sides. Explain your
(SB 14) answer.

24. **Write** Use the divisibility test to determine if 1248 is divisible by 2. Explain
(SB 4) your answer.

*25. **Geometry** The diagram shows a right triangle. The length of the hypotenuse is
(1) a member of which subset(s) of real numbers?

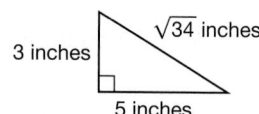

*26. **Multi-Step** The diagram shows a rectangle.
(1)
    a. Find the area of the rectangle.

    b. The number of square feet is a member of which subset(s) of real numbers?

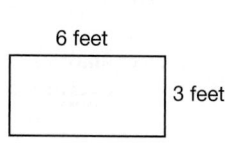

27. (**Lunar Rover**) The surface-speed record set by the lunar rover on the moon is
(SB 2) 10.56 miles per hour. At that speed, how far would the rover travel in 3.5 hours?

28. **Write** Use the divisibility test to determine if 207 is divisible by 3. Explain
(SB 4) your answer.

29. (**Swimming**) Vidiana and Jaime went swimming before school. Vidiana swam $\frac{3}{5}$ mile
(SB 1) and Jaime swam $\frac{4}{7}$ mile. Write a comparison to show who swam farther. Use <, >, or =.

*30. (**Banking**) Shayla is balancing her checkbook. Which subset of real numbers best
(1) describes her balance?

Understanding Variables and Expressions

Warm Up

1. Vocabulary When two numbers are multiplied, the result is called
(SB 2) the _____. (*quotient, product*)

Add.

2. $\frac{2}{5} + \frac{1}{3}$
(SB 3)

3. $654.1 + 78.39$
(SB 2)

Multiply.

4. $4.5(0.23)$
(SB 2)

5. $\frac{3}{8}\left(\frac{2}{9}\right)$
(SB 3)

New Concepts

A symbol, usually a letter, used to represent an unknown number is called a **variable**. In the algebraic expression $4 + x$, x is a variable. The number 4 in this expression does not change value. A quantity whose value does not change is called a **constant**.

Example 1   **Identifying Variables and Constants**

Identify the constants and the variables in each expression.

a. $6 - 3x$

SOLUTION

The numbers 6 and 3 are constants because they never change. The letter x is a variable because it represents an unknown number.

b. $71wz + 28y$

SOLUTION

The numbers 71 and 28 are constants because they never change. The letters w, y, and z are variables because they represent unknown numbers.

The expression $4xy$ can also be written as $4 \cdot x \cdot y$. When two or more quantities are multiplied, each is a **factor** of the product. The numeric factor of a product including a variable is called the numeric coefficient, or simply the **coefficient**.

Math Reasoning

Connect What other term can be used to describe the coefficient in the expression $5mn$?

coefficient

$\downarrow$

4xy

factors

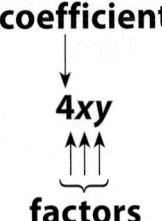

Example 2 Identifying Factors and Coefficients in Expressions

Identify the factors and coefficients in each expression.

a. $7vw$

SOLUTION

The factors are 7, v, and w. The coefficient is 7.

b. $-5rst$

SOLUTION

The factors are -5, r, s, and t. The coefficient is -5.

c. $\dfrac{y}{3}$

SOLUTION

The factors are $\frac{1}{3}$ and y. The coefficient is $\frac{1}{3}$.

d. cd

SOLUTION

The factors are c and d. The expression cd has an implied coefficient of 1.

Hint

$\dfrac{y}{3} = \dfrac{1}{3}y$

$cd = 1cd$

Parts of an expression separated by $+$ or $-$ signs are called **terms of an expression.** A term that is in parentheses such as $(y + 2)$ can include a plus or minus sign.

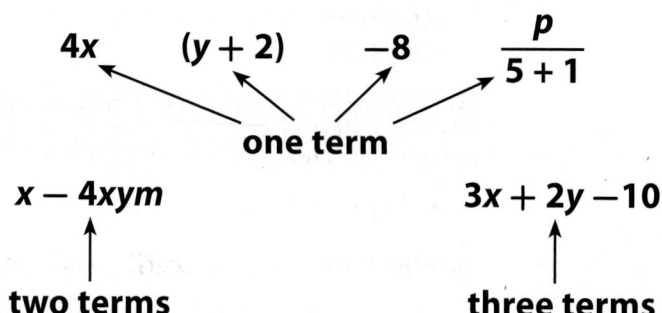

You can refer to a particular term of an expression by its placement within the expression. The terms of an expression are numbered from left to right, beginning with the first term.

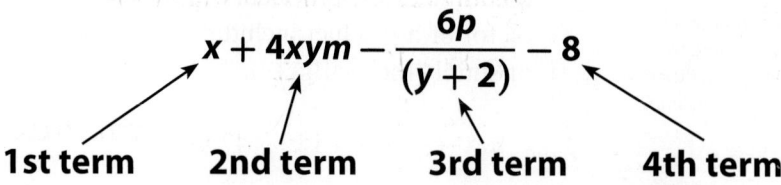

Example 3   **Identifying Terms**

Identify the terms in each expression.

a. $6xy + 57w - \dfrac{24x}{5y}$

SOLUTION

The first term is $6xy$.

The second term is $57w$.

The third term is $\dfrac{24x}{5y}$.

b. $m + 3mn - \dfrac{5t}{(d + 8)} - 9$

SOLUTION

The first term is m.

The second term is $3mn$.

The third term is $\dfrac{5t}{(d + 8)}$.

The fourth term is 9.

Example 4   **Application: Telecommunications**

The local telephone company uses the expression below to determine the monthly charges for individual customers.

$$0.1m + 4.95$$

a. How many terms are in the expression?

SOLUTION There are two terms.

b. Identify the constant(s).

SOLUTION The constants are 0.1 and 4.95.

c. Identify the variable(s).

SOLUTION The variable is m.

Lesson Practice

Identify the constants and variables in each expression.
(Ex 1)

   a. $65qrs + 12x$ **b.** $4gh - 71yz$

Identify the factors and coefficients in each expression.
(Ex 2)

   c. $17def$ **d.** $\dfrac{uv}{4}$

   e. $-3st$ **f.** abc

Identify the terms in each expression.
(Ex 3)

   g. $8v - 17yz + \dfrac{63b}{4gh}$

   h. $\dfrac{(4 + 2x)}{38q} + 18s - 47jkl$

Bill's Bikes uses the expression below to calculate rental fees.
(Ex 4)

$$6.50 + 3.25h - 0.75b$$

   i. How many terms are in the expression?

   j. Identify the constants.

   k. Identify the variables.

Find the GCF of each pair of numbers.

1. 24, 32
(SB 9)

2. 28, 42
(SB 9)

Find the LCM of each group of numbers.

3. 9, 12
(SB 10)

4. 3, 5, 6
(SB 10)

Multiply or divide.

5. $\dfrac{3}{4} \cdot \dfrac{8}{15}$
(SB 3)

6. $\dfrac{7}{15} \div \dfrac{21}{25}$
(SB 3)

Identify the coefficients and variables in each expression.

*7. $rst - 12v$
(2)

*8. $2xy + 7w - 8$
(2)

*9. $47s + \dfrac{2}{5}t$
(2)

Identify the following statements as true or false. Explain your choice.

*10. Verify All whole numbers are natural numbers.
(1)

11. Verify All integers are real numbers.
(1)

12. Verify A number can be a member of the set of rational numbers and the set of irrational numbers.
(1)

13. Multi-Step Use the following set of data.
(SB 29)

$$3, 6, 4, 3, 6, 5, 6, 7, 4, 3, 2, 4, 6$$

   a. What is the frequency of each number?

   b. Display the set of data in a line plot.

14. All natural numbers are members of which other subsets of real numbers?
(1)

15. Measurement Add $7\dfrac{3}{8}$ meters $+ 6\dfrac{1}{3}$ meters. Does the sum belong to the set of rational numbers, integers, or whole numbers?
(1, SB 3)

16. Find the prime factorization of 153.
(SB 12)

17. Verify True or False: An obtuse triangle can have more than one obtuse angle. Explain your choice.
(SB 13)

18. Geometry A line can be classified as a _____ angle.
(SB 13)

19. Write Use the divisibility test to determine if 2345 is divisible by 4. Explain your answer.
(SB 4)

20. Write 0.003 as a percent. If necessary, round to the nearest tenth.
(SB 5)

21. Use braces and digits to designate the set of whole numbers.
(1)

22. The set {1, 2, 3,...} represents what set of numbers?
(1)

*23. **Multiple Choice** What is the second term in the expression
(2)
$$\sqrt{8} + \frac{gh}{5} + (3x + y) + 15gh?$$

A $(3x + y)$ **B** $15gh$ **C** $\sqrt{8}$ **D** $\dfrac{gh}{5}$

*24. (**Astronomy**) To calculate the amount of time it takes for a planet to travel around
(2)
the sun, you use the following expression: $\frac{2\pi r}{v}$. Which values are constants, which
are variables, and which are coefficients?

*25. (**Entertainment**) Admission price for a matinee movie is \$5.75 for children and \$6.25
(2)
for adults. Brad uses the expression $\$5.75c + \$6.25a$ to calculate the cost for his
family. What are the variables in the expression?

*26. **Error Analysis** The surface area of a rectangular prism is $2lw + 2lh + 2wh$. Two
(2)
students determined the variables in the formula. Which student is correct? What
was the error of the other student?

Student A	Student B
variables: $2lw, 2lh$	variables: l, w, h

*27. (**Cost Analysis**) A large medical organization wants to put two cylindrical aquariums
(2)
in the pharmacy area. It will cost the pharmacy 53 cents per cubic inch of
aquarium. This is the formula for figuring out the cost: $P = (\pi r^2 h)(\$0.53)$.
a. Find the coefficients of the expression.

b. Find the variables of the expression.

28. **Multiple Choice** Which shape is not a parallelogram?
(SB 14)
A square **B** rectangle **C** trapezoid **D** rhombus

*29. (**Cycling**) A bicycle shop uses the expression $\$5 + \$2.25h$ to determine the charges
(2)
for bike rentals. How many terms are in the expression?

30. (**Attendance**) The attendance clerk keeps records of students' attendance. Which
(1)
subset of real numbers would include the number of students in attendance each
school day?

Simplifying Expressions Using the Product Property of Exponents

Warm Up

1. *(2)* **Vocabulary** In the term $4x$, x is the _____. (*variable, coefficient*)

Simplify.

2. *(SB 2)* $(1.2)(0.7)$

3. *(SB 2)* $(0.5)(11)(0.9)$

4. *(SB 3)* $\left(\dfrac{2}{3}\right)\left(\dfrac{6}{7}\right)$

5. *(SB 3)* $\left(\dfrac{1}{2}\right)\left(\dfrac{4}{5}\right)\left(\dfrac{15}{16}\right)$

New Concepts

An exponent can be used to show repeated multiplication.

$$\text{base} \longrightarrow 5^3 \longleftarrow \text{exponent}$$

The **base of a power** is the number used as a factor. If the **exponent** is a natural number, it indicates how many times the base is used as a factor.

Words	Power	Multiplication	Value
five to the first power	5^1	5	5
five to the second power or five squared	5^2	$5 \cdot 5$	25
five to the third power or five cubed	5^3	$5 \cdot 5 \cdot 5$	125
five to the fourth power	5^4	$5 \cdot 5 \cdot 5 \cdot 5$	625

Caution

Be careful not to multiply the base and the exponent when simplifying powers.

Online Connection
www.SaxonMathResources.com

Example 1 Simplifying Expressions with Exponents

Simplify each expression.

a. 7^3

SOLUTION

The exponent 3 indicates that the base is a factor three times.

7^3

$= 7 \cdot 7 \cdot 7$

$= 343$

b. $(0.3)^4$

SOLUTION

The exponent 4 indicates that the base is a factor four times.

$(0.3)^4$

$= (0.3)(0.3)(0.3)(0.3)$

$= 0.0081$

Math Reasoning

Generalize Examine the powers of 10. What pattern do you see?

c. $\left(\dfrac{1}{2}\right)^5$

SOLUTION

The exponent 5 indicates that the base is a factor five times.

$$\left(\dfrac{1}{2}\right)^5$$

$$= \dfrac{1}{2} \cdot \dfrac{1}{2} \cdot \dfrac{1}{2} \cdot \dfrac{1}{2} \cdot \dfrac{1}{2}$$

$$= \dfrac{1}{32}$$

d. 10^3

SOLUTION

The exponent 3 indicates that the base is a factor three times.

$$10^3$$

$$= 10 \cdot 10 \cdot 10$$

$$= 1000$$

The product of powers whose bases are the same can be found by writing each power as repeated multiplication.

$$5^4 \cdot 5^5 = (5 \cdot 5 \cdot 5 \cdot 5) \cdot (5 \cdot 5 \cdot 5 \cdot 5 \cdot 5) = 5^9$$

The sum of the exponents in the factors is equal to the exponent in the product.

Product Property of Exponents
If m and n are real numbers and $x \neq 0$, then
$x^m \cdot x^n = x^{m+n}.$

Example 2 **Applying the Product Property of Exponents**

Simplify each expression.

a. $x^5 \cdot x^7 \cdot x^2$

SOLUTION

Since each of the factors has the same base, the exponents can be added to find the power of the product.

$$x^{5+7+2} = x^{14}$$

b. $m^3 \cdot m^2 \cdot m^4 \cdot n^6 \cdot n^7$

SOLUTION

The first three factors have m as the base. The exponents can be added to find the product of those three factors. The last two factors have n as the base. The exponents can be added to find the product of the last two factors.

$$m^{3+2+4} \cdot n^{6+7} = m^9 n^{13}$$

Math Reasoning

Estimate Use the order of magnitude to estimate 1,127,000 times 108.

The **order of magnitude** is defined as the nearest power of ten to a given quantity. The order of magnitude can be used to estimate when performing calculations mentally.

Example 3 Application: Speed of a Supercomputer

In 2006, the fastest supercomputer's performance topped out at about one PFLOPS. One PFLOPS is equal to 10^3 TFLOPS. Each TFLOPS is equal to 10^{12} FLOPS. What was the computer's speed in FLOPS?

SOLUTION

Understand

$1 \text{ PFLOPS} = 10^3 \text{ TFLOPS}$

$1 \text{ TFLOPS} = 10^{12} \text{ FLOPS}$

Find the number of FLOPS in one PFLOPS.

Plan

Write an expression to find the number of FLOPS in one PFLOPS.

Solve

To find the speed in FLOPS, find the product of the number of TFLOPS, 10^3, and the number of FLOPS in a TFLOPS, 10^{12}.

$10^3 \cdot 10^{12}$

$= 10^{3+12}$

$= 10^{15}$

The computer performed at a speed of 10^{15} FLOPS.

Check

$$10^3 \cdot 10^{12} \stackrel{?}{=} 10^{15}$$

$$(10 \cdot 10 \cdot 10)(10 \cdot 10 \cdot 10 \cdot 10 \cdot 10 \cdot 10 \cdot 10 \cdot 10 \cdot 10 \cdot 10 \cdot 10 \cdot 10) \stackrel{?}{=} 10^{15}$$

$$10^{15} = 10^{15} \quad \checkmark$$

Lesson Practice

Simplify each expression.

a. 6^4
(Ex 1)

b. $(1.4)^2$
(Ex 1)

c. $\left(\dfrac{2}{5}\right)^3$
(Ex 1)

d. 10^6
(Ex 1)

e. $w^3 \cdot w^5 \cdot w^4$
(Ex 2)

f. $y^6 \cdot y^5 \cdot z^3 \cdot z^{11} \cdot z^2$
(Ex 2)

g. If a supercomputer has a top speed of one EFLOPS which is equal to 10^9 GFLOPS, and if one GFLOPS is 10^9 FLOPS, what is the computer's speed in FLOPS?
(Ex 3)

Practice Distributed and Integrated

Find the GCF for each pair of numbers.

1. 15, 35
(SB 9)

2. 32, 48
(SB 9)

Find the LCM for each group of numbers.

3. 8, 12
(SB 10)

4. 2, 4, 7
(SB 10)

Multiply or divide.

5. $\dfrac{9}{16} \cdot \dfrac{12}{15}$
(SB 3)

6. $\dfrac{6}{15} \div \dfrac{24}{30}$
(SB 3)

Identify the coefficients and variables in each expression.

7. $6mn + 4b$
(2)

8. $5j - 9cd + 2$
(2)

9. $23t + \dfrac{4}{7}w$
(2)

Identify the following statements as true or false. Explain your choice.

*10. **Verify** All real numbers are integers.
(1)

11. **Verify** All natural numbers are whole numbers.
(2)

12. **Verify** All irrational numbers are real numbers.
(2)

Complete the comparisons. Use <, >, or =.

13. $42.53 \bigcirc 42.35$
(SB 1)

14. $\dfrac{5}{9} \bigcirc \dfrac{7}{12}$
(SB 1)

15. Add $1\dfrac{1}{8} + 7\dfrac{2}{5}$.
(SB 3)

 16. **Measurement** Use braces and digits to designate the set of integers. Which
(1) measurement can be described by the set of integers: temperature or volume?

17. Find the prime factorization of 98.
(SB 12)

*18. **Error Analysis** Two students are trying to simplify the expression $x^2 \cdot x^5$. Which
(3) student is correct? Explain the error.

Student A	Student B
$x^2 \cdot x^5$	$x^2 \cdot x^5$
$x^{2 \cdot 5} = x^{10}$	$x^{2+5} = x^7$

19. **Verify** True or False: A rhombus is always a square. Explain your choice.
(SB 14)

20. **Write** Use the divisibility test to determine if 306 is divisible by 6. Explain your
(SB 4) answer.

*21. The expression 3^6 indicates the number of times 3 is used as a factor.
(3) **a.** Which number in the expression is the base?

b. Which number is the exponent?

c. What is the simplified value of this expression?

*22. Multiple Choice MFLOPS, TFLOPS, and PFLOPS are used to measure the speed
(3) of a computer. One PFLOP is equal to 10^3 TFLOPS. Each TFLOP is equal to 10^6
MFLOPS. How many MFLOPS are in a PFLOP?

   A 10^{18} **B** 10^9 **C** 10^6 **D** 10^3

*23. (Cooking) A cooking magazine advertises 4^4 recipes in every issue. How many
(3) recipes are in 4^2 issues?

*24. Multi-Step A business is worth 10^6 dollars this year. The business expects to be 10^3
(3) more valuable in five years.

   a. Simplify 10^3 to determine how many times more valuable the business
will be.

   b. What will the business be worth in five years? Express your answer in
exponential form, then simplify your answer.

*25. (Population) The population of Bridgetown triples every decade. If the population
(3) in the year 2000 was 25,000, how many people will be living in Bridgetown
in 2030?

26. Multiple Choice Which triangle is a right triangle?
(SB 13)

   A a triangle with angle measures of 45°, 45°, and 90°

   B a triangle with angle measures of 40°, 110°, and 30°

   C a triangle with angle measures of 55°, 45°, and 80°

   D a triangle with angle measures of 60°, 60°, and 60°

*27. (Bacteria) The population of a certain bacteria doubles in size every 3 hours. If
(3) a population begins with one bacterium, how many will there be after one day?
Simplify the expression $1 \cdot (2)^8$ to determine the population after one day.

28. Geometry You can calculate the area of a trapezoid using the following equation:
(2) $A = h \times \frac{b_1 + b_2}{2}$. Identify the constant(s) in the equation.

*29. (Aquarium) A fish tank is in the shape of a cube. Each side measures 3 feet. What is
(SB 26) the volume of the fish tank?

*30. (Remodeling) Vanessa is remodeling her bathroom. She uses the expression $2l + 2w$
(2) to determine the amount of wallpaper border she needs.

   a. How many terms are in the expression?

   b. What are the variables?

Using Order of Operations

Warm Up

1. **Vocabulary** A(n) _____ can be used to show repeated multiplication.
(3)

Simplify.

2. $28.75 + 13.5$
(SB2)

3. $89.6 - 7.4$
(SB2)

4. $\dfrac{2}{3} \cdot \dfrac{9}{16}$
(SB3)

5. $4\dfrac{1}{5} \div 3\dfrac{1}{2}$
(SB3)

New Concepts

To **simplify** an expression means to perform all indicated operations. Simplifying an expression could produce multiple answers without rules concerning the order in which operations are performed. Consider the example below.

Method 1: $\dfrac{2 \cdot (3)^2}{6} = \dfrac{2 \cdot 9}{6} = \dfrac{18}{6} = 3$

Method 2: $\dfrac{2 \cdot (3)^2}{6} = \dfrac{(2 \cdot 3)^2}{6} = \dfrac{6^2}{6} = \dfrac{36}{6} = 6$

To avoid confusion, mathematicians have agreed to use the order of operations. The **order of operations** is a set of rules for simplifying expressions. Method 1 followed the order of operations.

Order of Operations
1. Work inside grouping symbols.
2. Simplify powers and roots.
3. Multiply and divide from left to right.
4. Add and subtract from left to right.

Example 1 Simplifying Expressions with Parentheses

Simplify. Justify each step.

$(10 \cdot 3) + 7 \cdot (5 + 4)$

SOLUTION

Write the expression. Then use the order of operations to simplify.

$(10 \cdot 3) + 7 \cdot (5 + 4)$

$= 30 + 7 \cdot 9$ Simplify inside the parentheses.

$= 30 + 63$ Multiply.

$= 93$ Add.

Online Connection
www.SaxonMathResources.com

Example 2 Simplifying Expressions with Exponents

Simplify each expression. Justify each step.

a. $4^3 + 9 \div 3 - 2 \cdot (3)^2$

SOLUTION Write the expression. Then use the order of operations to simplify.

$4^3 + 9 \div 3 - 2 \cdot (3)^2$

$= 64 + 9 \div 3 - 2 \cdot 9$ Simplify exponents.

$= 64 + 3 - 18$ Multiply and divide from left to right.

$= 49$ Add and subtract from left to right.

b. $\dfrac{(2 \cdot 3 - 2)^2}{2}$

SOLUTION Write the expression. Then use the order of operations to simplify.

$\dfrac{(2 \cdot 3 - 2)^2}{2}$

$= \dfrac{(6 - 2)^2}{2}$ Multiply inside the parentheses.

$= \dfrac{(4)^2}{2}$ Subtract inside the parentheses.

$= \dfrac{16}{2}$ Simplify the exponent.

$= 8$ Divide.

Hint

Remember to use the order of operations inside parentheses as well.

Example 3 Comparing Expressions

Compare the expressions. Use $<$, $>$, or $=$.

$(1.5 + 3) \div 9 + 3^3 \bigcirc \dfrac{(18 + 8)}{2} - 8 \div 4$

SOLUTION

Use the order of operations to simplify the two expressions.

$(1.5 + 3) \div 9 + 3^3$ $\dfrac{(18 + 8)}{2} - 8 \div 4$

$= (4.5) \div 9 + 3^3$ $= \dfrac{26}{2} - 8 \div 4$

$= 4.5 \div 9 + 27$ $= 13 - 8 \div 4$

$= 0.5 + 27$ $= 13 - 2$

$= 27.5$ $= 11$

Hint

Remember to compare the original expressions in the inequality.

Since $27.5 > 11$, $(1.5 + 3) \div 9 + 3^3 \;\ovee\; \dfrac{(18 + 8)}{2} - 8 \div 4$.

Example 4 Application: Comparing a Crop Circle to a Soccer Field

A crop circle in a wheat field has a diameter of 100 yards. Its area is $3.14 \cdot \left(\frac{100}{2}\right)^2$ square yards. A World Cup soccer field is 70 yards by 110 yards. Its area is $(70 \cdot 110)$ square yards. How much larger is the crop circle than the soccer field?

Hint

Remember that the formula for the area of a circle is πr^2.

SOLUTION

Find each area and subtract to find the difference.

Area of crop circle: $3.14 \cdot \left(\frac{100}{2}\right)^2$

Area of soccer field: $(70 \cdot 110)$

Difference in area: $3.14 \cdot \left(\frac{100}{2}\right)^2 - (70 \cdot 110)$

Simplify the expression.

$3.14 \cdot \left(\frac{100}{2}\right)^2 - (70 \cdot 110)$

$= 3.14 \cdot (50)^2 - (7700)$ Evaluate inside the parentheses.

$= 3.14 \cdot 2500 - 7700$ Simplify the exponent.

$= 7850 - 7700$ Multiply.

$= 150$ Subtract.

The crop circle is 150 yd^2 larger than the soccer field.

Lesson Practice

    a. Simplify $45 - (2 + 4) \cdot 5 - 3$. Justify each step.
  (Ex 1)

Simplify each expression. Justify each step.
(Ex 2)

    b. $9 \cdot 2^3 - 9 \div 3$

    c. $\dfrac{15 - 3^2 + 4 \cdot 2}{7}$

    d. Compare the expressions. Use $<$, $>$, or $=$.
  (Ex 3)

        $\dfrac{1}{4} + 3^2 + 6 \bigcirc 5 - 2 + 2 \cdot 4 + 3 \div 9$

Caution

Do not forget to cube $\frac{3}{2}$ in the expression for the model moon's volume.

    e. Jonah is making a model of the moon using plastic foam. He uses
  (Ex 4) the formula $\frac{4}{3}\pi r^3$ to find the volume. The model moon's radius is $\frac{3}{2}$ inches. What is the volume of the model moon? Give the answer in terms of π.

Add, subtract, multiply, or divide.

1. $2\frac{1}{4} + 4\frac{1}{2}$
(SB 3)

2. $5\frac{2}{5} - 3\frac{1}{4}$
(SB 3)

3. $1\frac{3}{4} + 4\frac{1}{8} - 2\frac{1}{2}$
(SB 3)

4. $4\frac{1}{3} \div 2\frac{1}{6}$
(SB 3)

5. $3.519 \div 0.3$
(SB 2)

6. $4.16 \cdot 2.3$
(SB 2)

7. How many terms are in the algebraic expression $14x^2 + 7x + \frac{x}{4}$?
(2)

8. Find the prime factorization of 225.
(SB 12)

9. Write Use the divisibility test to determine if 124,302 is divisible by 3. Explain
(SB 4) your answer.

10. Represent the following numbers as being members of set L: $-15, 1, 7, 3, -8, 7, 0,$
(1) 12, 6, 12

*11. Verify True or False: All whole numbers are integers. Explain your answer.
(1)

*12. To which set(s) of numbers does $\sqrt{5}$ belong?
(1)

13. Write $\frac{1}{6}$ as a percent. If necessary, round to the nearest tenth.
(SB 5)

14. Write $\frac{5}{9}$ as a percent. If necessary, round to the nearest tenth.
(SB 5)

*15. Compare $3 \cdot 4^2 + 4^2 \bigcirc 3 \cdot (16 + 16)$ using $<, >,$ or $=$. Explain.
(4)

16. Multiple Choice Which triangle is an obtuse triangle?
(SB 13)
  A a triangle with angle measures of 45°, 45°, and 90°

  B a triangle with angle measures of 40°, 120°, and 20°

  C a triangle with angle measures of 55°, 45°, and 80°

  D a triangle with angle measures of 60°, 60°, and 60°

17. Display the following set of data in a line plot:
(SB 29)

$$6, 7, 8, 4, 5, 4, 3, 4, 5, 3, 2, 6, 2, 7$$

18. Verify True or False: A square is a rectangle. Explain your choice.
(SB 14)

19. Measurement Subtract $15\frac{1}{3}$ yards $- 7\frac{4}{5}$ yards.
(SB 3)

20. Error Analysis Two students determine the prime factorization of 108. Which
(SB 12) student is correct? Explain the error.

Student A	Student B
$108 = 2 \cdot 2 \cdot 3 \cdot 3 \cdot 3$	$108 = 2^2 \cdot 3^3$

21. Write Use the divisibility test to determine if 1116 is divisible by 9. Explain
(SB 4) your answer.

22. $\frac{n}{6} + 3xy - 19$
(2)

   a. Find the variables of the expression.

   b. Find the terms of the expression.

*23. (**Biology**) A survey found that there were 1100 gray wolves in Minnesota in 1976.
(4) By 2003, the number of gray wolves had increased to 2300. What was the average growth of the wolf population in one year? (Round to the nearest whole number.)

*24. Multiple Choice A bouquet is made from nine red roses that cost $1.75 each and
(4) five white roses that cost $1.50 each. Use the expression $9 \cdot (\$1.75) + 5 \cdot (\$1.50)$ to find the cost of the bouquet.

   A $31.00   **B** $23.25

   C $25.25   **D** $21.75

*25. A can of soup in the shape of a cylinder has a radius of
(4) 3.8 cm and a height of 11 cm. What is the surface area of the can to the nearest tenth? Use 3.14 for π.

$r = 3.8$ cm

$h = 11$ cm

*26. Multi-Step Two friends compare the amount of change they
(4) have in their pockets. Ashley has 12 nickels, 2 dimes, and 4 quarters. Beto has 10 nickels, 4 dimes, and 3 quarters. Who has more money?

   a. Write an expression to represent the value of Ashley's money. (Hint: Use 10¢ to represent the value of each dime, 5¢ for each nickel, and so on). Simplify the expression.

   b. Write an expression to represent the value of Beto's money. Simplify the expression.

   c. Compare the value of money that each friend has. Who has more?

*27. (**School Supplies**) Anthony had 10 packages of markers. Each package contained
(4) 8 markers. He gave 2 packages to each of the other 3 people in his group. Use the expression $8(10 - 3 \cdot 2)$ to determine how many markers Anthony kept for himself.

28. Geometry Use the cube shown to write a formula for the volume
(3) of any cube.

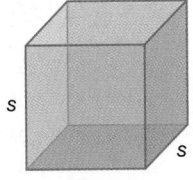

*29. (**Temperature**) The hottest day in Florida's history was 109°F,
(4) which occurred on June 29, 1931 in Monticello. Use the expression $\frac{5}{9}(F - 32)$ to convert this temperature to degrees Celsius. Round your answer to the nearest tenth of a degree.

s

s

s

*30. (**Billing**) Each month Mrs. Li pays her phone company $28 for phone service and
(4) $0.07 per minute for long-distance calls. Use the expression $28 + 0.07\,m$ to find the amount she was billed if her long-distance calls totaled 223 minutes.

Finding Absolute Value and Adding Real Numbers

Warm Up

1. **Vocabulary** The set of _____ (*integers*, *real numbers*) includes all
(1) rational or irrational numbers.

Simplify.

2. $54.2 - 27.38$
(SB 2)

3. $\dfrac{1}{2} + \dfrac{3}{8}$
(SB 3)

4. $1.09 + 76.9$
(SB 2)

5. $\dfrac{3}{4} - \dfrac{3}{8}$
(SB 3)

New Concepts

The **absolute value** of a number is the distance from the number to zero on a
number line. The absolute value of 4 is written $|4|$.

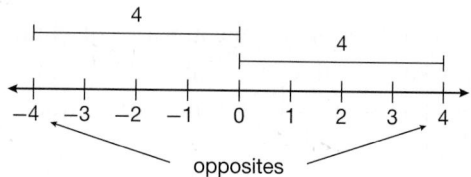

$$|-4| = 4 \qquad\qquad |4| = 4$$

Absolute Value
The absolute value of a number *n* is the distance from *n* to 0 on a number line.

Example 1 Finding the Absolute Value

Simplify.

a. $|0|$

SOLUTION

The absolute value of 0
is 0.

b. $|7.12|$

SOLUTION

The distance from 7.12 to 0 is 7.12.
So the absolute value is 7.12.

c. $\left|1 - \dfrac{3}{4}\right|$

SOLUTION

First simplify within the
absolute-value bars. Then
find the absolute value.

$$\left|1 - \frac{3}{4}\right| = \left|\frac{1}{4}\right| = \frac{1}{4}$$

d. $-|11 - 2|$

SOLUTION

First simplify within the
absolute-value bars. Then find the
absolute value.

$$-|11 - 2| = -|9| = -9$$

Reading Math

Read $-|9|$ as the
opposite of the absolute
value of 9.

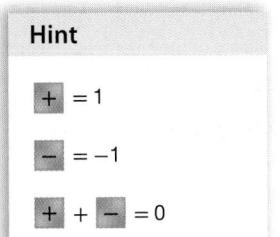
Exploration **Modeling Real Number Addition**

Find the sum $-5 + 3$.

Model -5 and 3 using algebra tiles.

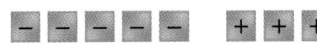

Group positive and negative tiles to make zero pairs.

Count the remaining tiles.

$$-5 + 3 = -2$$

Model $-5 + 3$ on a number line.

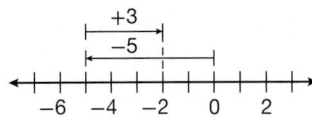

Use algebra tiles to find the sum. Then model each problem on a number line.

a. $4 + (-3)$ **b.** $-2 + -6$ **c.** $(-7) + 7$

Generalize Determine whether each statement is true or false. Provide a counterexample for false statements.

d. The sum of two positive numbers is always positive.

e. The sum of two negative numbers is always negative.

f. The sum of a positive and a negative number is always negative.

The sum of two numbers can also be found using the rules for adding real numbers. These rules apply to all real-number addends.

Rules for Adding Real Numbers
Adding Numbers With the Same Sign
To add numbers with the same sign, add their absolute values. The sum will have the same sign as the addends.
Examples $3 + 2 = 5$ $-3 + (-2) = -5$
Adding Numbers With Different Signs
To add numbers with different signs, find the difference of their absolute values. The sum will have the sign of the addend with the greater absolute value.
Examples $3 + (-2) = 1$ $(-3) + 2 = -1$

Example 2 Adding Real Numbers

Find the sum.

a. $(-12) + 21$

SOLUTION Since the numbers have different signs, find the difference of their absolute values. The sum is positive because $|-12| < |21|$.

$(-12) + 21 = 9$

b. $(-19) + (-8)$

SOLUTION Since the numbers have the same sign, find the sum of their absolute values. The sum is negative because both addends are negative.

$(-19) + (-8) = -27$

c. $(3.2) + (-5.1)$

SOLUTION Since the numbers have different signs, find the difference of their absolute values. The sum is negative because $|3.2| < |-5.1|$.

$(3.2) + (-5.1) = -1.9$

d. $\left(-\frac{3}{5}\right) + \left(-\frac{1}{5}\right)$

SOLUTION Since the numbers have the same sign, find the sum of their absolute values. The sum is negative because both addends are negative.

$\left(-\frac{3}{5}\right) + \left(-\frac{1}{5}\right) = \left(-\frac{4}{5}\right)$

Example 3 Identifying Sets of Real Numbers Closed Under Addition

Determine whether each statement is true or false. Give a counterexample for false statements.

a. The set of integers is closed under addition.

SOLUTION The statement is true because the sum of any two integers will be an integer.

b. The set of real numbers is closed under addition.

SOLUTION The statement is true because the sum of any two real numbers will be a real number.

Example 4 Application: Football

On the first down, the Cougars lost 4 yards. They gained 7 yards on the second down. Use addition to find the total number of yards lost or gained on the first two downs.

SOLUTION A loss of 4 yards can be expressed as -4.

$(-4) + 7 = 3$

The Cougars gained a total of 3 yards on the first two downs.

Simplify.
(Ex 1)

a. $|-3.4|$

b. $\left|\dfrac{6}{7}\right|$

c. $\left|14 + (-22)\right|$

d. $-|7 + 16|$

Find the sum.
(Ex 2)

e. $(-23.4) + 18.72$

f. $\left(-\dfrac{2}{3}\right) + \left(-\dfrac{1}{6}\right)$

Determine whether each statement is true or false. Give a counterexample for false statements.
(Ex 3)

g. The set of rational numbers is closed under addition.

h. The set of positive integers is closed under addition.

i. The temperature at 7:00 p.m. was 34°F. The temperature fell 12°F by
(Ex 4) midnight. Use addition to find the temperature at midnight.

Practice   **Distributed and Integrated**

Add, subtract, multiply, or divide.

1. $1\dfrac{1}{6} + 3\dfrac{1}{3}$
(SB 3)

2. $2\dfrac{3}{8} - 1\dfrac{1}{4}$
(SB 3)

3. $3\dfrac{2}{3} + 1\dfrac{5}{8} - 1\dfrac{3}{4}$
(SB 3)

4. $3\dfrac{1}{3} \div 1\dfrac{3}{5}$
(SB 3)

5. $1.506 \div 0.2$
(SB 2)

6. $2.89 \cdot 1.2$
(SB 2)

7. How many terms are in the algebraic expression $2x^2 + 3x + 7$?
(2)

8. Find the prime factorization of 150.
(SB 12)

9. Write Use the divisibility test to determine if 125,000 is divisible by 10.
(SB 4) Explain your answer.

10. Model Represent the following numbers as being members of set L: $-12, 0, -8, 4,$
(1) $-4, 4, 0, 8, 8, 12$.

11. Verify True or False: All integers are rational numbers. Explain your answer.
(1)

12. Error Analysis Student A said that $\dfrac{\sqrt{2}}{1}$ is a rational number. Student B said that it is
(1) an irrational number. Which student is correct? Explain your answer.

13. Write $\dfrac{5}{8}$ as a decimal and a percent.
(SB 5)

14. Measurement Order the lengths 1.25 yards, 3 feet, $1\dfrac{1}{3}$ yards from least to greatest.
(SB 1)

15. Write 7% as a fraction in simplest form and as a decimal.
(SB 5)

16. Formulate Write an equation using absolute values to represent the sentence.
(5) "The distance from -11 to 0 is 11."

17. **Multiple Choice** Which angle measures form an acute triangle?
(SB 13)

    A 45°, 45°, and 90°   **B** 40°, 110°, and 20°

    C 55°, 45°, and 80°   **D** 30°, 30°, and 120°

18. Estimate: $1.48 + $0.12 − $0.27.
(SB 8)

19. **Write** Use the definition of absolute value to write $|-5| = 5$ in words.
(5)

20. **Verify** True or False: A rectangle is a parallelogram. Explain your choice
(SB 14)

*21. **Geometry** The hypotenuse squared (c^2) can be determined by solving for $a^2 + b^2$ in
(4) the Pythagorean Theorem. Using the order of operations, decide if the expression $(a + b)$ should be determined before a^2?

*22. (**Weather**) One winter day the temperature rose 29°F from a low of −3°F in the
(5) morning. What was the day's high temperature?

*23. (**Football**) On the first down, the Tigers gained 8 yards. Then they were pushed back
(5) for a loss of $13\frac{1}{2}$ yards on the second down. Write and solve an addition problem to find the total number of yards lost or gained on the first two downs.

*24. **Multiple Choice** Which of these sets of numbers is closed under addition?
(5)

    A integers   **B** rational numbers

    C real numbers   **D** all of these

*25. **Multi-Step** Airplane A took off from an airport that is 43 feet below sea level, and
(5) then climbed 20,512 feet to its cruising altitude. Airplane B took off at the same time from an airport that was 1924 feet above sea level, and then climbed 18,527 feet to its cruising altitude. Which airplane is currently cruising at a higher altitude?

*26. (**Banking**) Martha had $500 in her checking account. She made a withdrawal of $34.65.
(5) Write and solve an addition problem to find Martha's balance after the withdrawal.

*27. **Multi-Step** A china cup-and-saucer set sells for $15.25 and a plate sells for $25.
(4) A woman buys 3 cup-and-saucer sets and 4 plates. If she pays a 5% sales tax, how much does she pay for her purchase?

    a. Determine how much the woman spends before sales tax. Use the expression $3 \cdot (\$15.25) + 4 \cdot (\$25)$ to solve.

    b. How much does she pay with sales tax included? Round your answer to the nearest hundredth. Use the expression $\$145.75 + (0.05) \cdot (\$145.75)$ to solve.

*28. (**Stocks**) Stock in the ABC Company fell 12.67 points on Monday and 31.51 points
(5) on Tuesday. Determine the total change in the stock for the two days.

*29. **Multiple Choice** Which expression correctly represents 1.6^5?
(3)

    A $1.6 \times 1.6 \times 1.6 \times 1.6 \times 1.6$ **B** $1.6 + 1.6 + 1.6 + 1.6 + 1.6$

    C $0.6 \times 0.6 \times 0.6 \times 0.6 \times 0.6 + 1$ **D** $1 \times 1 \times 1 \times 1 \times 1 + 0.6$

*30. (**Temperature**) At midnight the temperature was −7°F. By noon the temperature had
(5) risen 23°F. What was the temperature at noon?

Subtracting Real Numbers

Warm Up

1. Vocabulary The _____ of a number is the distance from the
$^{(1)}$ number to 0 on a number line.

Simplify.

2. $86.9 - 18.94$
$_{(SB\,2)}$

3. $\dfrac{1}{3} + \dfrac{4}{9}$
$_{(SB\,3)}$

4. $41.06 + 83.7$
$_{(SB\,2)}$

5. $\dfrac{5}{6} - \dfrac{5}{12}$
$_{(SB\,3)}$

New Concepts

Two numbers with the same absolute value but different signs are called **opposites.** Another name for the opposite of a number is **additive inverse.** The sum of a number and its opposite is 0.

Inverse Property of Addition
For every real number a, $a + (-a) = (-a) + a = 0$.
Example $5 + (-5) = 0$

Addition and subtraction are inverse operations. Subtracting a number is the same as adding the inverse of the number.

Rules for Subtracting Real Numbers
To subtract a number, add its inverse. Then follow the rules for adding real numbers.
Example $3 - 5 = 3 + (-5) = -2$

Example 1 Subtracting Real Numbers

Find each difference.

a. $(-12) - 21$

SOLUTION

$(-12) - 21$

$(-12) + (-21) = -33$

b. $(-19) - (-8)$

SOLUTION

$(-19) - (-8)$

$(-19) + (+8) = -11$

c. $3.2 - (-5.1)$

SOLUTION

$3.2 - (-5.1)$

$3.2 + (+5.1) = 8.3$

d. $\left(-\dfrac{3}{5}\right) - \left(-\dfrac{1}{5}\right)$

SOLUTION

$\left(-\dfrac{3}{5}\right) - \left(-\dfrac{1}{5}\right)$

$\left(-\dfrac{3}{5}\right) + \left(+\dfrac{1}{5}\right) = -\dfrac{2}{5}$

Math Reasoning

Analyze What is the meaning of $-(-8)$?

Online Connection
www.SaxonMathResources.com

Example 2 Determining Closure Over Subtraction

Determine whether each statement is true or false. Give a counterexample for false statements.

a. The set of integers is closed under subtraction.

SOLUTION

The statement is true because the difference of any two integers will be an integer.

b. The set of real numbers is closed under subtraction.

SOLUTION

The statement is true because the difference of any two real numbers will be a real number.

Example 3 Application: Dive Depth

Nayip collected a water sample at a depth of 23 meters from the surface. He descended another 12 meters to collect a plant sample. Where was Nayip in relation to the surface when he retrieved the plant sample?

SOLUTION

A depth of 23 meters can be written as (-23).

$(-23) - 12$

$= (-23) + (-12)$

$= -35$

Nayip was at 35 meters below the surface when he collected the plant sample.

Lesson Practice

Find each difference.
(Ex 1)

   a. $14 - (-22)$ **b.** $(-7) - 16$

   c. $(-23.4) - 18.72$ **d.** $\left(-\frac{2}{3}\right) - \left(-\frac{1}{6}\right)$

Determine whether each statement is true or false. Give a counterexample for false statements.
(Ex 2)

   e. The set of whole numbers is closed under subtraction.

   f. The set of rational numbers is closed under subtraction.

   g. On January 23, 1960, the Trieste dove to a record depth of 37,800 feet below sea level. The record set previously, on January 7th of the same year, was 13,800 feet less than the dive on January 23rd. What was the record set on January 7th in relation to sea level?
(Ex 3)

Add, subtract, multiply, or divide.

1. $5\frac{1}{3} \div 2\frac{1}{3}$
(SB 3)

2. $40\frac{1}{8} - 21\frac{1}{4}$
(SB 3)

3. $5\frac{2}{3} + 2\frac{5}{6} + (-2\frac{1}{6})$
(5)

4. $1\frac{2}{3} \div 1\frac{1}{4} \cdot 1\frac{1}{2}$
(SB 3)

5. $0.74 \div 0.2 \cdot 0.3$
(SB 2)

6. $5.4 \cdot 0.3 \div 0.4$
(SB 2)

7. $1.24 \cdot 0.2 \div 0.1$
(SB 2)

8. $112.4 \div 3.2$
(SB 2)

9. Find the prime factorization of 592.
(SB 12)

10. Find the prime factorization of 168.
(SB 12)

11. Model Display the following set of data in a line plot.
(SB 29)

$$8, 6, 9, 7, 5, 4, 6, 7, 9, 8, 5, 6, 6, 8$$

12. Write Use the divisibility test to determine if 2326 is divisible by 3. Explain your
(SB 4) answer.

13. Write 6% as a fraction in simplest form and as a decimal.
(SB 5)

14. Measurement Write 1.25 feet as a fraction in simplest form and compare it to $\frac{5}{3}$ feet.
(SB 5) Which is greater?

15. Write $\frac{3}{5}$ as a decimal and as a percent.
(SB 5)

16. Multiple Choice What is the value of the expression below?
(4)
$$\frac{(3 \cdot 20 + 2 \cdot 20) \cdot 6 - 20}{10^2}$$

   A 2.8   **B** 58   **C** -14 **D** 5.8

17. Simplify $\dfrac{(45 + 39 + 47 + 40 + 33 + 39 + 41)}{(2 \cdot 2)^2 - 12}$.
(4)

*18. Multiple Choice Which of these differences will be negative?
(6)
   A $-4.8 - (-5.2)$ **B** $4.8 - 5.2$

   C $4.8 - 3.2$ **D** $6.7 - (-7.8)$

*19. (Football) Ryan's varsity football team is on its own 25-yard line. The quarterback
(6) stumbles for a loss of 15 yards. What line is Ryan's varsity football team on now?

*20. Geometry If one angle in a triangle measures 105.5°, and another measures 38.2°,
(6) what is the measurement of the third angle? Use the expression $180 - 105.5 - 38.2$ to solve.

*21. (Temperature) On a winter day, a wind gust makes the temperature in Antarctica
(6) feel sixteen degrees colder than the actual temperature. If the temperature is $-5°C$, how cold did it feel?

*22. (**Consumer Math**) Leila issued a check for $149.99 and deposited $84.50 in her
(6) account. What is the net change in her account?

23. **Multiple Choice** Which triangle is an equiangular triangle?
(SB 13) **A** a triangle with angle measures of 45°, 45°, and 90°

B a triangle with angle measures of 60°, 60°, and 60°

C a triangle with angle measures of 55°, 35°, and 90°

D a triangle with angle measures of 30°, 30°, and 120°

24. (**Boating**) The tour boat can leave the dock only if the level of the lake is no more
(5) than 2 feet below normal. Before the recent rainfall, the level of the lake was
$5\frac{1}{3}$ feet below normal. After the recent rainfall, the level of the lake rose $3\frac{1}{4}$ feet.
Can the tour boat leave the dock? Explain.

*25. **Geometry** The triangle inequality is a theorem from geometry stating that for any
(5) two real numbers a and b, $|a + b| \leq |a| + |b|$. Verify the triangle inequality by
simplifying $|-18.5 + 4.75| \leq |-18.5| + |4.75|$.

*26. **Error Analysis** Two students solved this problem. Which student is correct? Explain
(5) the error.

The elevator started on the second floor and went up 8 floors, then down 11 floors
to the garage level, and then up 6 floors. Which floor is the elevator on now?

Student A	Student B
$2 + 8 + (-11) + 6 = 5$ The 5th floor	$2 + 8 - (-11) + 6 = 27$ The 27th floor

27. **Multi-Step** A bit is a binary digit and can have a value of either 0 or 1. A byte is a
(3) string of 8 bits.
   a. Write the number of bits in one byte as a power of 2.

   b. Write 32 as a power of 2.

   c. Write the number of bits in 32 bytes as a power of 2.

*28. $16c + (-4d) + \frac{8\pi}{15} + 21efg$
(2)
   a. Find the coefficients of the expression.

   b. Find the number of terms in the expression.

   c. **Justify** Rewrite the expression so that there are no parentheses. Justify your change.

*29. **Multiple Choice** What subset of numbers does the number $-9.0909090909\overline{09}$ belong to?
(1) **A** integers   **B** irrational numbers

   C natural numbers   **D** rational numbers

*30. (**Oceanography**) The Pacific Ocean has an average depth of 12,925 feet, while the
(6) Atlantic Ocean has as average depth of 11,730 feet. Find the difference in average
depths.

Simplifying and Comparing Expressions with Symbols of Inclusion

Warm Up

1. **Vocabulary** A _____ is used to represent an unknown number.
(2)

Simplify.

2. $-1.5 + 3^2 - (3 - 5)$
(4)

3. $12 - 4 \cdot 0.5 + (3.4 - 1.7)$
(4)

4. $\left(\dfrac{2}{3}\right)^2 - \left(\dfrac{1}{3}\right)^2 + \dfrac{5}{6}$
(4)

New Concepts

A mathematical expression can include numbers, variables, operations, and symbols of inclusion. Symbols of inclusion, such as fraction bars, absolute-value symbols, parentheses, braces, and brackets indicate which numbers, variables, and operations are parts of the same term. An example is shown below.

$$\left(\frac{2x}{3} + 3\frac{1}{5}\right) - 2y$$

The expression inside the parentheses is considered a single term. To simplify an expression with multiple symbols of inclusion, begin inside the innermost symbol of inclusion and work outward.

Example 1 Expressions with Absolute-Value Symbols and Parentheses

Simplify each expression.

a. $9 - |4 - 6|$

SOLUTION

$9 - |4 - 6|$	
$= 9 - |-2|$	Subtract inside absolute-value symbols.
$= 9 - 2$	Simplify the absolute value.
$= 7$	Subtract.

b. $5 \cdot 2 + [3 + (6 - 8)]$

SOLUTION Begin simplifying inside the innermost symbol of inclusion.

$5 \cdot 2 + [3 + (6 - 8)]$	
$= 5 \cdot 2 + [3 + (-2)]$	Subtract inside parentheses.
$= 5 \cdot 2 + 1$	Add inside brackets.
$= 10 + 1$	Multiply.
$= 11$	Add.

Math Language

( )	parentheses
[ ]	brackets
{ }	braces
$\frac{a}{b}$	fraction bar
$|x|$	absolute-value symbols

Online Connection
www.SaxonMathResources.com

It is important to follow the order of operations at all times, even when working inside symbols of inclusion.

Example 2 Simplifying Expressions with Brackets

Simplify.

$$3 + 5 \cdot [(9 - 3)^2 - 6]$$

SOLUTION

Begin inside the innermost symbol of inclusion and work outward.

$$3 + 5 \cdot [(9 - 3)^2 - 6]$$

$= 3 + 5 \cdot [6^2 - 6]$	Simplify inside the parentheses.
$= 3 + 5 \cdot [36 - 6]$	Evaluate the exponent.
$= 3 + 5 \cdot 30$	Subtract inside the brackets.
$= 3 + 150$	Multiply.
$= 153$	Add.

To simplify a rational expression such as $\frac{6 \cdot 3}{4 - 2}$, the numerator and denominator must be simplified first.

Example 3 Simplifying Expressions with Rational Numbers

Simplify. Justify each step.

$$\left[5 \cdot (4 + 2)^2\right] + \frac{4 \cdot 5}{2}$$

SOLUTION

Justify each step using the order of operations or mathematical properties.

$$\left[5 \cdot (4 + 2)^2\right] + \frac{4 \cdot 5}{2}$$

$= \left[5 \cdot (6)^2\right] + \frac{4 \cdot 5}{2}$	Add inside the parentheses.
$= \left[5 \cdot 36\right] + \frac{4 \cdot 5}{2}$	Simplify the exponent.
$= 180 + \frac{4 \cdot 5}{2}$	Multiply inside the brackets.
$= 180 + \frac{20}{2}$	Simplify the numerator.
$= 180 + 10$	Simplify the fraction.
$= 190$	Add.

Example 4 Compare Expressions with Symbols of Inclusion

Compare the expressions. Use $<$, $>$, or $=$.

$$12 + [5(7 - 5)^3 - 14] \;\bigcirc\; [(9 - 5)^2 + 7] - 3^3$$

SOLUTION Simplify each expression. Then compare.

$$12 + [5(7-5)^3 - 14] \qquad [(9-5)^2 + 7] - 3^3$$
$$= 12 + [5(2)^3 - 14] \qquad = [(4)^2 + 7] - 3^3$$
$$= 12 + [5 \cdot 8 - 14] \qquad = [16 + 7] - 3^3$$
$$= 12 + [40 - 14] \qquad = 23 - 3^3$$
$$= 12 + 26 \qquad = 23 - 27$$
$$= 38 \qquad = -4$$

Since $38 > -4$, $12 + [5(7-5)^3 - 14]$ $\bigcirc$ $[(9-5)^2 + 7] - 3^3$.

Graphing Calculator

Enter the expression $10 + 8 \div 2^2$ into your calculator. If the calculator follows the order of operations, the answer will be 12.

Example 5 **Application: Half Price Sale**

Beatrice wants to buy 3 DVDs marked $7 each and 4 CDs marked $12 each. Everything in the store is on sale for half off the marked price. Beatrice has $31.50 to spend and a coupon good for $1 off each CD. Use the expression below to determine if Beatrice has enough money to buy all the items she wants.

$$\$31.50 - \left[\frac{3 \cdot \$7}{2} + \frac{4 \cdot \$12}{2} - (4 \cdot \$1) \right]$$

SOLUTION Begin inside the innermost symbols of inclusion to simplify the expression.

$$\$31.50 - \left[\frac{3 \cdot \$7}{2} + \frac{4 \cdot \$12}{2} - (4 \cdot \$1) \right]$$

$$= \$31.50 - \left[\frac{3 \cdot \$7}{2} + \frac{4 \cdot \$12}{2} - \$4 \right] \qquad \text{Multiply inside the parentheses.}$$

$$= \$31.50 - \left[\frac{\$21}{2} + \frac{\$48}{2} - \$4 \right] \qquad \text{Simplify the numerators.}$$

$$= \$31.50 - [\$10.50 + \$24 - \$4] \qquad \text{Simplify the fractions.}$$

$$= \$31.50 - \$30.50 \qquad \text{Simplify inside the brackets.}$$

$$= \$1.00 \qquad \text{Subtract.}$$

Beatrice has enough money.

Lesson Practice

Simplify each expression.
(Ex 1)

a. $12 + |5 - 11|$

b. $5(8 + 4) \div (15 - 5 - 4)$

c. $5 + [6 \cdot (2^3 + 4)]$

d. **Justify** Simplify the expression. Justify each step.
(Ex 3)

$$4(1 + 2)^2 \div 6 + \frac{8 \cdot 3}{2}$$

e. Compare the expressions. Use <, >, or =.
(Ex 4)
$$(13 + 5) - [5 \cdot 2^2] \bigcirc [(7 + 11) - 5] - 2^3.$$

f. (Health) Body Mass Index (BMI) is the relation of weight to height. The
(Ex. 5) expression $\left(\dfrac{W}{H^2}\right) \cdot 703$, where W is weight in pounds and H is height in
inches, is used to calculate BMI. Explain the steps that are necessary to
simplify this expression.

Practice   Distributed and Integrated

Add, subtract, multiply, or divide.

1. $(5 + 2)^2 - 50$
(4)

2. $(3 - 5) + 7^2$
(4)

3. $3\dfrac{1}{3} - 1\dfrac{1}{6} - 5\dfrac{1}{4}$
(6)

4. $2\dfrac{1}{3} \cdot 3\dfrac{1}{4} \cdot 1\dfrac{1}{2}$
(SB 3)

5. $(0.56 + 0.3) \cdot 0.2$
(4)

6. $3.25 \cdot 0.4 + 0.1$
(4)

7. $1.2 \div 0.1 \div 0.1$
(SB 2)

8. $20.2 \cdot 0.1 \cdot 0.1$
(SB 2)

9. Verify True or False: All whole numbers are counting numbers. If true, explain
(1) your answer. If false, give a counterexample.

10. The set $\{..., -3, -2, -1, 0, 1, 2, 3, ...\}$ represents which set of numbers?
(1)

11. Justify True or False: An obtuse triangle has two obtuse angles. Explain your choice.
(SB 13)

12. Find the prime factorization of 207.
(SB 12)

13. Find the prime factorization of 37.
(SB 12)

14. Write Use the divisibility test to determine if 10,048 is divisible by 8. Explain.
(SB 4)

15. Write 0.345 as a fraction in simplest form and as a percent.
(SB 5)

16. Write 0.07% as a fraction in simplest form and as a decimal.
(SB 5)

*17. Evaluate $(|-3| \cdot 4) + \left[\left(\dfrac{1}{2} + \dfrac{1}{4}\right) \div \dfrac{1}{3}\right].$
(7)

*18. Compare: $\dfrac{1}{3} + \dfrac{1}{5} \cdot \dfrac{2}{15} \bigcirc \left(\dfrac{1}{3} + \dfrac{1}{5}\right) \cdot \dfrac{2}{15}.$
(7)

*19. (Temperature) The following two formulas are used to convert degrees Celsius (°C) to
(7) degrees Fahrenheit (°F) and vise versa: $C = \dfrac{5}{9}(F - 32)$ and $F = \dfrac{9}{5}C + 32$. Explain
how the equations are different.

*20. (Fencing) The diagram represents the fencing around a backyard. The fence
(7) is formed with parallel lines and a half-circle. Write and solve an equation
to determine how many feet of fencing are needed. Round the answer to the
nearest tenth.

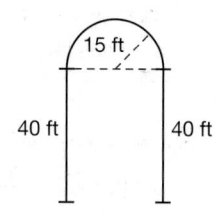

*21. Multiple Choice Simplify $[(10-8)^2-(-1)]+(5-3)$.
(7)
  A -38 **B** 7 **C** -80 **D** 37

*22. (**Manufacturing**) A company produces two different types of 6-sided boxes. Box A is
(7) 12 inches long, 12 inches wide, and 12 inches tall. Box B is 16 inches long,
16 inches wide, and 6.75 inches tall. Both boxes have the same volume, but the
company wants to know which box uses less material to produce.

  a. Write and solve an expression to find the surface area of Box A.

  b. Write and solve an expression to find the surface area of Box B.

  c. Compare the box sizes. Which box uses less material?

*23. Multi-Step A ball is dropped from a height of 25.6 feet. After it hits the ground, it
(6) bounces to 12.8 feet and falls back to the ground. Next it bounces to 6.4 feet and
falls back to the ground. Then it bounces to 3.2 feet and falls back to the ground.

  a. Find the difference in heights between each consecutive bounce.

  b. If the pattern continues, will the ball ever stop bouncing? Explain.

24. Geometry What is the perimeter of the rectangle?
(6)

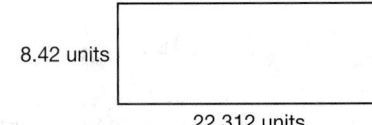

8.42 units

22.312 units

25. Measurement A valley is 250 below sea level and a small hill is 78 feet above sea
(5) level. Solve $|-250|+78$ to determine the distance from the bottom of the valley
to the top of the hill.

*26. (**Transportation**) In the last hour, 7 planes have landed at the airport and 11 planes
(5) have taken off. Use addition to find the change in the total number of planes at
the airport in the last hour.

27. Error Analysis The temperature in the morning was $-18°F$. It increased by $5°$ by noon
(4) and dropped $10°$ in the evening. Two students determined the temperature in the
evening. Which student is correct? Explain the error.

Student A	Student B
$-18+5+10=-3$	$-18+5+(-10)=-23$

*28. (**Meteorology**) The water level of the reservoir in Purcellville, Virginia was 2 feet
(6) below normal. After a heavy rainstorm, the water level increased to 5 feet above
normal. Write and solve a subtraction problem to find the change in the water
level caused by the rainstorm.

29. Multiple Choice Which term in the expression $\frac{\sqrt{9}ny}{nx}+a^2-\frac{n}{4}+\frac{3\pi}{8}$ contains an
(1) irrational constant?

  A $\dfrac{\sqrt{9}ny}{nx}$ **B** $\dfrac{3\pi}{8}$ **C** $\dfrac{n}{4}$ **D** a^2

*30. Geometry The measure of each interior angle of a hexagon is given by the
(7) expression $\dfrac{180(6-2)°}{6}$. What is the measure of an interior angle of a
hexagon?

Using Unit Analysis to Convert Measures

1. Vocabulary The amount of space a solid figure occupies is called
(SB 26)   the _____ (*area, volume*).

Simplify.

2. $\dfrac{7}{12} \cdot \dfrac{36}{49}$
(SB 3)

3. $\dfrac{8}{9} \cdot \dfrac{15}{36}$
(SB 3)

4. $\dfrac{2}{5} \cdot \dfrac{15}{16} \cdot \dfrac{6}{7}$
(SB 3)

5. $\dfrac{12}{13} \cdot \dfrac{1}{4} \cdot \dfrac{39}{48}$
(SB 3)

New Concepts

Unit analysis is a process for converting measures into different units. A unit ratio, or conversion factor, compares 2 measures that name the same amount.

$$\frac{12 \text{ in.}}{1 \text{ ft}} \qquad \frac{1 \text{ m}}{100 \text{ cm}} \qquad \frac{3 \text{ ft}}{1 \text{ yd}}$$

Since the amounts used in a unit ratio are equal to each other, a unit ratio is always equal to 1. Since the product of 1 and a number is that number, a unit ratio multiplied by a measure will always name the same amount.

> **Example 1** **Converting Units of Length**
>
> A cheetah ran at a rate of 105,600 yards per hour. How fast did the cheetah run in miles per hour?
>
> **SOLUTION** Find a unit ratio and multiply.

Hint

A mile is equal to 1760 yards.

$\dfrac{105{,}600 \text{ yd}}{1 \text{ hour}} = \dfrac{? \text{ mi}}{1 \text{ hour}}$ Identify known and missing information.

$105{,}600 \text{ yd} \rightarrow ? \text{ mi}$ Write the conversion.

$1 \text{ mi} = 1{,}760 \text{ yd}$ Equate units.

$\dfrac{1 \text{ mi}}{1760 \text{ yd}}$ Write a unit ratio.

$\dfrac{105{,}600 \text{ yd}}{1 \text{ hr}} \cdot \dfrac{1 \text{ mi}}{1760 \text{ yd}}$ Write the multiplication sentence.

$= \dfrac{\overset{60}{\cancel{105{,}600}} \text{ yd}}{1 \text{ hr}} \cdot \dfrac{1 \text{ mi}}{\underset{1}{\cancel{1760 \text{ yd}}}}$ Cancel out common factors.

$= \dfrac{60 \text{ mi}}{1 \text{ hr}}$ Multiply.

$\dfrac{105{,}600 \text{ yd}}{1 \text{ hr}} = \dfrac{60 \text{ mi}}{1 \text{ hr}}$ Write the ratio of miles per hour.

Online Connection
www.SaxonMathResources.com

The cheetah ran at a rate of 60 miles per hour.

If a measure of length changes, then the unit analysis occurs in one dimension. If a measure of area changes, the units for the dimensions of both length and width must change.

Draw two congruent squares with side lengths of 3 inches on a sheet of paper. Label the sides of the first square 1 yard. Divide both the length and width of the second square into 3 equal sections. This will divide the square into 9 congruent smaller squares. Label the sides of the second square 3 feet.

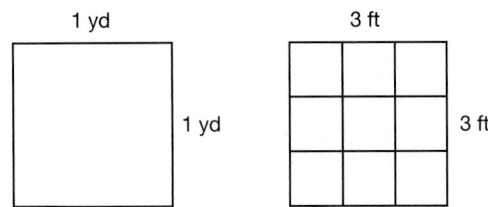

a. What is the area of the first square? Show your calculation.

b. What is the area of the second square? Show your calculation.

c. Write two unit ratios for converting between feet and yards.

d. Which unit ratio should be used for converting yards to feet? Explain your choice.

e. **Justify** Use a unit ratio to convert the area of the first square into square feet. Show your calculation.

f. **Write** Why is it necessary to multiply by the unit ratio twice to convert square yards to square feet?

Extend the example of the area of squares to the volume of cubes. Draw two cubes, one with dimensions of 1 yard and one with dimensions of 3 feet.

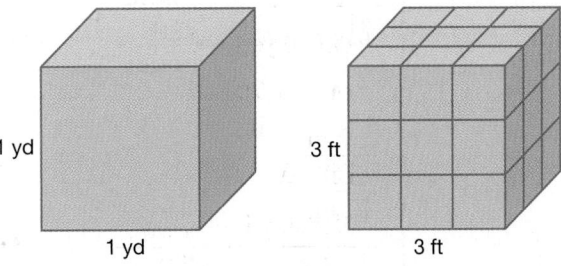

Math Reasoning

Write How could a single unit ratio be used to perform the area conversion?

g. What is the volume of the first cube? Show your calculation.

h. What is the volume of the second cube? Show your calculation.

i. **Justify** Use a unit ratio to convert the volume of the first cube into cubic feet. Show your calculation.

j. **Write** Why is it necessary to multiply by the unit ratio three times to convert cubic yards to cubic feet?

Example 2 Converting Units of Area

A gym measures 8.5 meters by 14 meters. The owner bought mats to cover the floor. Each mat is 110 centimeters square. If 95 mats were purchased, are there enough mats to cover the floor?

SOLUTION Find the area and convert the unit of measure.

$8.5 \text{ m} \cdot 14 \text{ m} = 119 \text{ m}^2$	Find the area of the room.
$119 \text{ m}^2 \rightarrow ? \text{ cm}^2$	Write the conversion.
$1 \text{ m} = 100 \text{ cm}$	Equate units.
$\dfrac{100 \text{ cm}}{1 \text{ m}}$	Write a unit ratio.
$119 \text{ m} \cdot \text{m} \cdot \dfrac{100 \text{ cm}}{1 \text{ m}} \cdot \dfrac{100 \text{ cm}}{1 \text{ m}}$	Write the multiplication sentence.
$= 119 \, \cancel{\text{m}} \cdot \cancel{\text{m}} \cdot \dfrac{100 \text{ cm}}{1 \, \cancel{\text{m}}} \cdot \dfrac{100 \text{ cm}}{1 \, \cancel{\text{m}}}$	Cancel out common factors.
$= \dfrac{119 \cdot 100 \text{ cm} \cdot 100 \text{ cm}}{1} = 1{,}190{,}000 \text{ cm}^2$	Multiply.
$95(110 \text{ cm} \cdot 110 \text{ cm}) = 1{,}149{,}500 \text{ cm}^2$	Find the area of 95 mats.
$1{,}149{,}500 \text{ cm}^2 < 1{,}190{,}000 \text{ cm}^2$	Compare the areas.

The area covered by 95 mats is less than the area of the floor, so there are not enough mats to cover the floor.

> **Math Reasoning**
>
> Each mat is 110 **centimeters square.** This means that the length and width are 110 centimeters each.

Example 3 Application: Converting Units of Volume

A hose with a flow rate of 41,472 cubic inches per hour is filling up a pool. The volume of the pool is 1,104 cubic feet. How many hours will it take to fill the pool?

SOLUTION Find the volume and convert the unit of measure.

$\dfrac{41{,}472 \text{ in}^3}{1 \text{ hour}} \rightarrow \dfrac{? \text{ ft}^3}{1 \text{ hour}}$	Identify known and missing information.
$1 \text{ ft} = 12 \text{ in.}$	Equate units.
$\dfrac{1 \text{ ft}}{12 \text{ in.}}$	Write a unit ratio.
$\dfrac{41{,}472 \text{ in.} \cdot \text{in.} \cdot \text{in.}}{1 \text{ hr}} \cdot \dfrac{1 \text{ ft}}{12 \text{ in.}} \cdot \dfrac{1 \text{ ft}}{12 \text{ in.}} \cdot \dfrac{1 \text{ ft}}{12 \text{ in.}}$	Write the multiplication sentence.
$= \dfrac{\overset{24}{\cancel{41{,}472}} \, \cancel{\text{in.}} \cdot \cancel{\text{in.}} \cdot \cancel{\text{in.}}}{1 \text{ hr}} \cdot \dfrac{1 \text{ ft}}{\underset{1}{\cancel{12 \text{ in.}}}} \cdot \dfrac{1 \text{ ft}}{\underset{1}{\cancel{12 \text{ in.}}}} \cdot \dfrac{1 \text{ ft}}{\underset{1}{\cancel{12 \text{ in.}}}}$	Cancel out common factors.
$= \dfrac{24 \text{ ft} \cdot \text{ft} \cdot \text{ft}}{1 \text{ hr}} = \dfrac{24 \text{ ft}^3}{1 \text{ hr}}$	Multiply.
$1{,}104 \div 24 = 46 \text{ hours}$	

It will take 46 hours to fill the pool.

> **Math Reasoning**
>
> **Analyze** Compare the process of converting feet to inches with the process of converting feet per minute to inches per minute.

Unit analysis can be used for more than just converting units of length. It can also be used to convert units of mass, density, temperature, capacity, or even money. In economics, the value of money is defined by what people are willing to exchange for it. This means that the value of a currency can change relative to the value of other currencies. An exchange-rate listing shows what a currency is worth compared to other currencies at that moment.

Example 4 Foreign Travel: Converting Units of Currency

Jared and his family are going on a vacation to Europe. He takes \$225 with him. He needs to exchange this amount for its equivalent value in euros. If the current exchange rate is 1 euro = \$1.36, what is the value of Jared's \$225 in euros?

SOLUTION

Convert the unit of measure.

$225 \text{ dollars} \rightarrow ? \text{ euros}$ Write the conversion.

$1 \text{ euro} = 1.36 \text{ dollars}$ Equate units.

$\dfrac{1 \text{ euro}}{1.36 \text{ dollars}}$ Write a unit ratio.

$225 \text{ dollars} \cdot \dfrac{1 \text{ euro}}{1.36 \text{ dollars}}$ Write the multiplication sentence.

$= 165.44 \text{ euros}$ Multiply and cancel.

Check Since a euro is worth more than a dollar, Jared should have fewer euros than dollars after the exchange.

$225 > 165.44$ The answer is reasonable.

Hint

Choose a unit conversion factor that cancels the units you want to change and replaces them with the units you want.

Lesson Practice

a. A Mourning Dove can reach speeds up to 35 miles per hour. How fast is this in feet per hour?
(Ex 1)

b. An interior wall measures 4.5 yards by 3.25 yards. What is the size of the wall in square feet?
(Ex 2)

c. Della has a small bag containing 50 cubic centimeters of potting soil. Her planter has a volume of 46,300 cubic millimeters. Does Della have enough soil to fill the planter? Explain.
(Ex 3)

d. Arthur just returned from London. He has 16 British pounds to convert to American dollars. If the exchange rate is 1 pound = \$2.016, what is the value of Arthur's 16 pounds in dollars?
(Ex 4)

Add, subtract, multiply, or divide.

1. $4\frac{1}{3} \div 1\frac{1}{3} + 3\frac{1}{3}$
(4)

2. $2\frac{3}{8} - 1\frac{3}{4} \div 1\frac{1}{2}$
(4)

3. $2\frac{2}{3} + 1\frac{5}{6} - 6\frac{3}{4}$
(6)

4. $3\frac{1}{3} \div 1\frac{1}{4} \cdot \frac{1}{2}$
(4)

5. $0.37 \div 0.2 \cdot 0.1$
(6)

6. $1.74 \cdot 0.3 \div 0.2$
(SB 2)

7. Given the sets $A = \{1, 3, 5\}$, $B = \{0, 2, 4, 6\}$, and $C = \{1, 2, 3, 4\}$, are the
(1) following statements true or false?

   a. $A \cup B = \{0, 1, 2, 3, 4, 5, 6\}$

   b. $A \cap B = \{0, 1, 2, 3, 4, 5, 6\}$

   c. $B \cup C = \{2, 4\}$

   d. $A \cap C = \{1, 3\}$

8. Compare the expressions using $<$, $>$, or $=$. Explain.
(4)

$$8^2 \div 4 - 6^2 \bigcirc (6 \cdot 7 \cdot 5) \div 6 - 15$$

9. Draw a line plot for the frequency table.
(SB 29)

Number	2	3	4	5	6	7
Frequency	4	3	2	1	4	3

10. Subtract $78\frac{2}{5} - 14\frac{7}{10}$.
(SB 2)

11. Find the prime factorization of 484.
(SB 12)

12. Write Use the divisibility test to determine if 22,993 is divisible by 5. Explain your
(SB 4) answer.

13. Write 125% as a fraction in simplest form and as a decimal.
(SB 5)

14. Convert 105 kilometers per hour to kilometers per minute.
(8)

*15. Convert 74 square meters to square centimeters.
(8)

*16. (Camping) Norman's camping tent has a volume of 72,576 cubic inches. What is the
(8) volume of the tent in cubic feet?

17. Multiple Choice Which of these differences will be positive?
(6)

   A $-\frac{1}{2} - \frac{1}{8}$
      B $\frac{9}{12} - 1$

   C $\frac{5}{7} - \frac{3}{10}$
      D $-\frac{14}{15} - \left(\frac{4}{15}\right)$

18. Error Analysis Two students used unit analysis to convert a measurement of length.
(8) Which student is correct? Explain the error.

Student A	Student B
1 cm = 10 mm 5540 mm = 5540 mm × $\frac{1 \text{ cm}}{10 \text{ mm}}$ 5540 mm = 554 cm	1 cm = 10 mm 5540 mm = 5540 mm × $\frac{10 \text{ mm}}{1 \text{ cm}}$ 5540 mm = 55400 cm

*19. Multiple Choice Which one of the following ratios can be used to convert 120 cm
(8) into an equivalent measure in inches? (Hint: There are 2.54 cm in one inch.)

A $\frac{2.54 \text{ cm}}{1 \text{ in.}}$

B $\frac{1 \text{ in.}}{2.54 \text{ cm}}$

C $\frac{2.54 \text{ cm}}{1 \text{ in.}} \cdot \frac{2.54 \text{ cm}}{1 \text{ in.}}$

D $\frac{1 \text{ in.}}{2.54 \text{ cm}} \cdot \frac{1 \text{ in.}}{2.54 \text{ in.}}$

*20. (Weather Forecasting) One knot is exactly 1.852 kilometers per hour. The highest
(8) wind gust for the day was measured at 38 knots.

a. How many km/hr was the recorded wind gust? (Hint: 1 knot = 1.852 km/hr)

b. How many mph was the recorded wind gust? (Hint: 1 mi = 1.609 km)

*21. Multi-Step How can you find the area of the triangle in square inches?
(8)

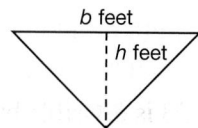

a. Write a formula for computing the area of the triangle in units of square feet.

b. Write a new formula that computes the area of the triangle in units of square inches.

c. What is the area of the triangle in square inches if $b = 3$ ft and $h = 2.2$ ft?

*22. (Chemistry) Water has a density of 1 gram per cubic centimeter. What is the density
(8) of water in grams per cubic inch?

*23. Justify True or False: A right triangle has one right angle, one obtuse angle, and
(SB 13) one acute angle. If false, explain why.

24. Error Analysis Student A and Student B simplified the expression $\frac{24}{8} + (2 + 4)^2$.
(7) Which student is correct? Explain the error.

Student A	Student B
$\frac{24}{8} + (2+4)^2$	$\frac{24}{8} + (2+4)^2$
$3 + 6^2$	$3 + (2 + 16)$
$3 + 36 = 39$	$3 + 18 = 21$

25. Geometry A square pyramid has a base with edges of 8 inches and a height of
(7) 12 inches.

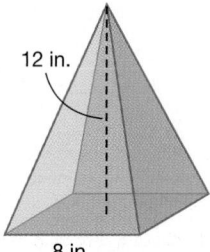

12 in.

8 in.

a. Use the following formula to find the volume: $V = \frac{1}{3}s^2h$.

b. Analyze Which term did you simplify first? Why?

*26. (Economics) Use the table of the Profit and Loss Report of ABC Company. What
(6) was the total profit or loss for the year? [( ) indicates a loss.]

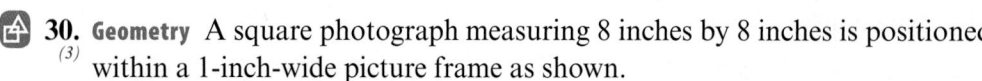

	1st Quarter	2nd Quarter	3rd Quarter	4th Quarter
Profit or Loss	$6 million	($3.5 million)	($2 million)	$5 million

*27. Multi-Step Two groups of students measured the length of a tabletop. Group A's
(5) measurement was $56\frac{3}{4}$ inches. Group B's measurement was $57\frac{3}{4}$ inches. If the
actual length of the tabletop was $57\frac{1}{2}$ inches, which group's measurement had the
smaller error?

28. Error Analysis Two students simplified an expression containing an exponent.
(3) Which student is correct? Explain the error.

Student A	Student B
$b^2 \cdot c^2 \cdot c \cdot b^2 \cdot b =$	$b^2 \cdot c^2 \cdot c \cdot b^2 \cdot b =$
$b^2 \cdot b^2 \cdot b \cdot c^2 \cdot c = b^5c^3$	$b^2 \cdot b^2 \cdot b \cdot c^2 \cdot c = b^4c^2$

29. (Speed) A giraffe can run 32 miles per hour. What is the speed in feet per hour?
(8)

30. Geometry A square photograph measuring 8 inches by 8 inches is positioned
(3) within a 1-inch-wide picture frame as shown.

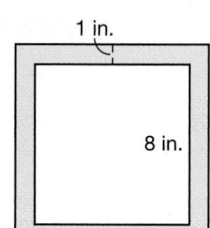

1 in.

8 in.

a. What is the area of the photograph?

b. What is the combined area of the photograph and frame?

c. What is the area of the frame alone?

d. If the 1-inch-wide frame is replaced with a 2-inch-wide frame, how much more
wall space will be needed to hang the framed photograph?

LESSON
9

Evaluating and Comparing
Algebraic Expressions

Warm Up

1. Vocabulary When two numbers are divided, the result is called
(2) the _____. (*quotient, product*).

Simplify.

2. $x^5 b^2 \cdot 3b^3 x$
(3)

3. $\dfrac{4^3}{2^3} + 7^2$
(4)

4. $\dfrac{5^3}{3^2 + 4^2}$
(4)

5. $32 \div \left[2 \cdot (8 - 7)\right]$
(7)

New Concepts

Any expression containing only numbers and operations is a **numeric expression**. An **algebraic expression** is an expression with variables and/or numbers that uses operations (e.g., $+$, $-$, $\times$, or $\div$). An algebraic expression is also called a variable expression.

Math Language

Evaluate means to substitute values for the variables and to simplify using the order of operations.

Example 1 **Evaluating Algebraic Expressions**

Evaluate the expression when $x = 3$ and $a = 1$.

$3x - 4x + ax$

SOLUTION Substitute 3 for x and 1 for a in the expression. Then simplify.

$3x - 4x + ax$

$= 3 \cdot 3 - 4 \cdot 3 + 1 \cdot 3$

$= 9 - 12 + 3$

$= 0$

When the variables in algebraic expressions have exponents, it is helpful to write the value in parentheses.

Example 2 **Evaluating Algebraic Expressions with Exponents**

Evaluate the expression for $y = 2$ and $z = 4$.

$3(z - y)^2 - 4y^3$

SOLUTION Substitute 2 for y and 4 for z in the expression. Then simplify.

$3(z - y)^2 + 4y^3$

$= 3(4 - 2)^2 - 4(2)^3$

$= 3(2)^2 - 4(2)^3$

$= 3 \cdot 4 - 4(8)$

$= 12 - (32)$

$= -20$

Online Connection
www.SaxonMathResources.com

Two algebraic expressions are equivalent if they can be simplified to the same value. For example, $2 \cdot 2 - 1$ is equivalent to $15 \div 5$. Both expressions have a simplified value of 3.

Example 3 Comparing Algebraic Expressions

Compare the expressions when $a = 4$ and $b = 3$. Use $<$, $>$, or $=$.

$$3a^2 + 2b - 4b^3 \bigcirc 2a^2b^2$$

SOLUTION Simplify the expression on the left and then compare.

$$
\begin{array}{ll}
3a^2 + 2b - 4b^3 & 2a^2b^2 \\
3(4)^2 + 2(3) - 4(3)^3 & 2(4)^2(3)^2 \\
= 3(16) + 2(3) - 4(27) & = 2(16)(9) \\
= 48 + 6 - 108 & = 288 \\
= 54 - 108 & \\
= -54 &
\end{array}
$$

Since $-54 < 288$, $3a^2 + 2b - 4b^3 < 2a^2b^2$ when $a = 4$ and $b = 3$.

Many real-world situations can be described using math. Algebraic expressions can be used to represent relationships between quantities.

Example 4 Application: Phone Charges

A cell phone company charges a $20 monthly fee and then 45 cents per minute. The company uses the expression $20 + 0.45m$ to find the total amount to charge for each month. How much would the company charge for 200 minutes?

SOLUTION Substitute 200 for m in the expression and simplify.

$$
\begin{aligned}
& 20 + 0.45m \\
&= 20 + 0.45(200) \\
&= 20 + 90 \\
&= 110
\end{aligned}
$$

The cell phone company would charge $110.

> **Math Reasoning**
>
> **Analyze** In the expression $20 + 0.45m$, what does the variable m represent?

Lesson Practice

Evaluate each expression for the given values.

a. $3x - 4b + 2bx$; $x = 10$, $b = 2$
(Ex 1)

b. $2ab - 4a^2 + 10$; $a = -1$, $b = 8$
(Ex 2)

c. Compare the expressions when $x = 2$ and $y = 5$. Use $<$, $>$, or $=$.
(Ex 3)
$$(6x^2 + y^3) - 3x^6 \bigcirc 8x^4 - y^3$$

d. (**Climate**) The lowest recorded temperature is $-89.4°C$ in Antarctica.
(Ex 4) The expression $\frac{9}{5}C + 32$ can be used to convert Celsius measurements to Fahrenheit. What is the lowest recorded temperature in degrees Fahrenheit?

Add, subtract, multiply, or divide.

1. $4\frac{1}{3} \div 2\frac{1}{3}$
(SB 3)

2. $42\frac{3}{8} - 21\frac{3}{4}$
(SB 3)

3. $1\frac{2}{3} + 2\frac{5}{6}$
(SB 3)

4. $2\frac{2}{3} \div 1\frac{3}{4}$
(SB 3)

5. $0.75 \div 0.2$
(SB 2)

6. $1.74 \div 0.3$
(SB 2)

7. $1.25 \cdot 0.2$
(SB 2)

8. 12.2×3.2
(SB 2)

9. Verify True or False: A square is a rhombus. Explain your choice.
(SB 14)

10. Simplify $4[(6-4)^3 - 5]$.
(7)

11. Convert 1.86 km^2 to m^2.
(8)

*12. Evaluate the expression $14c + 28 - 12cd$ for the given values $c = 4$ and $d = 5$.
(9)

13. A straight angle measures _____.
(SB 13)

14. Find the prime factorization of 125.
(SB 12)

*15. Find the value of the expression $\frac{t-36}{36} + l$ if $t = 72$ and $l = 1$.
(9)

16. Multiple Choice Evaluate the expression $14 + \frac{36}{9} \cdot (2 + 5)$.
(7)

   A 126   **B** 21   **C** 42   **D** 140

17. Simplify $(3 + 12) + (|-4| - 2)^3 + 1$.
(7)

*18. (**Flight**) A rocket is fired upward at an initial speed of 112 feet per second (ft/sec). It
(9) travels at a speed of $112 - 32t$ ft/sec, where t is the flight time in seconds.
   a. What is the rocket's speed after 1 second?
   b. What is the rocket's speed after 2 seconds?

*19. (**Canoeing**) Rachel wants to rent a canoe for 3 hours. Use the expression
(9) $\$6.50 + \$1.75h$, where h represents the number of hours, to calculate the cost
of renting the canoe.

*20. Error Analysis Two students were asked to evaluate $\frac{y^2}{-x}$ when x is 5 and y is -5.
(9) Which student is correct? Explain the error.

Student A	Student B
$\frac{y^2}{-x} = \frac{-5^2}{-(5)} = \frac{-25}{-5} = 5$	$\frac{y^2}{-x} = \frac{(-5)^2}{-(5)} = \frac{25}{-5} = -5$

*21. Data Analysis The variance of a set of data can be found with the expression $\frac{s}{n}$,
(9) where s is the sum of the squared deviation and n is the total number of data items
in the set. What is the variance for a set of data with 12 items and a sum of the
squared deviations equal to 30?

*22. **(Sports)** In volleyball, the statistic for total blocks at the net is calculated with the
(9) expression $s + 0.5a$, where s is the number of solo blocks and a is the number
of assisted blocks. What is the total-blocks statistic for a player who has 80 solo
blocks and 53 assisted blocks?

23. **Write** Use the divisibility test to determine if 224 is divisible by 6. Explain
(SB 4) your answer.

24. Write 35.2% as a fraction in simplest form and as a decimal.
(SB 5)

*25. **Multi-Step** The rectangle has dimensions measured in centimeters. What
(8) is the ratio of the area of the rectangle in centimeters to the area of the
rectangle in millimeters?

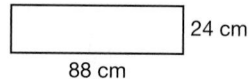

a. Calculate the area of the rectangle.

b. Find the area of the rectangle in square millimeters.

c. Find the ratio of square centimeters to square millimeters for the rectangle.

*26. **Geometry** A right circular cylinder has a base radius of 56 mm and a height of
(8) 128 mm. What is its volume in cubic centimeters? Round the answer to the
nearest hundredth. Use 3.14 for π.

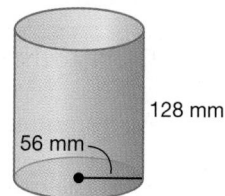

27. **(Loans)** The formula for long-term loans is $F = P(1 + i)^{n \div 12}$, where F is the future
(7) value of money, P is the present value, i is the interest rate, and n is the length of
time the money is borrowed in months. When solving this equation for F, what
step would you perform after adding 1 and i?

28. **(Golf)** Below is Rickie's golf score for two golf tournaments. What is the difference
(6) in his final score for the 1st and 2nd tournament?

1st Tournament	1	−2	−3	2
2nd Tournament	−2	−1	1	−1

29. **Error Analysis** Two students were asked to evaluate $(30 − 10)^2$. Student A answered
(4) 400, and Student B answered −70. Which student is correct? Explain the error.

Student A	Student B
$(30 - 10)^2$	$(30 - 10)^2$
$= 20^2$	$= (30 - 10 \cdot 10)$
$= 400$	$= (30 - 100)$
	$= -70$

*30. **(Typing)** Jared can type 35 words per minute. Use the expression $35m$ to find the
(9) number of words he can type in 15 minutes.

Adding and Subtracting Real Numbers

Warm Up

1. Vocabulary Any real number that cannot be written as a quotient of
(1) integers is called a(n) _____ number.

Simplify.

2. $(25 \div 5) - (30 \div 10)$
(4)

3. $-4 + (-9) + (-6)$
(5)

4. $(2.45 + 5.75) - (4.85 - 3.75)$
(4)

5. $(j^4 k^5)(4kj^2)(3k^3)$
(3)

New Concepts

When solving a problem containing addition and subtraction of signed numbers, begin by writing the problem as addition only. Next, group and add the terms with like signs. Then add the terms with unlike signs.

Example 1 **Adding and Subtracting Fractions and Decimals**

Simplify.

a. $-\dfrac{1}{5} + \dfrac{3}{5} - \dfrac{2}{5} - \left(-\dfrac{4}{5}\right)$

SOLUTION

$-\dfrac{1}{5} + \dfrac{3}{5} - \dfrac{2}{5} - \left(-\dfrac{4}{5}\right)$

$= -\dfrac{1}{5} + \dfrac{3}{5} + \left(-\dfrac{2}{5}\right) + \dfrac{4}{5}$ Write the problem as addition.

$= -\dfrac{1}{5} + \left(-\dfrac{2}{5}\right) + \dfrac{3}{5} + \dfrac{4}{5}$ Group the terms with like signs.

$= -\dfrac{3}{5} + \dfrac{7}{5}$ Add numbers with like signs.

$= -\dfrac{4}{5}$ Add.

b. $3.16 + (-1.22) - 4.73 + 5.6$

SOLUTION

$3.16 + (-1.22) - 4.73 + 5.6$

$= 3.16 + (-1.22) + (-4.73) + 5.6$ Write the problem as addition.

$= 3.16 + 5.6 + (-1.22) + (-4.73)$ Group the terms with the same signs.

$= 8.76 + (-5.95)$ Add numbers with like signs.

$= 2.81$ Add.

Hint

Use the rules below for adding integers.

1. Like signs: Add and keep the sign.

2. Unlike signs: Subtract and keep the sign of the greater absolute value.

Online Connection
www.SaxonMathResources.com

Order the numbers from least to greatest.

$$\frac{7}{8}, -2, 0.125, \frac{1}{2}$$

SOLUTION

Use a number line to order the numbers. Place each number on the number line.

To order these numbers from least to greatest, read the numbers on the number line from left to right.

$$-2, 0.125, \frac{1}{2}, \frac{7}{8}$$

Complete the comparison. Use $<$, $>$, or $=$.

$$\frac{3}{8} + \left(-\frac{5}{8}\right) - \frac{1}{8} \bigcirc -2.75 + 6.25 - 3.75$$

SOLUTION

Simplify each expression. Then compare.

$$\frac{3}{8} + \left(-\frac{5}{8}\right) - \frac{1}{8}$$

$$= \frac{3}{8} + \left(-\frac{5}{8}\right) + \left(-\frac{1}{8}\right)$$

$$= \frac{3}{8} + \left(-\frac{6}{8}\right)$$

$$= -\frac{3}{8}$$

$$-2.75 + 6.25 - 3.75$$
$$= -2.75 + 6.25 + (-3.75)$$
$$= -2.75 + (-3.75) + 6.25$$
$$= -6.50 + 6.25$$
$$= -0.25$$

> **Hint**
>
> Convert $-\frac{3}{8}$ to a decimal or -0.25 to a fraction to make comparing the values easier.

Since $-\frac{3}{8} < -0.25$, $\frac{3}{8} + \left(-\frac{5}{8}\right) - \frac{1}{8} \;\textless\; -2.75 + 6.25 - 3.75$.

Carly invested $250 in two accounts. The table below shows the ending balance per quarter.

	1st Quarter	2nd Quarter	3rd Quarter	4th Quarter
Investment A	$255.75	$258.81	$260.25	$262.99
Investment B	$260.66	$274.22	$268.92	$290.07

a. Which investment grew more?

SOLUTION

Find the differences and compare.

Investment A	Investment B
$262.99 − $250 = $12.99	$290.07 − $250 = $40.07

Investment B grew more.

b. In which quarter did Investment B grow the most?

SOLUTION

$260.66 − $250.00 = $10.66

$274.22 − $260.66 = $13.56

$268.92 − $274.22 = −$5.30

$290.07 − $268.92 = $21.15

The greatest difference is $21.15, which occurred in the 4th quarter.

Lesson Practice

Simplify.

(Ex 1)
a. $\dfrac{4}{9} + \dfrac{2}{9} - \dfrac{5}{9}$ **b.** $16.21 - 21.54 + 12.72$

c. Order the numbers from least to greatest.
(Ex 2)

$$\dfrac{3}{4}, -1, 0.85, \dfrac{5}{8}$$

d. Complete the comparison. Use <, >, or = .
(Ex 3)

$$3.2 + (-2.8) - 5.2 \; \bigcirc \; \dfrac{7}{12} - \dfrac{5}{12} + \left(-\dfrac{11}{12}\right)$$

e. Jonah ran a race in 32.68 seconds. Jarrod finished 1.92 seconds before
(Ex 4) Jonah. Gayle finished 3.01 seconds after Jonah. How many seconds did
it take Gayle to run the race?

Practice   Distributed and Integrated

Add, subtract, multiply, or divide.

1. $\dfrac{1}{2} + \dfrac{3}{5}$
(SB 3)

2. $15\dfrac{1}{3} - 7\dfrac{4}{5}$
(SB 3)

3. $3\dfrac{2}{3} \cdot 2\dfrac{1}{4}$
(SB 3)

4. $3\dfrac{2}{5} \div 1\dfrac{2}{3}$
(SB 3)

5. $78\dfrac{2}{5} - 14\dfrac{7}{10}$
(SB 3)

6. $2\dfrac{1}{3} \cdot 1\dfrac{1}{4}$
(SB 3)

7. $10.2 \cdot 3.15$
(SB 2)

8. $20.46 \div 2.2$
(SB 2)

9. $12.3 \cdot 2.02$
(SB 2)

10. $0.8 \div 0.25$
(SB 2)

*11. Order from greatest to least: $\frac{6}{7}, \frac{3}{5}, \frac{1}{7}, -\frac{4}{3}$.
(10)

12. A(n) _____ angle measures less than 90°.
(SB 1)

13. Convert 8673 g to kg.
(8)

14. Convert 26 mi to km. Round your answer to the nearest tenth.
(8)

15. True or False: $(2 + 5) - (3 \cdot 4) = 2 + 5 - 3 \cdot 4$. Explain.
(4)

*16. **Multiple Choice** Simplify $1.29 + 3.9 - 4.2 - 9.99 + 6.1$.
(10)
A -2.9 **B** -1 **C** 1 **D** 2.9

*17. **Error Analysis** Which student is correct? Explain the error.
(10)

Student A	Student B
$1 - \left(\frac{1}{5} - \frac{2}{10} - \frac{1}{10}\right)$	$1 - \left(\frac{1}{5} - \frac{2}{10} - \frac{1}{10}\right)$
$= 1 - \left(-\frac{1}{10}\right)$	$= 1 - \frac{1}{5} - \frac{2}{10} - \frac{1}{10}$
$= 1\frac{1}{10}$	$= \frac{1}{2}$

*18. (Time) A ship sailed northeast for $2\frac{1}{4}$ hours. It then sailed east for $1\frac{1}{3}$ hours.
(10) How much longer did it sail northeast than east?

19. **Model** Draw a line plot for the frequency table.
(SB 29)

Number	9	10	11	12	13	14
Frequency	4	3	2	1	0	4

*20. **Multi-Step** A map shows streets $\frac{1}{1000}$ of their size.
(9)
a. Write an expression that represents the real length of a block if the length of the block on the map is b.

b. Find the actual length of a block that is 0.4 feet on the map.

*21. **Geometry** A parallelogram has a base of z and a height of $2z$. Write an expression
(9) to find the area of the parallelogram. If z is equal to 12 cm, what is the area of the parallelogram?

22. **Error Analysis** Two students used unit analysis to convert a measurement of area
(8) to a different unit. Which student is correct? Explain the error.

Student A	Student B
1 ft = 12 in.	1 ft = 12 in.
$9 \text{ ft}^2 = 9 \text{ ft}^2 \times \frac{12 \text{ in.}}{1 \text{ ft}}$	$9 \text{ ft}^2 = 9 \text{ ft}^2 \times \frac{12 \text{ in.}}{1 \text{ ft}} \times \frac{12 \text{ in.}}{1 \text{ ft}}$
$9 \text{ ft}^2 = 108 \text{ in}^2$	$9 \text{ ft}^2 = 1{,}296 \text{ in}^2$

23. **(Meteorology)** When a weather system passes through, a barometer can be used to
(8) measure the change in atmospheric pressure in millimeters of mercury. What is the
pressure difference in inches of mercury for a measured change of +4.5 mm of
mercury? Round the answer to the nearest thousandth.

*24. **Multi-Step** A plot of land contains a rectangular building that is 9 yards
(7) long and 6 yards wide and a circular building with a diameter of 4 yards.

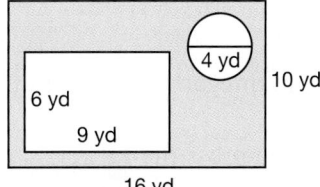

a. Write an expression for the area of the two buildings.

b. Write an expression and solve for how much area on the plot of land is
not being taken up by the buildings. Round the answer to the nearest
hundredth yard.

*25. **Error Analysis** Student A and Student B each added the numbers –4.8 and 3.6
(5) as shown below. Which student is correct? Explain the error.

Student A	Student B
$-4.8 + 3.6$	$-4.8 + 3.6$
$\lvert -4.8 \rvert = 4.8$	$\lvert -4.8 \rvert = 4.8$
$\lvert +3.6 \rvert = 3.6$	$\lvert +3.6 \rvert = 3.6$
4.8	4.8
$\underline{+3.6}$	$\underline{-3.6}$
8.4	1.2
8.4	-1.2

26. **(Banking)** Raul had $500 in his checking account. He wrote checks for $157.62
(5) and $43.96. Then he deposited $225. Find Raul's balance after these three
transactions.

27. **Write** Mutually exclusive means that two sets of numbers have no numbers in
(1) common. Name two subsets of real numbers that are mutually exclusive. Explain.

*28. **(Stocks)** Stock in the 123 Company fell 8.2 points on Monday and 5.3 points on
(5) Tuesday. On Wednesday the stock rose 9.1 points. Determine the total change
in the stock for the three days.

*29. **(Football)** The Rams gained 4 yards on the first down, lost 6 yards on the second
(5) down, and gained 14 yards on the third down. How many total yards did the
Rams gain on the three downs?

30. **Measurement** A kite flies 74 feet above the ground. The person flying the kite is
(10) 5 feet 6 inches tall. How far above the person is the kite?

Generating Random Numbers

Graphing Calculator Lab (*Use with Investigation 1*)

A set of random integers has no pattern. Some common methods for generating random integers include rolling a number cube or drawing numbers out of a hat. A graphing calculator can also be used to generate random integers.

Generate three random integers between 1 and 12.

1. Press **MATH** and then press the ▶ key three times to highlight PRB.

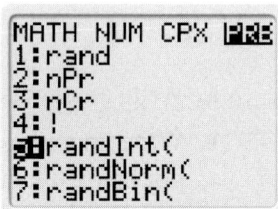

2. Select **5:randInt(** by pressing **5**.

3. Identify the range of values. The lowest possible value is 1 and the highest is 12. So, press **1** [,] **12** [)].

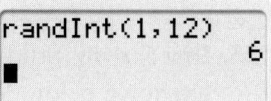

4. Press **ENTER** to generate one integer between 1 and 12. An integer between 1 and 12 is 6.

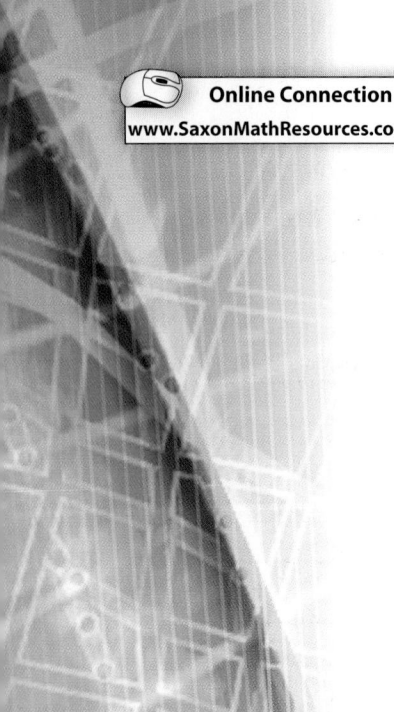

Online Connection
www.SaxonMathResources.com

5. Press **ENTER** two more times to generate two more integers between 1 and 12. Three integers between 1 and 12 are 6, 12, and 9.

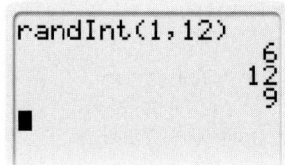

Lab Practice

Jared lost the number cubes to his favorite board game, but he does have his graphing calculator. According to the rules, the player should throw two number cubes and move the total number of spaces shown on the top faces of the cubes.

a. What range of numbers does a single number cube generate? What would Jared enter into the calculator to simulate a number cube?

b. How would Jared simulate rolling two number cubes? How would Jared know how many spaces to move?

c. Simulate Jared taking three turns. What number of spaces will he move in each turn? What is the total number of spaces moved?

Determining the Probability of an Event

Probability is the measure of how likely a given event, or outcome, will occur. The probability of an event can be written as a fraction or decimal ranging from 0 to 1, or as a percent from 0% to 100%.

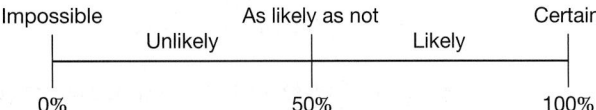

Range of Probability

Describe each of the events below as impossible, unlikely, as likely as not, likely, or certain.

1. Jake rolls a number less than 7 on a number cube.

2. February will have 30 days.

3. A tossed coin will land on tails.

4. Shayla correctly guesses a number between 1 and 100.

Experimental probability is the measure of how likely a given event will occur based on repeated trials.

$$\text{experimental probability} = \frac{\text{number of times an event occurs}}{\text{number of trials}}$$

Exploration Conducting Experiments to Find Probabilities

Place a small handful of colored squares into a paper sack. Draw out a square of paper without looking. Record the color in a frequency table like the one below.

Color	Tally	Frequency
Red		
Blue		
Green		
Yellow		

Repeat the experiment 50 times, replacing the square after each draw.

5. What is the experimental probability of drawing a red square? a blue square? a green square? a yellow square? Express each probability as a fraction and as a percent.

6. **Predict** Which color are you most likely to draw? Explain your reasoning.

Experimental probability is widely used in sports. In baseball, a player's batting average is the probability of a player getting a hit based on his previous at bats. It is typically expressed as a decimal to the thousandths place. For instance, if a player has made 3 hits after coming to bat 10 times, his batting average is .300.

7. (Sports) If a player gets 8 hits in 25 at bats, what is the probability that he will get a hit on his next at bat? Express the answer as a decimal number to the thousandths place.

In addition to sports, experimental probability is often used in banking, insurance, weather forecasting, and business.

8. (Quality Assurance) A piston manufacturer is concerned with the likelihood of defects, as this affects costs and profits. The manufacturer inspects 250 pistons and finds that 8 have defects.

   a. What is the probability a piston will have a defect? Express the probability as a percent.
   b. If the same manufacturer produces 3000 pistons, about how many will likely have defects?
   c. **Evaluate** Pistons sell for $35 and it costs $25 in materials to make each piston. How much profit would the manufacturer likely make on 3000 pistons if defective ones cannot be sold?

A **random event** is an event whose outcome cannot be predicted. For example, drawing a card labeled 8 from a bin of cards, each labeled with a number from 1 to 100, represents a random event. An experiment could be conducted to determine the experimental probability of drawing a card labeled 8, however, it is not always practical to conduct an experiment to determine an experimental probability. In some instances it makes sense to perform a **simulation** of a random event using models such as number cubes, spinners, coins, or random number generators.

(Exploration) **Using a Simulation to Find Probabilities**

Saxon O's cereal is having a contest. Each box of cereal contains a prize piece and claims that 1 in 8 pieces is a winner. Conduct a simulation to determine the experimental probability of winning a prize piece within 50 boxes of cereal.

To simulate this problem, use the digits 1 through 8, with 1 representing a winning prize piece. Use your calculator to generate 50 random numbers.

9. According to your simulation, what is the probability of winning a prize in the Saxon O's contest? Express your answer as a fraction and as a percent.

10. **Verify** How does your answer in problem **9** compare to the likelihood stated on the cereal box?

Describe each of the following events as impossible, unlikely, as likely as not, likely, or certain.

a. Gavin rolls an even number on a number cube.

b. In the northern hemisphere, the temperature will get above 90°F in the month of July.

c. The first person that Sonya meets is a left-handed person.

d. A player with a batting average of .875 gets a hit on his next at bat.

Jamie spun a game spinner and recorded the results in the table.

Outcome	Frequency
A	9
B	6
C	10

e. What is the probability of landing on A? on B? on C? Express each probability as a fraction and as a percent.

f. **Predict** Which letter will Jamie most likely spin? Explain your reasoning.

g. (Sports) If a baseball player has 18 hits in 50 at bats, what is the probability that he will get a hit in his next at bat? Express your answer as a decimal number in the thousandths place.

h. According to a survey at Johnson High School, 1 in 4 students has a part-time job. Conduct a simulation to determine the experimental probability of a student having a part-time job in a random group of 25 students.

Multiplying and Dividing Real Numbers

Warm Up

1. **Vocabulary** Two numbers with the same absolute value but different signs
₍₆₎ are called _____ (*integers, opposites*).

Simplify each expression.

2. $(-4) + (-4) + (-4)$
₍₅₎

3. $-8 - 8 - 8 - 8 - 8 - 8$
₍₆₎

4. 5^4
₍₃₎

5. 2^5
₍₃₎

New Concepts

The sum of three 2's is 6 and the sum of two 3's is 6.

$$2 + 2 + 2 = 6 \qquad 3 + 3 = 6$$

Multiplication is a way to show repeated addition of the same number. The repeated addition above can be shown as multiplication of the same number.

$$3 \cdot 2 = 6 \qquad \text{or} \qquad 2 \cdot 3 = 6$$

The properties of real numbers apply to all real numbers, rational and irrational. Use these properties when evaluating and simplifying numeric and algebraic expressions.

The table shows some properties of multiplication when a and b are real numbers.

Math Reasoning

Analyze How are the Identity Property of Multiplication and the Identity Property of Addition alike?

Properties of Real Numbers
Multiplication Property of -1
For every real number a,
$$a \cdot -1 = -1 \cdot a = -a$$
Example $\qquad 9 \cdot -1 = -1 \cdot 9 = -9$
Multiplication Property of Zero
For every real number a,
$$a \cdot 0 = 0$$
Example $\qquad 9 \cdot 0 = 0$
Inverse Property of Multiplication
For every real number a, where $a \neq 0$,
$$a \cdot \frac{1}{a} = \frac{1}{a} \cdot a = 1$$
Example $\qquad 3 \cdot \frac{1}{3} = \frac{1}{3} \cdot 3 = 1$

Online Connection
www.SaxonMathResources.com

To multiply signed numbers, use the rules in the table below.

Multiplying Signed Numbers
The product of two numbers with the same sign is a positive number.   **Examples** $\quad\quad (3)(4) = 12 \quad\quad\quad (-5)(-3) = 15$
The product of two numbers with opposite signs is a negative number.   **Examples** $\quad\quad (-2)(4) = -8 \quad\quad\quad 6(-2) = -12$

Example 1 Multiplying Rational Numbers

Simplify each expression. Justify your answer.

a. $4(-8)$

SOLUTION

$4(-8) = -32 \quad\quad$ The product of two numbers with opposite signs is negative.

b. $(-6)(-0.7)$

SOLUTION

$(-6)(-0.7) = 4.2 \quad$ The product of two numbers with the same sign is positive.

To raise a number to a power, use repeated multiplication to simplify.

Example 2 Raising a Number to a Power

Simplify each expression.

a. $(-3)^4$

SOLUTION

$(-3)^4$

$= (-3)(-3)(-3)(-3) \quad\quad$ Use repeated multiplication.

$= 81$

b. $(-3)^3$

SOLUTION

$(-3)^3$

$= (-3)(-3)(-3) \quad\quad$ Use repeated multiplication.

$= -27$

c. -3^4

SOLUTION

-3^4

$= -1 \cdot 3^4$

$= -1[(3)(3)(3)(3)] \quad\quad$ Use repeated multiplication.

$= -1(81) \quad\quad$ Find the product inside the brackets.

$= -81 \quad\quad$ Multiplication Property of -1

To divide signed numbers, use the rules in the table below.

Dividing Signed Numbers
The quotient of two numbers with the same sign is a positive number.
Examples $\quad 6 \div 3 = 2 \qquad\qquad\qquad -8 \div (-2) = 4$ $\qquad\qquad\quad \dfrac{6}{3} = 2 \qquad\qquad\qquad\quad \dfrac{-8}{-2} = 4$
The quotient of two numbers with opposite signs is a negative number.
Examples $\quad 10 \div (-5) = -2 \qquad\qquad -12 \div 3 = -4$ $\qquad\qquad\quad \dfrac{10}{-5} = -2 \qquad\qquad\qquad -\dfrac{12}{3} = -4$

Example 3 **Dividing Real Numbers**

Simplify each expression. Justify your answer.

a. $-16 \div (-2)$

SOLUTION

$-16 \div (-2) = 8$ $\qquad$ The quotient of two numbers with the same sign is positive.

b. $2.8 \div (-7)$

SOLUTION

$2.8 \div (-7) = -0.4$ $\qquad$ The quotient of two numbers with opposite signs is negative.

Dividing by a number a is the same as multiplying by the **reciprocal** $\frac{1}{a}$, or **multiplicative inverse,** of the divisor.

$$12 \div 2 = 12 \cdot \frac{1}{2} = 6$$

The reciprocal of 2 is $\frac{1}{2}$. Multiplying 12 by $\frac{1}{2}$ is the same as dividing 12 by 2.

Example 4 **Dividing Positive and Negative Fractions**

Evaluate each expression.

a. $-\dfrac{2}{3} \div \left(-\dfrac{3}{4}\right)$

SOLUTION

$-\dfrac{2}{3} \div \left(-\dfrac{3}{4}\right)$

$-\dfrac{2}{3} \cdot \left(-\dfrac{4}{3}\right)$ $\qquad$ Multiply by the reciprocal of $-\frac{3}{4}$.

$-\dfrac{2}{3} \cdot \left(-\dfrac{4}{3}\right) = \dfrac{8}{9}$ $\qquad$ The product of two fractions with the same sign is positive.

Reading Math

You can write $-\frac{3}{5}$ as $\frac{-3}{5}$ or $\frac{3}{-5}$.

b. $\frac{2}{9} \div \left(-\frac{3}{5}\right)$

SOLUTION

$\frac{2}{9} \div \left(-\frac{3}{5}\right)$

$\frac{2}{9} \cdot \left(-\frac{5}{3}\right)$ Multiply by the reciprocal of $-\frac{3}{5}$.

$\frac{2}{9} \cdot \left(-\frac{5}{3}\right) = -\frac{10}{27}$ The product of two fractions with different signs is negative.

Example 5   Application: Cave Exploration

The Voronya Cave in Abkhazia, Georgia is the deepest known cave in the world. At an elevation of -2140 meters, Voronya is a challenge for experienced cavers. If it takes 8 days to travel to the bottom of the cave, what is the average number of meters the cavers would travel each day?

SOLUTION

Write an expression.

elevation of cave		number of days to travel
-2140 m	$\div$	8 days

$-2140 \div 8 = -267.5$

The cavers would travel an average of -267.5 meters per day.

Lesson Practice

Simplify each expression. Justify your answer.
(Ex 1)

    a. $9(-0.8)$

    b. $-12(-2.5)$

Simplify each expression.
(Ex 2)

    c. $(-4)^3$

    d. $(-8)^4$

    e. -5^4

Simplify each expression. Justify your answer.
(Ex 3)

    f. $-105 \div (-7)$

    g. $63.9 \div (-3)$

Evaluate each expression.
(Ex 4)

    h. $-\frac{4}{5} \div \left(-\frac{9}{10}\right)$ **i.** $\frac{3}{8} \div \left(-\frac{3}{4}\right)$

    j. (Science) During a cold spell in January 1989, Homer, Alaska, recorded
(Ex 5) a low temperature of $-24°F$. The city of Bethel, Alaska, recorded a low temperature twice as cold as the low in Homer. What was the temperature in Bethel, Alaska?

*1. **Verify** True or False: The product of a number and its reciprocal is equal to one.
(11) Verify your answer.

*2. Simplify $-(-4)^2$.
(11)

3. **Error Analysis** Which student is correct? Explain the error.
(10)

Student A	Student B
$\left(\dfrac{11}{12} - \dfrac{2}{4} - \dfrac{1}{3}\right) + \dfrac{11}{12}$	$\left(\dfrac{11}{12} - \dfrac{2}{4} - \dfrac{1}{3}\right) + \dfrac{11}{12}$
$= \dfrac{1}{12} + \dfrac{11}{12}$	$= \dfrac{8}{12} + \dfrac{11}{12}$
$= 1$	$= \dfrac{19}{12}$

4. Simplify $\dfrac{2 \cdot 14 + 3 \cdot 7}{71 - 15}$.
(4)

5. Draw a line plot for the frequency table.
(SB 29)

Number	5	6	7	8	9	10
Frequency	4	2	0	1	0	3

6. A(n) _____ angle measures more than 90° and less than 180°.
(SB 13)

7. Evaluate $3(x + 4) + y$ when $x = 8$ and $y = 7$.
(9)

8. Evaluate the expression $3x^2 + 2(x - 1)^3$ for the given value $x = 6$.
(9)

9. **Multiple Choice** Which rate is the fastest?
(8)
   A 660 ft/15 s

   B 645 ft/11 s

   C 616 ft/12 s

   D 1100 ft/30 s

10. **Justify** Simplify $5 + \dfrac{9}{3}\left[4\left(\dfrac{1}{2} + 4\right)\right]$. Justify each step.
(7)

*11. **Multiple Choice** The temperature at noon was 20°C. The temperature fell 2 degrees
(11) every hour until 3 a.m. the next day. What was the temperature at 11 p.m. that
evening?
   A 22°C

   B −2°C

   C −30°C

   D −22°C

*12. (**Physics**) The magnitude of the instant acceleration of an object in uniform circular
$_{(9)}$ motion is found using the formula $a = \frac{v^2}{r}$, where r is the radius of the circle and v is
the constant speed. Evaluate $a = \frac{v^2}{r}$ if $v = 35$ cm/s and $r = 200$ cm.

*13. (**Retailing**) A grocery store is having a sale on strawberries. Suppose 560 pints of
$_{(11)}$ strawberries are sold at a loss of $0.16 for each pint. How much money does the
store lose on the sale of the strawberries?

*14. (**Ocean Travel**) The deepest point of the Kermandec trench in the Pacific Ocean
$_{(11)}$ is 10,047 meters below sea level. A submarine made two dives from above
the deepest point of the trench at a rate of 400 meters per minute. The first
of the two dives was 10 minutes long and the second was 4 minutes. How far
did the submarine travel in each dive?

15. Add $-1.06 + 2.01 + 4.13$.
$_{(10)}$

16. Multi-Step A purple string is 0.99 m long. A green string is 0.23 m long. What is
$_{(10)}$ the difference in length of the two pieces?

   a. Estimate Estimate the difference using fractions.

   b. Find the exact value of the difference using fractions.

17. Error Analysis Two students solved a homework problem as shown below. Which
$_{(9)}$ student is correct? Explain the error.

Student A	Student B
Evaluate $3g - 4(g + 2b)$; $g = 9$ and $b = 4$. $3(9) - 4(9 + 2(4))$ $27 - 4(17)$ $23(17)$ 391	Evaluate $3g - 4(g + 2b)$; $g = 9$ and $b = 4$. $3(9) - 4(9 + 2(4))$ $27 - 4(17)$ $27 - 68$ -41

18. (**Science**) Scientists can use the expression $2.6f + 65$ to estimate the height of a
$_{(9)}$ person if they know the length of the femur bone, f. What is the approximate
height of a person if the femur bone is 40 centimeters long?

19. Error Analysis The highest point in North America, Mount McKinley, in the
$_{(6)}$ Alaska Range, is 20,320 feet above sea level. The lowest point in North America
is 282 feet below sea level and is in Death Valley in California. Which student
correctly calculated the difference in elevations? Explain the error.

Student A	Student B
$20,320 - 282$ $20,320 + (-282)$ $20,038$ feet	$20,320 - (-282)$ $20,320 + (+282)$ $20,602$ feet

20. **Probability** Describe each of the events below as impossible, unlikely, as likely as not, likely, or certain.
(Inv.1)

   a. Joshua rolls an odd number on a standard number cube.

   b. Maria's birthday is September 31st.

   c. The basketball team has won 11 of their last 12 games. The team will win the next game.

Simplify each expression.

*21. $5(-2)$
(11)

*22. $(-3)(-5)$
(11)

23. $-|-15 + 5|$
(5)

*24. $(-3)(-6)(-2)(5)$
(11)

*25. $(3)(5)$
(11)

26. **Geometry** Can the perimeter of a rectangle be any integer value?
(1)

27. **Model** Mary is playing a board game using a number cube to decide the number of spaces she moves. She moves forward on an even number and backward on an odd number. Her first 5 rolls were 4, 2, 3, 6, 1.
(10)

   a. Model her moves on a number line with zero being the starting point.

   b. Using addition and subtraction, write an expression showing her moves.

   c. At a the end of 5 rolls, how many spaces is she away from the starting point?

*28. **Analyze** Jan bought 2 yards of ribbon. She needs 64 inches of ribbon to make a bow. Does she have enough ribbon? Explain your answer.
(8)

29. **Meteorology** A meteorologist reported the day's low temperature of $-5°F$ at 7 a.m. and the day's high temperature of $20°F$ at 5 p.m. How much did the temperature rise from 7 a.m. to 5 p.m.?
(6)

30. **Phone Charges** Fast Talk Phone Company charges an initial fee of $20 plus 10¢ per minute used. The total bill is expressed as $20 + 0.10m$, where m is the minutes used. If 200 minutes are used, what is the amount of the bill?
(9)

Using the Properties of Real Numbers to Simplify Expressions

Warm Up

1. **Vocabulary** A(n) _____ expression is an expression with constants
   (9) and/or variables that uses the operations $+$, $-$, $\times$, or $\div$.

2. Simplify $6 - |-6| + (-4)$.
   (5)

3. Divide $-\dfrac{4}{5} \div \left(-\dfrac{8}{9}\right)$.
   (11)

4. Evaluate $2|y| - 2|x| + m$ for $x = -1.5$, $y = -3$, and $m = -1.3$.
   (9)

New Concepts

The properties of real numbers are used to simplify expressions and write equivalent expressions. The table shows properties of addition and multiplication when a, b, and c are real numbers.

Math Language

0 is the **additive identity**.

1 is the **multiplicative identity**.

Properties of Addition and Multiplication
Identity Property of Addition
For every real number a, $\qquad$ $a + 0 = a$ $\qquad\qquad$ Example: $5 + 0 = 5$
Identity Property of Multiplication
For every real number a, $\qquad$ $a \cdot 1 = a$ $\qquad\qquad$ Example: $5 \cdot 1 = 5$
Commutative Property of Addition
For every real number a and b, $\qquad$ $a + b = b + a$ $\qquad\qquad$ Example: $5 + 2 = 2 + 5$ $\qquad\qquad\qquad\qquad$ $7 = 7$
Commutative Property of Multiplication
For every real number a and b, $\qquad$ $a \cdot b = b \cdot a$ $\qquad\qquad$ Example: $5 \cdot 2 = 2 \cdot 5$ $\qquad$ $ab = ba$ $\qquad\qquad\qquad\qquad$ $10 = 10$
Associative Property of Addition
For every real number a, b, and c, $\qquad$ $(a + b) + c = a + (b + c)$ $\qquad$ Example: $(1 + 2) + 3 = 1 + (2 + 3)$ $\qquad$ $a + b + c = a + b + c$ $\qquad\qquad\qquad\qquad$ $3 + 3 = 1 + 5$ $\qquad\qquad\qquad\qquad\qquad\qquad$ $6 = 6$
Associative Property of Multiplication
For every real number a, b, and c, $\qquad$ $(a \cdot b) \cdot c = a \cdot (b \cdot c)$ $\qquad$ Example: $(1 \cdot 2) \cdot 3 = 1 \cdot (2 \cdot 3)$ $\qquad$ $abc = abc$ $\qquad\qquad\qquad\qquad$ $2 \cdot 3 = 1 \cdot 6$ $\qquad\qquad\qquad\qquad\qquad\qquad$ $6 = 6$

Online Connection
www.SaxonMathResources.com

Example 1 | Identifying Properties

Example 1 | Identifying Properties

Identify the property illustrated in each equation.

Hint

Compare the left side of the equation to the right side. Determine what changes have been made.

a. $1 \cdot 8 = 8$

SOLUTION Since 8 is multiplied by 1, its value does not change. This is the Identity Property of Multiplication.

b. $13 + 5 = 5 + 13$

SOLUTION The order of the terms is changed. This is the Commutative Property of Addition.

c. $(3 \cdot 4) \cdot 7 = 3 \cdot (4 \cdot 7)$

SOLUTION The terms and the order are not changed; only the grouping of the factors is changed. This is the Associative Property of Multiplication.

Math Reasoning

Analyze Why does the Commutative Property not apply to subtraction?

d. $(12 + 9) + 5 = (9 + 12) + 5$

SOLUTION The terms are the same and the same two terms are grouped. However, the order of the grouped terms has changed. This is the Commutative Property of Addition.

Example 2 | Using Properties to Justify Statements

Tell whether each statement is true or false. Justify your answer using the properties. Assume all variables represent real numbers.

a. $gh = hg$

SOLUTION The statement is true. It illustrates the Commutative Property of Multiplication.

Check Substitute a value for each variable to determine whether the statement is true.

Let $g = 6$ and $h = 7$.

$6 \cdot 7 \stackrel{?}{=} 7 \cdot 6$

$42 = 42$ ✓

Write

Explain why it is necessary to substitute only one value for the variable to show that the statement is false.

b. $b + 1 = b$

SOLUTION The statement is false. To illustrate the Identity Property of Addition, the equation should be $b + 0 = b$.

Check Substitute a value for the variable to determine whether the statement is true.

Let $b = 13$.

$13 + 1 \neq 13$ ✗

c. $d + (e + f) = (d + e) + f$

SOLUTION Substitute a value for the variables to determine whether the statement is true.

Let $d = 5$, $e = 7$, and $f = 9$.

$$5 + (7 + 9) \overset{?}{=} (5 + 7) + 9$$
$$5 + 16 \overset{?}{=} 12 + 9$$
$$21 = 21 \quad \checkmark$$

The statement is true by the Associative Property of Addition.

Example 3 Justifying Steps to Simplify an Expression

Simplify each expression. Justify each step.

a. $16 + 3x + 4$

SOLUTION

$16 + 3x + 4$

$= 3x + 16 + 4$ Commutative Property of Addition

$= 3x + (16 + 4)$ Associative Property of Addition

$= 3x + 20$ Add.

b. $(25) \cdot y \cdot \left(\dfrac{1}{25}\right)$

SOLUTION

$(25) \cdot y \cdot \left(\dfrac{1}{25}\right)$

$= (25) \cdot \left(\dfrac{1}{25}\right) \cdot y$ Commutative Property of Multiplication

$= 1 \cdot y$ Multiply

$= y$ Identity Property of Multiplication

Caution

Don't skip or combine steps. For each property necessary to simplify the expression, a step must be shown.

Example 4 Application: Consumer Math

Envelopes, pens, and correction tape can be purchased at an office supply store for the following prices respectively: $2.85, $5.35, and $2.15. Find the total cost of the supplies. Justify each step.

SOLUTION

$\$2.85 + \$5.35 + \$2.15$

$= \$2.85 + \$2.15 + \$5.35$ Commutative Property of Addition

$= (\$2.85 + \$2.15) + \$5.35$ Associative Property of Addition

$= \$5.00 + \$5.35$ Add within the parentheses.

$= \$10.35$ Add.

The supplies will cost $10.35.

Identify each property illustrated.

(Ex 1)

   a. $5 + (9 + 8) = (5 + 9) + 8$

   b. $0 + 10 = 10$

   c. $15 \cdot 3 = 3 \cdot 15$

   d. $17 \cdot 1 = 17$

Tell whether each statement is true or false. Justify your answer using the properties. Assume all variables represent real numbers.

(Ex 2)

   e. $(ab)c = a(bc)$

   f. $m - z = z - m$

   g. $w + 0 = w$

Simplify each expression. Justify each step.

(Ex 3)

   h. $18 + 7x + 4$

   i. $\frac{1}{3}d \cdot 3$

   j. Erasers, markers, and paper can be purchased at the school store for
(Ex 4) the following prices, respectively: $1.45, $3.35, and $2.65. Find the total
cost of the supplies. Justify each step.

*1. Identify the property illustrated in the equation $100 \cdot 1 = 100$.
(12)

Simplify each expression.

2. $-18 \div 3$ **3.** $|12 - 30|$
(11)   *(5)*

4. $(-3)(-2)(-1)(-8)$
(11)

*5. True or False: $p(q + r) = (p + q)r$. Justify your answer using the properties.
(12)

6. Write a fraction equivalent to $\frac{2}{3}$.
(SB 7)

7. True or False: The sum of the measures of complementary angles is $90°$.
(SB 15)

*8. Multiple Choice Which equation demonstrates the Identity Property of
(12) Addition?

   A $a \cdot 0 = 0$

   B $a + 0 = a$

   C $a \cdot \frac{1}{a} = 1$

   D $a + 1 = 1 + a$

9. Add $\frac{11}{15} + \frac{1}{30} + \frac{3}{60}$.
(10)

10. Error Analysis Students were asked to simplify $\frac{5}{6} \div \left(-\frac{3}{2}\right)$. Which student is correct?
(11) Explain the error.

Student A	Student B
$\frac{5}{6} \div \left(-\frac{3}{2}\right)$	$\frac{5}{6} \div \left(-\frac{3}{2}\right)$
$= \frac{5}{6} \cdot \left(-\frac{2}{3}\right)$	$= \frac{5}{6} \cdot \left(-\frac{2}{3}\right)$
$= -\frac{5}{9}$	$= \frac{5}{9}$

*11. Jon has 5 marbles. His best friend gives him some more. Then he buys 15 more
(12) marbles. The expression $5 + x + 15$ shows the total number of marbles Jon now
has. Show two ways to simplify this expression and justify each step.

12. Multiple Choice What is the value of $\frac{(5x + x)^2(6 - x)}{x}$ when $x = 2$?
(9)
  A 288   **B** 200   **C** 400   **D** 28

*13. Find the value of $(4x^3y^2)^2$ when $x = 2$ and $y = 1$.
(9)

14. Convert 588 ounces to pounds. (Hint: 1 lb = 16 oz)
(8)

*15. Geometry A wall in a rectangular room is 12 feet by 8 feet. Jose calculated the area
(12) using the equations $A = 12 \cdot 8$ and $A = 8 \cdot 12$. Explain why each expression will
give him the same answer.

*16. (Interior Decorating) Tim is building a picture frame that is 10 inches long and
(12) 6 inches wide. He calculated the perimeter using $P = 2(10 + 6)$. His brother
calculated the perimeter for the same frame using $P = 2(6 + 10)$. Will the
measurements be the same? Explain.

*17. (Temperature) To convert a temperature from Celsius to Fahrenheit, Marc uses the
(12) formula $F = \frac{9}{5}C + 32$. He also uses the formula $F = 32 + \frac{9}{5}C$. Which calculation is
correct? Explain.

18. Geometry A rectangle is twice as long as it is wide. If the width of the
(11) rectangle measures 2.3 inches, what is the area of the rectangle?   2.3 in.   2.3 in.

19. Multi-Step In each of the first five rounds of a game; Tyra scored 28 points. In
(11) each of the next three rounds, she scored -41 points. Then she scored two rounds
of -16 points. What is the total number of points that Tyra scored? Explain.

*20. Multiple Choice Order from greatest to least: $\frac{1}{4}, 0.23, -0.24, \frac{1}{3}$.
(10)
  A $-0.24, 0.23, \frac{1}{4}, \frac{1}{3}$ **B** $\frac{1}{4}, \frac{1}{3}, 0.23, -0.24$

  C $-0.24, 0.23, \frac{1}{3}, \frac{1}{4}$ **D** $\frac{1}{3}, \frac{1}{4}, 0.23, -0.24$

21. (Sewing) Maria is sewing curtains that require 124 inches of ribbon trim. She can
(8) only buy the ribbon in whole yard lengths. How many yards does she need to buy?

22. **Error Analysis** Student A and Student B simplified the expression $9 - 4 \cdot 2$. Which student is correct? Explain the error.
(7)

Student A	Student B
$9 - 4 \cdot 2$	$9 - 4 \cdot 2$
$= 5 \cdot 2$	$= 9 - 8$
$= 10$	$= 1$

23. **Write** Explain how to use the order of operations to simplify $4(8 - 9 \div 3)^2$.
(4)

24. Simplify $x^2kxk^2x^2ykx^2$.
(3)

25. **Error Analysis** Two students evaluate the expression $4t + 5x - \frac{1}{x}$ when $x = 3$.
(2) Which student is correct? Explain the error.

Student A	Student B
$4t + 5x - \frac{1}{x}; x = 3$	$4t + 5x - \frac{1}{x}; x = 3$
$= 4t + 5(3) - \frac{1}{3}$	$= 4t + 53 - \frac{1}{3}$
$= 4t + 15 - \frac{1}{3}$	$= 4t + 52\frac{2}{3}$
$= 4t + 14\frac{2}{3}$	

26. (Savings Accounts) The table below shows the transactions Jennifer made to her
(10) savings account during one month. Find the balance of her account.

Jennifer's Bank Account

Beginning Balance	$396.25
Withdrawal	$150.50
Deposit	$220.00
Interest (deposit)	$8.00

*27. (Tug of War) In a game of Tug of War, Team A pulls the center of the rope three and
(10) a half feet in their direction. Then Team B pulls back five feet before Team A pulls for another eight feet. How far from the starting point is the center of the rope?

28. (Travel) Bill rides a bus for 2.5 hours to visit a friend. If the bus travels at
(11) about 60 to 63 miles per hour, how far away does Bill's friend live? (Hint: To find distance, multiply rate by time.)

29. **Justify** Simplify $2^2 + 24 - (3 - 12)$. Explain your steps.
(4)

30. **Verify** Give an example that illustrates that the sum of a number and its opposite
(6) is zero.

Calculating and Comparing Square Roots

Warm Up

1. **Vocabulary** The number that tells how many times the base of a power is
(3) used as a factor is called the _____ (*variable, exponent*).

Simplify each expression.

2. $-3 + (-4) - (-8)$
(10)

3. $[-(-4)^3]$
(11)

4. $a^3 \cdot x^4 \cdot x^8 \cdot a^4 \cdot z^4$
(3)

5. $\left(-\dfrac{2}{6}\right) \div \left(-\dfrac{3}{8}\right)$
(11)

New Concepts

A **perfect square** is a number that is the square of an integer. The product of an integer and itself is a perfect square.

$$2^2 = \quad\boxplus\quad\quad 3^2 = \quad\boxplus$$

A square root is indicated by a radical symbol $\sqrt{}$. A **radicand** is the number or expression under a radical symbol.

$$\sqrt{50} \qquad\qquad 2\sqrt{7}$$

50 is the radicand.   7 is the radicand.

The **square root** of x, written $\sqrt{x}$, is the number whose square is x.

$$4^2 = 16$$
$$\sqrt{16} = 4$$

A square number can only end with the digits: zero, one, four, five, six, and nine. However, not all numbers ending in these digits will be perfect squares.

> **Math Reasoning**
>
> **Formulate** What is the inverse of x^2?

Example 1   Finding Square Roots of Perfect Squares

a. Is the radicand in $\sqrt{50}$ a perfect square? Explain.

SOLUTION

50 is not a perfect square. There is no integer multiplied by itself that equals 50.

b. Is the radicand in $\sqrt{64}$ a perfect square? Explain.

SOLUTION

64 is a perfect square; $8 \cdot 8 = 8^2 = 64$. The product of an integer and itself is a perfect square.

> **Online Connection**
> www.SaxonMathResources.com

Not all numbers are perfect squares, but their square roots can be estimated.

Example 2 **Estimating Square Roots**

Estimate the value $\sqrt{50}$ to the nearest integer. Explain your reasoning.

SOLUTION

$\sqrt{50}$ is not a perfect square.

Determine which two perfect squares 50 falls between on the number line.

50 is between the perfect squares 49 and 64.

Then determine which perfect square $\sqrt{50}$ is closest to.

$\sqrt{50}$ is between the numbers 7 and 8 because $\sqrt{49} = 7$ and $\sqrt{64} = 8$.

$\sqrt{50}$ is closer to the number 7 because 50 is closer to 49 than 64.

$\sqrt{50} \approx 7$

When comparing expressions that contain radicals, simplify the expressions with radicals first. Next, perform any operations necessary. Then compare the expressions.

Example 3 **Comparing Expressions Involving Square Roots**

Compare the expressions. Use $<$, $>$, or $=$.
$$\sqrt{4} + \sqrt{36} \ \bigcirc \ \sqrt{9} + \sqrt{25}$$

SOLUTION

$\sqrt{4} + \sqrt{36} \ \bigcirc \ \sqrt{9} + \sqrt{25}$

$\quad 2 + 6 \ \bigcirc \ 3 + 5$ Simplify the expressions.

$\quad\quad 8 \ \bigcirc\!= \ 8$ Add.

Example 4 **Application: Ballroom Dancing**

The area of a dance floor that is in the shape of a square is 289 square feet. What is the side length of the dance floor? Explain.

SOLUTION

The side length can be found by finding the square root of the area.

Area of a square = side length × side length

$\quad\quad A = s^2$ Write the formula.

$\quad 289 = s^2$ Substitute 289 for A.

$\quad \sqrt{289} = s$ Find the square root of 289.

$\quad\quad 17 = s$

Each side length of the dance floor is 17 feet.

Math Reasoning

Analyze Is 1.44 a perfect square?

Caution

Square roots must be simplified before performing any other operations. For example, $\sqrt{4} + \sqrt{36} \neq \sqrt{40}$.

a. Is the radicand in $\sqrt{225}$ a perfect square? Explain.
(Ex 1)

b. Is the radicand in $\sqrt{350}$ a perfect square? Explain.
(Ex 1)

c. Estimate the value of $\sqrt{37}$ to the nearest integer. Explain your reasoning.
(Ex 2)

d. Compare the expressions. Use $<$, $>$, or $=$.
(Ex 3)
$$\sqrt{16} + \sqrt{441} \bigcirc \sqrt{81} + \sqrt{361}$$

e. The city park has a new sandbox in the shape of a square. The area of the sandbox is 169 square feet. What is the side length of the sandbox? Explain.
(Ex 4)

Practice   Distributed and Integrated

Simplify each expression.

1. $-16 \div -2$
(11)

2. $\dfrac{4 + 7 - 6}{2 + 7 - 3}$
(11)

3. $-2 + 11 - 4 + 3 - 8$
(6)

4. $(-2)(-3) + 11(2) - 3 - 6$
(6)

Evaluate each expression for the given values.

*5. $3p - 4g - 2x$ for $p = 2$, $g = -3$, and $x = 4$
(9)

6. $3xy - 2yz$ for $x = 3$, $y = 4$, and $z = 3$
(9)

*7. $\sqrt{40}$ is between which two whole numbers?
(13)

*8. Multiple Choice Which of the following numbers is a perfect square?
(13)

   A 200   **B** 289

   C 410   **D** 150

*9. Solve $b = \sqrt{4}$.
(13)

10. Model Draw a model to compare $\dfrac{5}{12}$ and $\dfrac{1}{3}$.
(10)

11. Convert 25 feet per hour to yards per hour.
(8)

12. True or False: The square root of any odd number is an irrational number. If false, provide a counterexample.
(1)

*13. **Multiple Choice** The area of a square is 392 square meters. The area of a second
square is half the area of the first square. What is the side length of the second
square?

A 14 meters

B ≈ 20 meters

C 196 meters

D 96 meters

*14. True or False: $xyz = yxz$. Justify your answer using the properties.
(12)

15. **Verify** Determine whether each statement below is true or false. If false,
(4) explain why.

   a. $4^2 + 15 \cdot 20$ is equal to 316.

   b. $(4 + 5)^2$ is the same as $4 + 5^2$.

16. **Multi-Step** Kristin has several ropes measuring $8\frac{1}{4}$ in., $8\frac{3}{16}$ in., $8\frac{5}{8}$ in., and $8\frac{1}{16}$ in.
(10) How should she order them from least to greatest?

   a. Find a common denominator for each measure.

   b. Order the measures from least to greatest.

17. Arrange in order from least to greatest:
(10)

$$1.11, \ 1.5, \ 1.09, \ 1.05$$

*18. Are the expressions $(20k^3 \cdot 5v^5)9k^2$ and $900k^3v^5$ equivalent? Explain.
(9)

*19. (Science) The Barringer Meteor Crater in Winslow, Arizona, is very close to a
(13) square in shape. The crater covers an area of about 1,690,000 square meters. What
is the approximate side length of the crater?

20. (Science) The time, t, in seconds it takes for an object dropped to travel a distance,
(13) d, in feet can be found using the formula $t = \frac{\sqrt{d}}{4}$. Determine the time it takes for
an object to drop 169 feet.

*21. **Multi-Step** The flow rate for a particular fire hose can be found using $f = 120\sqrt{p}$,
(13) where f is the flow rate in gallons per minute and p is the nozzle pressure in
pounds per square inch. When the nozzle pressure is 169 pounds per square inch,
what is the flow rate?

22. (World Records) The world's largest cherry pie was baked in Michigan. It had a
(1) diameter of 210 inches. If the diameter was converted to feet, would it be a
rational number? Explain.

23. Find the area of the shaded portion of the circle. The radius of the circle is
(4) 4 inches. (Use 3.14 for π.)

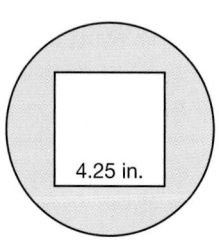

4.25 in.

24. (**Banking**) Frank deposited $104.67 into his bank account. Later that day, he spent
(5) $113.82 from the same account. Estimate the change in Frank's account balance
for that day.

25. Justify Simplify $52 + (1 + 3)^2 \cdot (16 - 14)^3 - 20$. Justify each step.
(7)

26. Error Analysis Two students simplify the expression $2 + 3x + 1$. Which student
(12) is correct? Explain the error.

Student A	Student B
$2 + 3x + 1$	$2 + 3x + 1$
$= 2 + 1 + 3x$	$= (2 + 3)x + 1$
$= (2 + 1) + 3x$	$= 5x + 1$
$= 3 + 3x$	

*27. Justify Arlene has 30 buttons and buys x packages of buttons. There are
(12) 7 buttons in each package. She uses 12 buttons. The number of buttons she now
has is represented by the expression $30 + 7x - 12$. Simplify the expression and
justify each step using the properties.

28. Multiple Choice Which of the following expressions will result in a negative
(11) number?

A $(-6)^2$

B $(-6) \div (-6)$

C $-\dfrac{3}{4}(6) \div (-4)$

D $-1 \cdot (-6)^2$

29. (**International Banking**) A Greek company needs to purchase some products from a
(8) U.S. corporation. First, the company must open an account in U.S. dollars. If the
account is to hold $1,295,800, how many drachma, the Greek currency, should the
company deposit? Use the exchange rate of one Greek drachma for every $0.004
in U.S. currency.

30. Probability Describe each of the following events as impossible, unlikely, as likely as
(Inv 1) not, likely, or certain.

a. Jim rolls a 10 on a standard number cube.

b. Sarah guesses a number correctly between 1 and 900.

c. Mayra dropped a coin and it landed heads up.

Determining the Theoretical Probability of an Event

Warm Up

1. **Vocabulary** _____ (*Closure, Probability*) is the measure of how likely
(Inv 1)   it is that an event will occur.

Simplify each expression.

2. $5 \times 7 - 27 \div 9 + 6$
(4)

3. $6.3 + (-2.4) + (-8.9)$
(10)

4. $6 + |-72| + |-5|$
(5)

5. Write a number to represent the opposite of "twelve floors up."
(6)

New Concepts

A **sample space** is the set of all possible outcomes of an event. For example, a toss of a fair coin has two equally likely outcomes. The two possible outcomes, heads and tails, is the sample space.

A **simple event** is an event having only one outcome. For example, rolling a 5 on a number cube is a simple event.

The **theoretical probability** of an outcome is found by analyzing a situation in which all outcomes are equally likely, and then finding the ratio of favorable outcomes to all possible outcomes. For example, the probability of tossing a coin and it landing on heads is $\frac{1}{2}$ or 0.5 or 50%.

> **Math Language**
>
> A fair coin has an equally likely chance of landing on heads or tails. The coin is not weighted so that one outcome is more likely than another.

Exploration Finding Theoretical Probability

Place 4 different-colored marbles in a sack. Without looking, draw one marble out of the sack. Record the color in a frequency table.

Color	Tally	Frequency
Red		
Green		
Yellow		
Blue		

> **Materials**
>
> • small paper sacks
> • colored marbles

a. Repeat the experiment 10 times, 20 times, 50 times and 100 times, replacing the marble after each draw.

b. Divide the number of times a red marble is picked by the total number of times you pick a marble. Write this as a probability.

c. **Generalize** What do you notice about the probabilities as the number of times you pick a marble is increased?

> **Online Connection**
> www.SaxonMathResources.com

Example 1   Identifying Sample Spaces

A number cube labeled 1–6 is rolled. List the outcomes for each event.

a. a number less than or equal to 3   **b.** an odd number

SOLUTION

$\{3, 2, 1\}$

SOLUTION

$\{1, 3, 5\}$

c. a number greater than 4

SOLUTION

$\{5, 6\}$

Theoretical probability can be determined using the following formula:

$$P(\text{event}) = \frac{\text{number of favorable outcomes}}{\text{total number of outcomes}}$$

A **complement of an event** is a set of all outcomes of an experiment that are not in a given event. For example, if heads is the desired event when tossing a coin, tails is the complement of the event. The sum of an event and its complement equals 1.

$$P(\text{event}) + P(\text{not event}) = 1$$
$$P(\text{not event}) = 1 - P(\text{event})$$

Example 2   Calculating Theoretical Probability

There are 4 green, 3 blue, and 3 red marbles in a bag.

Give each answer as a decimal and as a percent.

a. What is the probability of randomly choosing a red marble?

SOLUTION

$$P(\text{red}) = \frac{3 \text{ red marbles}}{10 \text{ marbles in all}}$$

$$P(\text{red}) = \frac{3}{10}$$

The probability of choosing a red marble is 0.3 or 30%.

b. What is the probability of randomly choosing a marble that is not green?

SOLUTION

$$P(\text{green marble}) + P(\text{not green marble}) = 1$$
$$P(\text{not green marble}) = 1 - P(\text{green marble})$$
$$P(\text{not green marble}) = 1 - \frac{4}{10}$$
$$P(\text{not green marble}) = \frac{6}{10} = \frac{3}{5}$$

The probability of not choosing a green marble is 0.6 or 60%.

Math Language

A spinner is divided into four equal parts: blue, yellow, green, and red. If the spinner lands on yellow, then the **outcome** is yellow.

Reading Math

The probability of an event can be written **P(event).** The probability of picking a red marble can be written *P*(red).

Hint

Probability can be expressed as a fraction, decimal, or percent.

Chance, like probability, is the likelihood of an event occurring.

Example 3 Calculating Chance

In a bucket there are 10 balls numbered as follows: 1, 1, 2, 3, 4, 4, 4, 5, 6, and 6. A single ball is randomly chosen from the bucket. What is the probability of drawing a ball with a number greater than 4? Is there a greater chance of drawing a number greater than 4 or a 1?

SOLUTION

$$P(\text{greater than } 4) = \frac{3}{10}$$ 3 out of the 10 balls have a number greater than 4.

The probability of drawing a ball with a number greater than 4 is 0.3, or 30%.

$$P(1) = \frac{2}{10} = \frac{1}{5}$$ 2 out of the 10 balls are numbered 1.

$$\frac{3}{10} > \frac{1}{5}$$ Compare $\frac{3}{10}$ and $\frac{1}{5}$.

There is a greater chance of drawing a number greater than 4 than drawing a 1.

Example 4 Application: State Fair

At a carnival game, you drop a ball into the top of the device shown below. As the ball falls, it goes either left or right as it hits each peg. In total, the ball can follow 16 different paths. The ball eventually lands in one of the bins at the bottom and you win that amount of money. (One path to $0 is shown.) What is the probability of winning $2?

SOLUTION

total number of paths = 16

number of paths to $2 bins = 2

$$P(\$2) = \frac{\text{number of paths to \$2 bins}}{\text{total number of paths to win}} = \frac{2}{16}$$

$$P(\$2) = \frac{1}{8}$$

The probability of winning $2 is $\frac{1}{8}$.

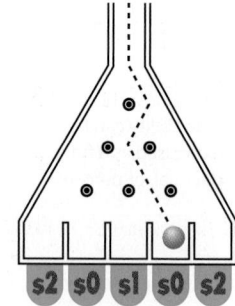

$2 $0 $1 $0 $2

Math Reasoning

Analyze If you drop the ball once, is there less than or greater than a 20% probability of not winning $2?

Lesson Practice

A number cube labeled 1–6 is rolled. List the outcome for each event.
(Ex 1)

   a. a number less than or equal to 4

   b. an even number

   c. a number greater than 2

There are 4 green, 3 blue, and 3 red marbles in a bag.
(Ex 2)

   d. What is the probability of randomly choosing a blue marble?

   e. What is the probability of randomly not choosing a red marble?

f. *(Ex 3)* Suppose there are 8 balls in a bucket numbered as follows; 1, 2, 3, 5, 5, 6, 7, and 7. A single ball is randomly chosen from the bucket. What is the probability of drawing a ball with a number less than 6? Do you have a greater chance of drawing a 7 or a 6?

g. *(Ex 4)* A 52-card deck has 4 kings in the deck. What is the probability of randomly drawing a king out of the deck?

Practice   Distributed and Integrated

*1. *(14)* A number cube labeled 1–6 is rolled three times. What is the probability that the next roll will produce a number greater than 4?

*2. *(14)* An jar contains 5 green marbles and 9 purple marbles. A marble is drawn and dropped back into the jar. Then a second marble is drawn and dropped back into the jar. Both marbles are green. If another marble is drawn, what is the probability that it will be green?

3. *(8)* Convert 20 inches to centimeters (2.54 cm = 1 in.).

4. *(8)* Convert 25 feet to centimeters. (Hint: Convert from feet to inches to centimeters.)

Simplify.

5. *(4)* $3 - 2 \cdot 4 + 3 \cdot 2$

6. *(11)* $-3(-2)(-3) - 2$

7. *(4)* $5(9 + 2) - 4(5 + 1)$

8. *(4)* $3(6 + 2) + 3(5 - 2)$

9. *(13)* Evaluate $\sqrt{31 + z}$ when $z = 5$.

10. *(10)* Use $<$, $>$ or $=$ to compare $\frac{4}{5}$ and $\frac{5}{6}$.

*11. *(13)* **Geometry** What is the length of the side of a square that has an area of 49 square centimeters?

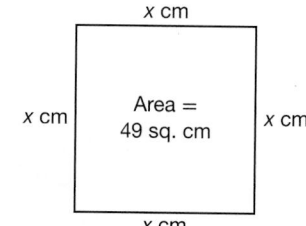

12. *(12)* **Multiple Choice** Which equation demonstrates the Associative Property of Addition?

A $(a + b) + c = a + (b + c)$

B $ab + c = ba + c$

C $a(b + c) = ab + ac$

D $a + (b + c) = a + (c + b)$

*13. **Justify** What must be true of each of the values of x and y if $-xy$ is positive? zero?
(11) negative?

14. Identify the property illustrated in the expression $5 \cdot 6 = 6 \cdot 5$.
(12)

*15. **Multiple Choice** A number cube labeled 1–6 is tossed. What is the theoretical
(14) probability of rolling an odd number?

 A $\dfrac{1}{2}$

 B $\dfrac{1}{3}$

 C $\dfrac{1}{4}$

 D $\dfrac{2}{3}$

*16. A letter is chosen at random from the word probability. What is the probability of
(14) randomly choosing the letter b?

*17. **Multiple Choice** A bag contains 4 blue, 6 red, 5 yellow, and 1 orange marble. What is
(14) the probability of randomly choosing a blue marble?

 A $\dfrac{1}{16}$

 B $\dfrac{4}{15}$

 C $\dfrac{1}{4}$

 D $\dfrac{4}{32}$

18. **Error Analysis** Students were asked to find the square root of 16. Which student is
(13) correct? Explain the error.

Student A	Student B
$\sqrt{16} = 4$	$\sqrt{16} = 8$
$4 \times 4 = 16$	$8 \times 2 = 16$

*19. (**Braking Distance**) The speed a vehicle was traveling when the brakes were first applied
(13) can be estimated using the formula $s = \sqrt{\dfrac{d}{0.04}}$, where d is the length of the vehicle's
skid marks in feet and s is the speed of the vehicle in miles per hour. Determine the
speed of a car whose skid marks were 4^2 feet long.

*20. (**Physics**) The centripetal force of an object in circular motion can be expressed as $\dfrac{mv^2}{r}$,
(9) where m is mass, v is tangential velocity, and r is the radius of the circular path.
What is the centripetal force of a 2-kg object traveling at 50 cm/s in a circular path
with a radius of 25 centimeters?

21. Verify Convert 2.35 pounds to ounces (1 lb = 16 oz). Check to see if your answer
(8) is reasonable.

22. Write If a computer program is designed to run until it reaches the end of the
(1) number pi (π), will the program ever end? Explain.

23. (Geography) The lowest point in elevation in the United States is Death Valley,
(1) California. Death Valley is 86 meters below sea level. Which set of numbers best
describes elevations in Death Valley?

24. (Temperature) To convert degrees Celsius to degrees Fahrenheit, use the
(2) equation $C = \frac{5}{9}(F - 32)$.

a. How many terms are in the expression $\frac{5}{9}(F - 32)$?

b. Identify the constants in the expression.

25. Simplify $-7 + 3 - 2 - 5 + (-6)$.
(6)

26. Error Analysis Ms. Mahoney, the algebra teacher, has two cakes that weigh 3 pounds
(4) and 5 pounds. She cuts the cakes into 16 equal pieces. She asks the students to
write an expression that represents the weight of each piece. Which student is
correct? Explain the error.

Student A	Student B
uses the expression $3 + 5 \div 16$	uses the expression $(3 + 5) \div 16$

27. Model While the Petersen family was waiting for their table, 9 people left the
(5) restaurant and 15 people entered. Find the sum of -9 and 15 to determine the
change in the number of people in the restaurant. Use algebra tiles to model the
situation.

28. Justify Simplify $22 - (-11) - 11 - (-22)$. Justify your answer.
(6)

29. Write Why is the order of operations important when simplifying an expression
(7) like $(5 + 7)^2 \div (14 - 2)$?

*30. (Landscaping) Tanisha is building a fence around a square flower bed that has an
(13) area of 144 square feet. How many feet of fencing does she need?

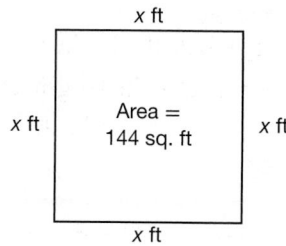

x ft

x ft   Area = 144 sq. ft   x ft

x ft

Using the Distributive Property to Simplify Expressions

Warm Up

1. **Vocabulary** In the expression $3x + 5$, $3x$ is a _____ (*variable, term*) of the expression.

Simplify each expression.

2. $5 - 7 + 5(3)$

3. $(-5) + (-2) + |(-5) + (-2)|$

4. Evaluate $7x + 4y$ for $x = 2.1$ and $y = -0.7$.

5. Find the product of $\frac{3}{8}$, $\frac{4}{5}$, and $\frac{2}{3}$.

New Concepts

The Distributive Property can be used to simplify expressions. Since subtraction is the same as adding the opposite, the Distributive Property will also work with subtraction.

The Distributive Property
For all real numbers a, b, c,
$$a(b + c) = ab + ac \text{ and } a(b - c) = ab - ac$$
Examples
$5(2 + 1) = 5 \cdot 2 + 5 \cdot 1 = 15 \qquad\qquad 5(2 - 1) = 5 \cdot 2 - 5 \cdot 1 = 5$

Example 1 Distributing a Positive Integer

Simplify each expression.

a. $6(4 + 8)$

SOLUTION

$6(4 + 8)$

$= 6(4) + 6(8)$ — Distribute the 6.

$= 24 + 48$ — Multiply.

$= 72$ — Add.

b. $4(5 - 3)$

SOLUTION

$4(5 - 3)$

$= 4(5) + 4(-3)$ — Distribute the 4.

$= 20 - 12$ — Multiply.

$= 8$ — Subtract.

Math Reasoning

Verify Use the order of operations to show that $4(5 - 3) = 8$.

Online Connection
www.SaxonMathResources.com

Use the Multiplication Property of -1 to simplify an expression like $-(5 + 2)$. Rewrite the expression as $-1(5 + 2)$ and then distribute.

Example 2 **Distributing a Negative Integer**

Simplify each expression.

Hint

The product of a real number and 1 is the real number.

a. $-(9 + 4)$

SOLUTION

$-(9 + 4)$

$= (-1)(9) + (-1)(4)$ Distribute.

$= -9 - 4$ Multiply.

$= -13$ Simplify.

b. $-9(-6 - 3)$

SOLUTION

$-9(-6 - 3)$

$= (-9)(-6) + (-9)(-3)$

$= 54 + 27$

$= 81$

The Distributive Property of Equality applies not only to numeric expressions but also to algebraic expressions.

Example 3 **Simplifying Algebraic Expressions**

Simplify each expression.

Reading Math

There are different ways to write the same expression:

$6 \cdot (5 - x)$
$(5 - x) \cdot 6$
$6(5 - x)$
$(5 - x)6$

a. $-4(x + 7)$

SOLUTION

$-4(x + 7)$

$= (-4)(x) + (-4)(7)$ Distribute.

$= -4x - 28$ Multiply.

b. $(5 - x)6$

SOLUTION

$(5 - x)6$

$= 6(5) + 6(-x)$

$= 30 - 6x$

Example 4 **Simplifying Algebraic Expressions with Exponents**

Simplify each expression.

a. $mn(mx + ny + 2p)$

SOLUTION

$mn(mx + ny + 2p)$

$= m^2nx + mn^2y + 2mnp$ Multiply.

Hint

When multiplying, add the exponents of powers with the same base.

$y(y^2) = y^{1+2} = y^3$

b. $-xy(y^2 - x^2z)$

SOLUTION

$-xy(y^2 - x^2z)$ Distribute.

$= (-xy)(y^2) + (-xy)(-x^2z)$ Combine like terms.

$= -xy^3 + x^3yz$

Example 5 Application: Landscaping

The turf on a football field is being replaced. The field is 300 feet long and 160 feet wide, not including the two end zones. Each end zone adds an additional 30 feet to the field's length. Write an expression using the Distributive Property to show the entire area of the field. Simplify the expression.

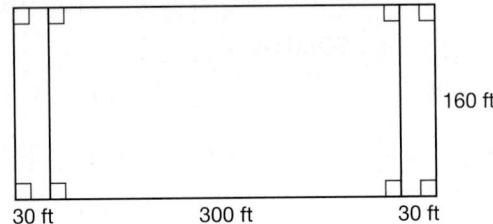

160 ft

30 ft   300 ft   30 ft

SOLUTION

width   ×   length

$= 160$ × $(30 + 300 + 30)$

$= 160(30 + 300 + 30)$

$= 160(30) + 160(300) + 160(30)$ Use the Distributive Property.

$= 4800 + 48{,}000 + 4800$ Multiply.

$= 57{,}600$ Add.

Check Use the order of operations.

$160(30 + 300 + 30)$ Perform the operation inside the parentheses.

$= 160(360)$ Multiply.

$= 57{,}600$ ✓

The area of the football field is $57{,}600 \text{ ft}^2$.

Lesson Practice

Simplify each expression.

a. $8(2 + 7)$
(Ex 1)

b. $4(6 - 2)$
(Ex 1)

c. $-(9 + 3)$
(Ex 2)

d. $-14(4 - 2)$
(Ex 2)

e. $-10(m + 4)$
(Ex 3)

f. $(7 - y)8$
(Ex 3)

g. $4xy^3(x^4y - 5x)$
(Ex 4)

h. $-2x^2m^2(m^2 - 4m)$
(Ex 4)

i. A group of 4 adults and 8 children are buying tickets to an amusement
(Ex 5) park. Tickets are $15 each. Write an expression using the Distributive Property to show the total cost of the tickets. Simplify the expression.

Evaluate.

1. $-7(-8 + 3)$
(15)

2. $5(-3 - 6)$
(15)

3. Evaluate $\sqrt{10,000}$.
(13)

4. Solve $c = \sqrt{25}$.
(13)

*5. Multi-Step In a shipment of 800 eggs, the probability of an egg breaking is $\frac{2}{25}$.
(14) How many are likely to be broken in the shipment? Justify the answer.

6. The digits 0, 1, 2, 3, 4, 5, 6, 7, 8 and 9 are written on cards that are shuffled
(14) and placed face down in a stack. One card is selected at random. What is the probability that the digit is odd and greater than 5?

*7. In a bucket there are 10 balls in a bucket numbered 1, 1, 2, 3, 4, 4, 4, 5, 6, and 6.
(14) A single ball is randomly chosen from the bucket. What is the probability of drawing a ball with a number less than 7? Explain.

*8. Multiple Choice Simplify the expression $-5(x + 6)$. Which is the correct
(15) simplification?

   A $-5 + x - 11$ **B** $-5x + 1$ **C** $-5x + 30$ **D** $-5x - 30$

*9. Find the value of y in the equation $18 - x = y$ if $x = -4$.
(6)

10. The water level of the reservoir in Austin, Texas, was 3 feet below normal. After a
(5) heavy rain storm, the water level increased to 5 feet above normal. How much did the rain storm change the water level?

11. Error Analysis Two students evaluated a numeric expression. Which student is
(15) correct? Explain the error.

Student A	Student B
$-8(-5 + 14)$	$-8(-5 + 14)$
$= 40 - 112$	$= -13 + 6$
$= -72$	$= -7$

12. Write Evaluate the expression $-8(9 - 15)$ using the Distributive Property. Explain.
(15)

*13. ⟨**Surveying**⟩ The county surveyed a piece of property and divided it into
(15) equal-sized lots. Use the diagram to write an expression that requires the Distributive Property to evaluate it. Evaluate the expression to find the total number of lots on the property.

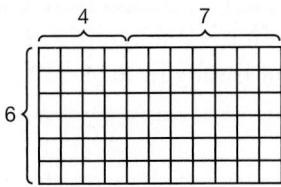

*14. True or False: $m + 0 = m$. Justify your answer using the properties.
(12)

15. Convert 3.4 yd^3 to ft^3.
(8)

16. Multi-Step Travis plans to divide his collection of baseball cards among
(15)   8 grandchildren. He will give each child the same number of cards. Each card
       is worth \$14. Write an expression to represent the value of each child's cards.
       Let c equal the total number of cards in Travis's collection.

17. (Budgeting) Kennedy's teacher asked her to plan the budget for the class party.
(15)   Kennedy began by writing the expression $g = b + 7$ to represent that the number
       of girls equals the number of boys plus seven. Each girl will need \$6. Write and
       simplify an algebraic expression that uses the Distributive Property to show the
       total cost for girls at the class party.

*18. If a number cube is rolled, what is the probability of it landing on the number
(14)   5 or 6?

*19. Error Analysis Two students are evaluating the expression $\sqrt{36 + z}$ for $z = 13$.
(13)   Which student is correct? Explain the error.

Student A	Student B
$\sqrt{36 + z}$	$\sqrt{36 + z}$
$= \sqrt{36 + 13}$	$= \sqrt{36} + z$
$= \sqrt{49}$	$= 6 + 13$
$= 7$	$= 19$

20. Justify The expression $6 \cdot 2 \cdot 4$ would be simplified from left to right using the order
(12)   of operations. What property would allow this expression to be simplified from
       right to left?

*21. (Investments) Susan invests the same amount of money in each of 7 stocks. In one
(12)   year, her money increased 8 times. The value of her investment is represented by
       the expression $7x \cdot 8$. Show two methods to simplify the expression and justify each
       step using the properties.

22. (Age) Rickie is $3\frac{3}{4}$ years older than Raymond. Raymond is $2\frac{1}{2}$ years younger
(10)   than Ryan. If Ryan is $14\frac{1}{4}$ years old, how old is Rickie?

23. Write Write the procedure for evaluating the expression $16f^2 g^3 - 4f^8 + 12$ for
(9) $f = 3$ and $g = 5$.

24. Model Use the number line to model $x - 8$ when $x = -6$.
(6)

25. (Astronomy) In astronomy, brightness is given in a value called magnitude. A
(3) -2-magnitude star is 2.512 times brighter than a -1-magnitude star, a
       -3-magnitude star is 2.512 times brighter than a -2-magnitude star, and so on.
       If Sirius is magnitude -1.5 and the full moon is magnitude -12.5, how much
       brighter is the full moon?

26. **Error Analysis** Student A and Student B each solved the absolute-value problem as
$^{(5)}$ shown below. Which student is correct? Explain the error.

Student A	Student B
$-\lvert 12 - 15 \rvert$	$-\lvert 12 - 15 \rvert$
$= -\lvert -3 \rvert$	$= -\lvert -3 \rvert$
$= -(3)$	$= \lvert +3 \rvert$
$= -3$	$= 3$

*27. Find the value of y for the given values of x in the equation $x - \lvert x - 2 \rvert = y$
$^{(6)}$ if $x = -3$.

28. **Verify** When simplified, will the expression $3 + \frac{2}{3} + \lvert -5 \rvert$ be positive or negative?
$^{(7)}$ Explain.

29. **Probability** Thomas spun a game spinner and recorded the results in the table below.
$^{(Inv\ 1)}$

Outcome	Frequency
Red	3
Blue	5
Yellow	9
Green	8

Use the table to find the experimental probability of each event. Express each
probability as a fraction and as a percent.

a. landing on red

b. landing on green

c. not landing on green

30. **Geometry** What is the perimeter of a square with an area of 121 sq. in.?
$^{(13)}$

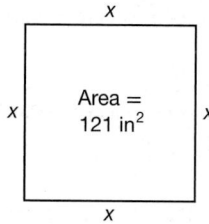

x

x Area = 121 in^2 x

x

Simplifying and Evaluating Variable Expressions

1. **Vocabulary** The set of whole numbers and their opposites $\{..., -4, -3,$
(6)
$-2, -1, 0, 1, 2, 3, 4,...\}$ is the set of _____.

Simplify.

2. $-ax^2(dx^3 - a^5x)$
(15)

3. $\sqrt{36} + \sqrt{81} - 4^2$
(13)

4. $[-(-5)] - |-7|$
(7)

5. Which value is equivalent to $\frac{9}{10}\left(-\frac{1}{12}\right)$?
(11)

    A $-\frac{49}{60}$ **B** $-\frac{3}{40}$ **C** $\frac{3}{60}$ **D** $\frac{3}{40}$

New Concepts To evaluate an expression that contains variables, substitute each variable in the expression with a given numeric value, and then find the value of the expression.

Example 1 **Evaluating Expressions with Two Variables**

Evaluate each expression for the given values of the variables.

a. $-a[-a(p - a)]$ for $a = 3$ and $p = 4$

SOLUTION

$-a[-a(p - a)]$

$= -3[-3(4 - 3)]$ Substitute each variable with the given value.

$= -3[-3(1)]$ Subtract.

$= -3[-3]$ Multiply inside the brackets.

$= 9$ Multiply.

Hint

Use parentheses when substituting a number for a variable, so that the negative signs and the subtraction signs are not confused.

b. $(-x + a) - (x - a)$ for $a = -2$ and $x = 7$

SOLUTION

$(-x + a) - (x - a)$

$= [-7 + (-2)] - [7 - (-2)]$ Substitute each variable with the given value.

$= [-7 + (-2)] - [7 + 2]$ Take the opposite of -2.

$= (-9) - (9)$ Evaluate inside the brackets.

$= -18$ Subtract.

Example 2 Evaluating Expressions with Three Variables

Evaluate each expression for the given values of the variables.

a. $(yx)(zyx)$ for $x = 2$, $y = -1$, and $z = 4$

SOLUTION

$(yx)(zyx)$

$= [(-1)(2)][(4)(-1)(2)]$ Substitute each variable with the given value.

$= (-2)(-8)$ Multiply inside the brackets.

$= 16$ Multiply.

b. $\dfrac{x(4ap)}{xp}$ for $a = 1$, $p = 5$, and $x = -3$

SOLUTION

$\dfrac{x(4ap)}{xp}$

$= \dfrac{(-3)(4)(1)(5)}{(-3)(5)}$ Substitute each variable with the given value.

$= \dfrac{-60}{-15} = 4$ Multiply and simplify.

An expression can be simplified before it is evaluated.

Example 3 Simplifying Before Evaluating Expressions

Simplify each expression. Then evaluate it. Justify each step.

a. $-x(y - 3) + y$ for $x = 0.5$ and $y = -1.75$

SOLUTION

$-x(y - 3) + y$

$= -xy + 3x + y$ Distributive Property

$= -(0.5)(-1.75) + 3(0.5) + (-1.75)$ Substitute.

$= 0.875 + 1.5 - 1.75$ Multiply and add.

$= 0.625$

b. $x(x + 2y) - x$ for $x = \dfrac{1}{2}$ and $y = \dfrac{1}{4}$

SOLUTION

$x(x + 2y) - x$

$= x^2 + 2xy - x$ Distributive Property

$= \left(\dfrac{1}{2}\right)^2 + 2\left(\dfrac{1}{2}\right)\left(\dfrac{1}{4}\right) - \left(\dfrac{1}{2}\right)$ Substitute.

$= \dfrac{1}{4} + \dfrac{1}{4} - \dfrac{1}{2} = 0$ Use order of operations to simplify.

Math Reasoning

Verify Evaluate Example 3a without simplifying first to show that the answer is the same.

Online Connection
www.SaxonMathResources.com

Example 4 **Evaluating Expressions with Exponents**

Evaluate each expression for the given values of the variables.

a. If $m = -2$ and $y = 2.5$, what is the value of ym^3?

SOLUTION

$$ym^3$$
$$= (2.5)(-2)^3 \qquad \text{Substitute each variable with the given value.}$$
$$= (2.5)(-8) \qquad \text{Evaluate the exponent.}$$
$$= -20 \qquad \text{Multiply.}$$

b. If $a = 3$ and $b = -1$, what is the value of $2\left(\frac{a}{5-b}\right)^2$?

SOLUTION

$$2\left(\frac{a}{5-b}\right)^2$$
$$= 2\left(\frac{3}{5-(-1)}\right)^2 \qquad \text{Substitute each variable with the given value.}$$
$$= 2\left(\frac{3}{5+1}\right)^2 \qquad \text{Take the opposite of } -1.$$
$$= 2\left(\frac{3}{6}\right)^2 \qquad \text{Perform operations inside the parentheses.}$$
$$= 2\left(\frac{1}{2}\right)^2 \qquad \text{Write the fraction in simplest form.}$$
$$= 2\left(\frac{1}{4}\right) \qquad \text{Evaluate the exponent.}$$
$$= \frac{1}{2} \qquad \text{Multiply.}$$

c. If $a = 3$, what is the value of $\left|(-a)^3\right|$?

SOLUTION

$$\left|(-a)^3\right|$$
$$= \left|(-3)^3\right| \qquad \text{Substitute the variable with the given value.}$$
$$= \left|(-3)(-3)(-3)\right| \qquad \text{Evaluate the exponent.}$$
$$= \left|-27\right| \qquad \text{Multiply.}$$
$$= 27 \qquad \text{Take the absolute value.}$$

Example 5 **Application: Investments**

A savings account increases as interest accumulates according to the formula $P_y = 1.04(P_{y-1})$, where P_y is the principal balance at the end of y years and P_{y-1} is the principal balance after $y - 1$ years. After 6 years, there is a principal balance of $1450.00. How much is the principal balance after 8 years?

SOLUTION

P_{7-1} or P_6	represents the principal balance after 6 years
P_{7-1} or $P_6 = \$1450$	
$P_7 = 1.04(P_{7-1})$	Write the formula for the principal balance after 7 years.
$P_7 = 1.04(1450)$	Substitute 1450 for P_{7-1}.
$P_7 = \$1508$	
$P_8 = 1.04(P_{8-1})$	Write the formula for the principal balance after 8 years.
P_{8-1} or P_7	represents the principal balance after 7 years
$P_8 = 1.04(1508)$	Substitute 1508 for P_{8-1}.
$P_8 = \$1568.32$	

Her principal balance is $1568.32 after 8 years.

Lesson Practice

Evaluate each expression for the given values of the variables.

a. $ax[-a(a - x)]$ for $a = 2$ and $x = -1$
(Ex 1)

b. $-b[-b(b - c) - (c - b)]$ for $b = -2$ and $c = 0$
(Ex 1)

c. $(5y)(2z)4xy$ for $x = 3$, $y = -1$, and $z = \dfrac{1}{2}$
(Ex 2)

d. $\dfrac{4rs}{6st}$ for $r = -1$, $s = -3$, and $t = -2$
(Ex 2)

Simplify each expression. Then evaluate for $a = 2$ and $b = -1$. Justify each step.
(Ex 3)

e. $-b(a - 3) + a$

f. $-a(-b - a) - b$

Evaluate each expression for the given values of the variable.
(Ex 4)

g. If $a = -2$ and $b = 25$, what is the value of $\dfrac{-b(a - 4) + b}{b}$?

h. If $x = -4$ and $y = -2$, what is the value of $\dfrac{x^2 - x|y|}{x^3}$?

i. A savings account grows according to the formula $P_y = 1.04(P_{y-1})$, where
(Ex 5) P_y is the principal balance at the end of y years and P_{y-1} is the principal balance after $y - 1$ years. After 6 years, there is a principal balance of $1600.00. How much is the principal balance after 8 years?

Simplify.

1. $2 + 5 - 3 + 7 - (-3) + 5$
(10)

2. $3(7) + 5 - 3 + 7 - 9 \div 2$
(4)

3. Represent the following numbers as being members of set K: $-2, -1, -4, -1, -3,$
(1) $-1, -5, -3$.

Determine if each statement is true or false. If true, explain why. If false, give a counterexample.

4. The set of whole numbers is closed under multiplication.
(1)

5. All integers are whole numbers.
(1)

Simplify by using the Distributive Property.

6. $-4y(d + cx)$
(15)

7. $(a + bc)2x$
(15)

Evaluate the expression for the given values.

*8. $pa[-a(-a)]$ when $p = 2$ and $a = -1$
(16)

*9. $x(x - y)$ when $x = \dfrac{1}{5}$ and $y = \dfrac{6}{5}$
(16)

*10. $\left(\dfrac{x - 3}{y}\right)^2$ when $x = -5$ and $y = 2$
(16)

11. $4(b + 1)^2 - 6(c - b)^4$ when $b = 2$ and $c = 7$
(9)

12. Geometry The measure of one side of a square is $5x + 1$ meters. What expression
(15) would be used for the perimeter of the square? Explain.

13. Identify the property illustrated in the equation $2 + (1 + 7) = (2 + 1) + 7$.
(12)

*14. Multiple Choice A fish tank empties at a rate of $v = 195 - 0.5t$, where v is the
(16) number of liters remaining after t seconds have passed. If the fish tank empties for 20 seconds, how many liters remain?

A 205 **B** 185

C 175 **D** 174.5

*15. Multi-Step A solid, plastic machine part is shaped like a cone that is 8 centimeters
(16) high and has a radius of 2 centimeters. A machinist has removed some of the plastic by drilling a cylindrical hole into the part's base. The hole is 4 centimeters deep and has a diameter of 1 centimeter.

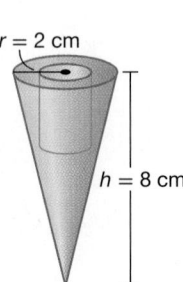

a. Determine the volume of the cone. Use the formula $V = \frac{1}{3}\pi r^2 h$.

b. Determine the volume of the cylindrical hole. Use the formula $V = \pi r^2 h$.

c. Determine the volume of the plastic machine part by subtracting the volume of the cylindrical hole from the volume of the cone.

*16. **(Chemistry)** Boyle's law relates the pressure and volume of a gas held at a constant
(16) temperature. This relationship is represented by the equation $P_f = \frac{P_i V_i}{V_f}$. In this
equation, P_i and V_i represent the gas's initial pressure and volume. P_f and V_f
represent the gas's final pressure and volume. What is the final pressure of the
gas if a 3-liter volume of gas at a pressure of 1 atmosphere is expanded to a final
volume of 6 liters?

*17. **(Investing)** Jamie wants to determine how much she should invest in a stock. She uses
(16) the equation for present value, $V_p = \frac{V_f}{(1 + i)^t}$, in which V_f is the future value, i is the
interest rate, and t is the number of years. How much should her present value be
if she wants the future value of the stock to be $2000 in 10 years at an interest rate
of 0.02? Round the answer to the nearest dollar.

*18. **Multiple Choice** Given the information in the table, which
(16) equation best relates x and y?

A $y = x^3 + 5$ **B** $y = \frac{x^2 + 5}{x}$

C $y = |x^3 + 5|$ **D** $y = \frac{x^3 + 5}{x}$

x	y
2	13
1	6
−1	4
−2	3

*19. **Measurement** A party planner use the equation $A = Nx^2$ to estimate how much cake
(16) is needed for a party with N guests, where x is the width of a square piece of cake.
If each piece of cake will be about 3 inches wide, approximate the area of the base
of a cake pan for the given number of guests.

a. 50 guests

b. 150 guests

c. 350 guests

*20. **Multi-Step** Two teams of students were riding bikes for charity. There were a total
(15) of b students on the blue team and they each rode 15 miles. There were a total of
r students on the red team and they each rode 3 miles. The students collected $2
for each mile.

a. Write an expression for the total number of miles ridden by both teams.

b. Write and simplify an expression that uses the Distributive Property to show the
total amount of money collected.

21. **Error Analysis** A bucket contains 10 balls numbered 1, 1, 2, 3, 4, 4, 4, 5, 6, and 6. A
(14) single ball is randomly chosen from the bucket. What is the probability of drawing
a ball with a number greater than or equal to 5? Which student is correct? Explain
the error.

Student A	Student B
$P(5 \text{ or } 6) = \frac{3}{10}$	$P(5 \text{ or } 6) = \frac{2}{10} \text{ or } \frac{1}{5}$

22. **Estimate** $\sqrt{36} + \sqrt{40} \bigcirc \sqrt{25} + \sqrt{80}$. Verify the answer.
(13)

23. Multi-Step John is using square ceramic floor tiles that are each 18 inches
(13) long. How many of these tiles will John need to cover a floor with an area
of 81 square feet?

24. (Oceanography) *Alvin* (DSV-2), a 16-ton manned research submersible, is used to
(11) observe life forms at depths of up to 8000 feet below sea level. After the hull was
replaced, *Alvin* was able to dive about 2.6 times the distance as before the hull
replacement. About how far was it able to travel after the hull was replaced?

25. Analyze What is the sign of the sum of -8 + 7? Explain how the sign is
(10) determined.

26. Write Why would you want to convert measures from one unit to another when
(8) working with a recipe found in a French cookbook?

27. Justify Evaluate $10(8-6)^3 + 4(|-5 + (-2)| + 2)$. Justify each step.
(7)

28. Error Analysis Two students wanted to find out the change in temperature in
(6) Calgary, Canada. It was -1°C in the morning and was -20°C by nighttime.
Which student is correct? Explain the error.

Student A	Student B
-20 - 1	-20 - (-1)
-20 + (-1)	-20 + 1
-21	-19

29. (Construction) A father builds a playhouse in the shape of a rectangular prism
(4) with a triangular prism on top, as shown in the figure. The volume of the
rectangular prism is $(10 \cdot 5.8 \cdot 8)$ ft³, and the volume of the triangular prism is
$[\frac{1}{2} \cdot (10 \cdot 5.8)] \cdot 4$ ft³. What is the volume of the whole structure?

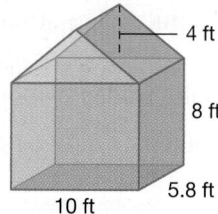

4 ft
8 ft
5.8 ft
10 ft

30. (Manufacturing) A manufacturing company produced 500 bowling balls in one day.
(Inv 1) Of those, 10 were found to be defective. The manufacturer sent a shipment of
250 balls to Zippy Lanes.

a. What is the experimental probability that a bowling ball with have a defect?

b. Predict the number of balls in the shipment to Zippy Lanes that will have a
defect.

Translating Between Words and Algebraic Expressions

1. Vocabulary An expression that has only numbers and operations is a
(9)
_____ (*numeric, variable*) expression.

Simplify each expression.

2. $5 - 7 + 5 - (-3)$
(6)

3. $(5 + 7)4 + 7(5 - 3)$
(15)

4. $(x^3 + m^5)x^2m^2$
(15)

5. Which value is equivalent to $-(-6)^3$?
(11)
    A -216 **B** 216 **C** 18 **D** -18

New Concepts   Algebraic expressions, or variable expressions, are expressions that contain at least one variable. A numeric expression contains only numbers and operations.

Translating Word and Phrases into Algebraic Expressions		
Words	**Phrases**	**Expressions**
Addition sum, total, more than, added, increased, plus	4 added to a number 7 increased by a number	$x + 4$ $7 + x$
Subtraction less, minus, decreased by, difference, less than	the difference of 5 and a number 8 less than a number	$5 - x$ $x - 8$
Multiplication product, times, multiplied	the product of a number and 12 a number times 3	$12(x)$ $3x$
Division quotient, divided by, divided into	the quotient of a number and 6 10 divided by a number	$x \div 6$ $\frac{10}{x}$

Hint

Remember that in multiplication, the coefficient is usually written before the variable.

Hint

"Years younger than" means less than.

Online Connection
www.SaxonMathResources.com

Example 1   **Translating Words into Algebraic Expressions**

Write an algebraic expression for each phrase.

a. y increased by 12

SOLUTION $y + 12$

b. the product of x and 4

SOLUTION $4x$

c. 8 less than the quotient of m and 15

SOLUTION $\frac{m}{15} - 8$

d. James is 6 years younger than Lydia, who is x years old. Write the expression that shows James's age.

SOLUTION If x represents Lydia's age, then $x - 6$ represents James's age.

Example 2   Translating Algebraic Expressions into Words

Use words to write each algebraic expression in two different ways.

a. $m + 7$

SOLUTION

7 more than m;

the sum of 7 and m

b. $y - 9$

SOLUTION

9 less than y;

the difference of y and 9

c. $5 \cdot n$

SOLUTION

the product of 5 and n;

5 times n

d. $x \div 3$

SOLUTION

x divided by 3;

the quotient of x and 3

e. $27 - \frac{1}{2}(18)$

SOLUTION

the difference of 27 and one-half of 18;

27 minus 18 divided by 2

Example 3   Application: Savings

Jayne is saving money to buy a car. She has x dollars saved and is saving y dollars per week. Write an algebraic expression to represent the total amount of money she will have saved after 52 weeks.

SOLUTION

dollars saved	dollars saved each week	amount saved after 52 weeks
x	y	$x + 52y$

Jayne will have $x + 52y$ dollars saved after 52 weeks.

Lesson Practice

Write each phrase as an algebraic expression.
(Ex 1)

a. the product of x and 8

b. 18 minus y

c. 7 more than 5 times x

d. Raquel is 2 years older than Monica, who is x years old. Write the expression that shows Raquel's age.

Use words to write each algebraic expression in two different ways.
(Ex 2)

e. $\dfrac{10}{s}$

f. $5 - r$

g. $3m + 7$

h. $\frac{3}{4}x + 9$

i. $\frac{x - 3}{2}$

j. (Savings) Jon has d dollars in a savings account. He withdraws x dollars
(Ex 3) each week for 15 weeks. Write an algebraic expression to represent the
amount of money that will be left in the savings account at the end of
the 15 weeks.

Practice   Distributed and Integrated

Expand each algebraic expression by using the Distributive Property.

1. $(4 + 2y)x$
(15)

2. $-2(x - 4y)$
(15)

3. Write What is a term of an algebraic expression?
(2)

4. Given the sets $A = \{-3, -2, -1\}$, $B = \{1, 2, 3\}$, and $C = \{-1, 1, -2, 2, -3, 3\}$,
(1) are the following statements true or false?

   a. $A \cap C = \{-3, -2, -1\}$

   b. $A \cap B = \{-3, -2, -1, 1, 2, 3\}$

   c. $B \cup C = \{-3, -2, -1, 1, 2, 3\}$

   d. $A \cup B = \{-3, -2, -1\}$

Write the algebraic expressions for each statement.

*5. three times the sum of the opposite of a number and -7
(17)

*6. 0.18 of what number is 4.68?
(17)

7. Add $4.7 + (-9.2) - 1.9$.
(10)

8. Compare $\sqrt{36} + \sqrt{121} \;\bigcirc\; \sqrt{100} + \sqrt{49}$ using $<$, $>$, or $=$.
(13)

9. Between which two whole numbers is $\sqrt{15}$?
(13)

10. Justify True or False: $k = 0 \cdot k$, where k is any real number except for zero. Justify your
(12) answer using the properties.

11. Evaluate $(a + 4)^3 + 5x^2$ when $a = -3$ and $x = -1$.
(16)

*12. Justify True or False: $yx^2m^3 = -4$ when $x = -1$, $y = 2$, and $m = -2$. Justify your
(16) answer.

*13. Translate $3(x + 6)$ into word form.
(17)

*14. Multiple Choice Which expression is the algebraic translation of "4 times the sum of
(17) 9 and g"?

   A $4 + 9g$ **B** $4(9 + g)$ **C** $4 \cdot 9g$ **D** $(4 + 9)g$

*15. **(Age)** Mary is one year younger than twice Paul's age. Write an expression for
(17)   Mary's age.

*16. **(Finance)** Miles spent $7 and then received a paycheck that doubled the money he
(17)   had left. Write an expression to represent how much money he has now.

*17. **Multi-Step** A produce stand sells apples and bananas. Apples cost $0.20 each and
(17)   bananas cost $0.10 each.

    a. Choose variables to represent apples and bananas.

    b. Write an expression to represent the total pieces of fruit.

    c. Write an expression to represent how much the fruit costs in dollars.

18. **Error Analysis** Students are asked to evaluate $\frac{x^2 - 4x}{xy}$ when $x = -2$ and $y = 3$. Which
(16)   student is correct? Explain the error.

Student A	Student B
$\dfrac{x^2 - 4x}{xy}$	$\dfrac{x^2 - 4x}{xy}$
$\dfrac{(-2)^2 - 4(-2)}{(-2)(3)}$	$\dfrac{(-2)^2 - 4(-2)}{(-2)(3)}$
$= \dfrac{4 + 8}{-6}$	$= \dfrac{-4 - (-8)}{-6}$
$= \dfrac{12}{-6} = -2$	$= \dfrac{4}{-6}$
	$= \dfrac{-2}{3}$

*19. **Geometry** The figure below has corners that are square and a curved section that
(16)   is a half circle. The dimensions given are in meters. What is the area of the figure?
Use 3.14 for π.

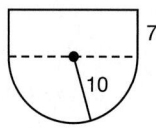

*20. **Multi-Step** A painter estimates that one gallon of a certain kind of paint will
(4)   cover 305 square feet of wall. How many gallons of the paint will cover the wall
described by the diagram below? (Dimensions given are in feet.)

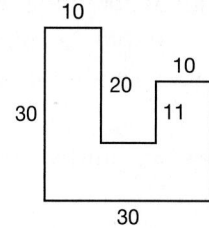

*21. Error Analysis Two students simplified an algebraic expression. Which student is
₍₁₅₎ correct? Explain the error.

Student A	Student B
$2r^3t\,(r^5t^2 + 4r^3t^3)$ $= 2r^{15}t^2 + 8r^9t^3$	$2r^3t\,(r^5t^2 + 4r^3t^3)$ $= 2r^8t^3 + 8r^6t^4$

22. Probability There are 400 students in the cafeteria. Of these students, 120 are
₍₁₄₎ tenth-graders. What is the probability of randomly selecting a tenth-grader?
Express the answer as a percent.

23. Error Analysis Two students simplify the expression $-7 - x + 7$. Which student is
₍₁₂₎ correct? Explain the error.

Student A	Student B
$-7 - x + 7$ $= x + (-7) + 7$ $= x + (-7 + 7)$ $= x + 0$ $= x$	$-7 - x + 7$ $= -7 + 7 - x$ $= (-7 + 7) - x$ $= 0 - x$ $= -x$

24. Justify Simplify $-\frac{2}{3} \div \left(-\frac{8}{9}\right)$. Show your steps.
₍₁₁₎

25. Write Must the algebraic expression $x + 7y$ have only one value? Explain.
₍₉₎

26. Measurement Madison used a scale and measured her weight at 85 pounds. How
₍₈₎ many kilograms does Madison weigh? (Hint: 1 kilogram $= 2.2$ pounds.)

27. (Energy Conservation) Wind turbines take the energy from the wind and convert it
₍₄₎ to electrical energy. Use the formula $P = ad^2v^3 \frac{\pi}{4} e$ to find the amount of available
energy in the air. Describe the steps you would take to simplify the formula.

28. (Finance) Tonia deposited a total of \$174.52 into her checking account. She also
₍₅₎ withdrew a total of \$186.15. Use addition to find the net change in Tonia's
checking account.

29. Justify What is the first step in simplifying the expression $2 \cdot 4 + 5^2 + (23 - 2)^2$?
₍₄₎

30. (Payroll Accounting) Employees at Wilkinson Glass Company earn x number of
₍₁₅₎ dollars per hour. Executives make y number of dollars per hour. Each employee
and executive works 40 hours per week. Write and simplify an algebraic expression
that uses the Distributive Property to show a weekly payroll for one employee and
one executive.

Combining Like Terms

1. Vocabulary A _____ (*constant, variable*) is a symbol, usually a letter
(2) used to represent an unknown number.

Simplify each expression.

2. $(0.2)^5$
(3)

3. $y^3 \cdot x^4 \cdot y^2 \cdot x^5 \cdot y$
(3)

4. Write the phrase "six more than twice a number" as an algebraic expression.
(17)

New Concepts

Two or more terms that have the same variable or variables raised to the same power are **like terms**. Terms with different variables or terms with the same variable or variables raised to a different power are **unlike terms**.

$$\boxed{3x^4} + 5y^4 + \boxed{5x^4}$$

Because the variable x has the same power, $3x^4$ and $5x^4$ are like terms. Because the variables are not the same, $5y^4$ and $5x^4$ are unlike terms. The coefficient is not used to establish whether the terms are like or unlike.

> **Hint**
>
> It may be helpful to circle, box, or underline the terms that are alike before combining like terms.

Example 1 Combining Like Terms Without Exponents

Simplify each expression.

a. $5x + 7x$

SOLUTION

$5x + 7x$

$= (5 + 7)x$ Use the Distributive Property.

$= 12x$ Simplify.

b. $-4y - (-3y) + 5y$

SOLUTION

$-4y - (-3y) + 5y$

$= (-4 + 3 + 5)y$ Take the opposite of -3, and then use the Distributive Property.

$= 4y$ Simplify.

> **Math Reasoning**
>
> **Justify** Why can the order of the factors in a term be rearranged?

c. $6xy - 3a + 4yx$

SOLUTION

$6xy - 3a + 4yx$

$= 6xy + 4yx - 3a$ Rearrange the terms.

$= 6xy + 4xy - 3a$ Rearrange the factors.

$= 10xy - 3a$ Add the like terms.

Example 2 Combining Like Terms With Exponents

Simplify each expression.

a. $x^5 + y^3 + x^5 + y^3$

SOLUTION

$$x^5 + y^3 + x^5 + y^3$$

$= x^5 + x^5 + y^3 + y^3$	Rearrange the terms.
$= (1 + 1)x^5 + (1 + 1)y^3$	Use the Distributive Property.
$= 2x^5 + 2y^3$	Simplify.

b. $3k^2 - 2k^2 + 4k^2 + 2kx^4 + kx^4$

SOLUTION

$$3k^2 - 2k^2 + 4k^2 + 2kx^4 + kx^4$$

$= (3 - 2 + 4)k^2 + (2 + 1)kx^4$	Use the Distributive Property.
$= 5k^2 + 3kx^4$	Simplify.

c. $2x^2y^3 + xy - 8y^3x^2 - 5yx$

SOLUTION

$$2x^2y^3 + xy - 8y^3x^2 - 5yx$$

$= 2x^2y^3 - 8y^3x^2 + xy - 5xy$	Rearrange the terms.
$= 2x^2y^3 - 8x^2y^3 + xy - 5xy$	Rearrange the factors.
$= (2 - 8)x^2y^3 + (1 - 5)xy$	Use the Distributive Property.
$= -6x^2y^3 - 4xy$	Simplify.

Example 3 Application: Measurement

Olympic competition offers three equestrian disciplines: dressage, show jumping, and endurance. The diagram represents the measurements for a regulation dressage arena.

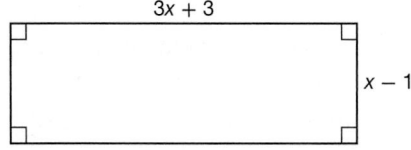

Find the perimeter of the arena as a simplified variable expression. Then evaluate the expression for $x = 19.5$ meters.

SOLUTION

$P = 2l + 2w$	Write the formula for the perimeter of a rectangle.
$P = 2(3x + 3) + 2(x - 1)$	Substitute for l and w.
$P = 6x + 6 + 2x - 2$	Use the Distributive Property.
$P = 8x + 4$	Combine like terms.
$P = 8(19.5) + 4$	Substitute 19.5 for x.
$P = 156 + 4 = 160$	Multiply. Then add.

The perimeter of the dressage arena is $8x + 4$ or 160 meters.

Simplify each expression.

a. $-2xy - 3x + 4 - 4xy - 2x$
(Ex 1)

b. $7m - (-8m) + 9m$
(Ex 1)

c. $3yac - 2ac + 6acy$
(Ex 1)

d. $x^4y + 3x^4y + 2x^4y$
(Ex 2)

e. $x^2y - 3yx + 2yx^2 - 2xy + yx$
(Ex 2)

f. $m^3n + m^3n - x^2y^7 + x^2y^7$
(Ex 2)

g. A triangular-shaped display case has the
(Ex 3) dimensions shown on the diagram. Find the perimeter of the display case as a simplified variable expression. Then evaluate the expression for $x = 2$ feet.

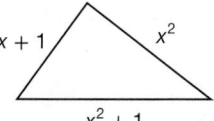

$x + 1$ x^2
$x^2 + 1$

Practice   **Distributed and Integrated**

1. Write an algebraic expression for this statement: The sum of 5 times a number and -8.
(17)

Simplify each expression by adding like terms.

*2. $m + 4 + 3m - 6 - 2m + mc - 4mc$
(18)

*3. $xy - 3xy^2 + 5y^2x - 4xy$
(18)

*4. **Multiple Choice** Simplify $2x^2 + 3x$.
(18)

   A $5x^2$ **B** $5x^3$

   C $6x^3$ **D** cannot be simplified

*5. (**Reading**) Two classes are keeping track of how many pages they can read. In one
(18) class, the boys read 15 pages per night and the girls read 12 pages per night. In another class, the boys read 7 pages per night and the girls read 9 pages per night. Each class has x girls and y boys.

   a. Write expressions representing the number of pages each class read per night.

   b. Write an expression for the number they read altogether.

6. **Justify** After doing three addition problems that included negative numbers, John
(5) found that all three answers were negative. John concluded that any addition problem involving a negative number must have a negative answer. Is John correct? Explain. Give a counterexample if necessary.

7. (**Geography**) The retention pond at Martha's summer home in Florida changed
(6) -3 inches every day for 5 days. After 5 days, the water level was -40 inches. What was the original water level 5 days ago?

8. (**Bowling**) A ten-pin bowling ball has a volume of about 5274 cm³. A candlepin bowling ball has a volume of about 48 in³. About how much greater is the volume of a ten-pin bowling ball than the volume of a candlepin bowling ball?
(8)

Simplify.

9. $\dfrac{-16 + 4}{2\left(\sqrt{13 - 4}\right)}$
(4, 13)

10. $-7 - (2^4 \div 8)$
(4, 13)

*11. $6bac - 7ac + 8acb$
(18)

*12. $2x^3y + 4x^3y + 9x^3y$
(18)

13. $\left| -15 + \sqrt{81} \right|^2$
(13)

14. $\dfrac{\sqrt{6 - 2}}{2 \cdot \left| -7 + 3 \right|}$
(13)

*15. (**Sewing**) Susan started with 11 bows. She can tie 4 bows per minute. Analise ties twice as many per minute.
(18)

    a. Write expressions representing the number of bows each girl will have after x minutes.

    b. Write an expression for the number they will have altogether after x minutes.

16. Multi-Step Marshall, Hank, and Jean are all cousins. Marshall is 3 years older than Hank. Hank is twice the age of Jean.
(17)

    a. Write expressions to represent the ages of the cousins. Assign the variable j to represent Jean.

    b. If Jean is 12 years old, how old are the other cousins?

    c. If Hank was 14, how old would Jean be?

*17. Justify Simplify $8x + x(2x + 5)$ and explain each step.
(18)

18. Evaluate $\dfrac{8ak}{4k(2a - 2c + 8)}$ when $a = \dfrac{1}{2}$, $c = 3$, and $k = -2$.
(16)

*19. True or False: $pm^2 - z^3 = 27$ when $p = -5$, $m = 0$, and $z = -3$. Justify your answer.
(16)

20. Error Analysis Two students are asked to evaluate $x^2y - |4x|^2z$ when $x = -2$, $y = \dfrac{1}{2}$, and $z = -1$. Which student is correct? Explain the error.
(16)

Student A	Student B
$x^2y - |4x|^2\,z$	$x^2y - |4x|^2\,z$
$(-2)^2\left(\dfrac{1}{2}\right) - |4(-2)|^2\,(-1)$	$(-2)^2\,(-1) - |4(-2)|^2\left(\dfrac{1}{2}\right)$
$= 4\left(\dfrac{1}{2}\right) - |-8|^2\,(-1)$	$= 4(-1) - |-8|^2\left(\dfrac{1}{2}\right)$
$= 2 - (8)^2\,(-1) = 66$	$= -4 - (8)^2\left(\dfrac{1}{2}\right) = -36$

21. Predict How can finding a common denominator tell you that $\dfrac{1}{9} - \dfrac{2}{20}$ will result in a positive number?
(10)

*22. Multi-Step Tamatha picks 10 peaches a minute for x minutes. Her grandmother picks 12 peaches a minute for 3 fewer minutes.
(18)

    a. Write an expression to represent the number of minutes the grandmother picks peaches.

    b. Write an expression for the number of peaches they pick together and then simplify.

23. Geometry Translate the Pythagorean Theorem into symbols. In a right triangle,
(17) the sum of the squares of the legs of the triangle is equal to the square of the hypotenuse. Let a and b be the legs of the triangle and c be the hypotenuse.

24. Measurement A railing is being built around a rectangular deck.
(17)

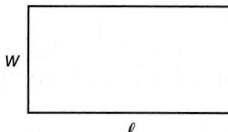

    a. Write an expression to represent the number of feet of railing needed.

    b. The width is doubled. The length is tripled. Write an expression to represent the number of feet of railing needed.

25. Multiple Choice Simplify the expression $7(10 - y)$. Which expression is correct?
(15)

    A $70 - y$ **B** $70 - 7y$

    C $70 - 7 + y$ **D** $70y - 7y$

26. Justify Simplify the expression $-m(mn^2 - m^2n)$ and explain your method for
(15) simplifying.

27. Probability A number is chosen at random from the numbers 1 through 5. What is
(14) the probability that an odd number will be chosen?

28. (Carpentry) A new company buys 140 square feet of carpet to cover the floor in one
(13) of its square offices. The carpet is 4 square feet too small. What is the length of the office floor?

29. Verify The Commutative Property states that $6 \cdot 4 = 4 \cdot 6$. Show that the
(12) Commutative Property does not apply to division.

30. Error Analysis Two students translate the phrase "the sum of the squares of 8 and p"
(17) into an algebraic expression. Which student is correct? Explain the error.

Student A	Student B
$(p + 8)^2$	$p^2 + 8^2$

Solving One-Step Equations by Adding or Subtracting

Warm Up

1. **Vocabulary** -4 and 4 are _____ because they have the same absolute value but different signs.
   (6)

2. Add $7.5 + (-1.25)$.
   (5)

3. Subtract $12.75 - (-1.05)$.
   (6)

4. Use $<$, $>$, or $=$ to compare $6x + 3$ and $-2x + 4$ when $x = -3$.
   (16)

5. Evaluate $w - (wy - y)$ for $w = -4$ and $y = -1$.
   (9)

   A 1 **B** -1 **C** -9 **D** 9

New Concepts

An **equation** is a statement that uses an equal sign to show that two quantities are equal. A **solution of an equation in one variable** is a value of the variable that makes the equation true.

Example 1   Identifying Solutions

State whether the value of the variable is a solution of the equation.

a. $x + 6 = 9$ for $x = 3$

SOLUTION

$$x + 6 = 9$$
$$(3) + 6 \stackrel{?}{=} 9 \qquad \text{Substitute 3 for } x.$$
$$9 = 9 \quad \checkmark$$

Solution, $3 + 6 = 9$

b. $x - 6 = 9$ for $x = 3$

SOLUTION

$$x - 6 = 9$$
$$(3) - 6 \stackrel{?}{=} 9 \qquad \text{Substitute 3 for } x.$$
$$-3 \neq 9 \quad ✗$$

Not a solution, $3 - 6 \neq 9$

> **Math Reasoning**
>
> **Verify** If the same quantity is added to both sides of $x - 7 = 15$, show that the resulting equation is equivalent to $x - 7 = 15$.

An equation is like a balance scale.

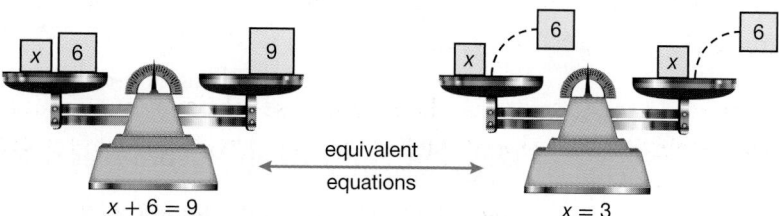

equivalent equations

$x + 6 = 9$ $x = 3$

The scale remains balanced when the same quantity is added to both sides, or when the same quantity is subtracted from both sides.

Equivalent equations have the same solution set. By adding or subtracting the same quantity from both sides of an equation, each equation remains equivalent to the original equation. Furthermore, each side of the equation remains balanced as the equation is solved.

Online Connection
www.SaxonMathResources.com

The Addition and Subtraction Properties of Equality hold for every real number a, b, and c.

Addition and Subtraction Properties of Equality
Addition Property of Equality
You can add the same number to both sides of an equation and the statement will still be true.
Examples $2 = 2$ $a = b$ $3 + 2 = 2 + 3$ $a + c = b + c$ $5 = 5$
Subtraction Property of Equality
You can subtract the same number from both sides of an equation and the statement will still be true.
Examples $10 = 10$ $a = b$ $10 - 4 = 10 - 4$ $a - c = b - c$ $6 = 6$

On the first page of the lesson the Subtraction Property of Equality is illustrated with balance scales. Below, the Addition Property of Equality is illustrated.

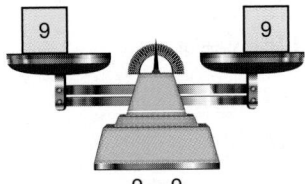
$9 = 9$

$2 + 9 = 9 + 2$

Inverse operations are operations that undo each other. To solve an equation, isolate the variable on one side of the equal sign by using inverse operations. Use the same inverse operation on each side of the equation.

Inverse Operations

Addition $\longleftrightarrow$ Subtraction

Multiplication $\longleftrightarrow$ Division

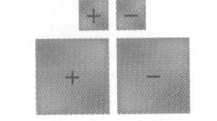
Exploration   Using Algebra Tiles to Model One-Step Equations

Use algebra tiles to model $x + 6 = 9$.

a. Model each side of the equation.

b. Isolate the x-tile. Add six negative 1-tiles to both sides. Remove pairs that equal zero.

c. What is the solution?

d. Use algebra tiles to model $x - 2 = 4$. What is the solution?

Example 2 — Solving Equations by Adding

Solve. Then check the solution.

a. $x - 3 = 12$

SOLUTION

$$x - 3 = 12$$
$$\underline{+3 = +3} \qquad \text{Add 3 to both sides to undo the subtraction.}$$
$$x = 15$$

Check Substitute 15 for x.

$$x - 3 \stackrel{?}{=} 12$$
$$(15) - 3 \stackrel{?}{=} 12$$
$$12 = 12 \quad \checkmark$$

b. $-15 = n - 8$

SOLUTION

$$-15 = n - 8$$
$$\underline{+8 = +8} \qquad \text{Add 8 to both sides.}$$
$$-7 = n$$

Check Substitute -7 for n.

$$-15 \stackrel{?}{=} (-7) - 8$$
$$-15 = -15 \quad \checkmark$$

Example 3 — Solve Equations by Subtracting

Solve.

a. $k + 7 = 13$

SOLUTION

$$k + 7 = 13$$
$$\underline{-7 = -7} \qquad \text{Subtract 7 from both sides.}$$
$$k = 6$$

b. $-21 = p + 9$

SOLUTION

$$-21 = p + 9$$
$$\underline{-9 = -9} \qquad \text{Subtract 9 from both sides.}$$
$$-30 = p$$

Example 4 Solve Fraction Equations by Adding or Subtracting

Solve.

$$x + \frac{1}{4} = -\frac{3}{8}$$

SOLUTION

$$x + \frac{1}{4} = -\frac{3}{8}$$

$$\underline{-\frac{1}{4} = -\frac{1}{4}} \qquad \text{Subtract } \frac{1}{4} \text{ from both sides.}$$

$$x = -\frac{5}{8}$$

Example 5 Application: Weather

On January 10, 1911, the temperature in Rapid City, South Dakota, fell 47°F in 15 minutes. What was the temperature at 7:00 a.m.?

Temperature in Rapid City, SD	
7:00 a.m.	
7:15 a.m.	8°F

SOLUTION

Let x = the temperature at 7:00 a.m.

Write an equation.

$$x - 47 = 8$$

$$\underline{+47 = +47} \qquad \text{To isolate the variable, add 47 to each side.}$$

$$x = 55$$

At 7:00 a.m. the temperature was 55°F.

Lesson Practice

State whether the value of each variable is a solution of the equation.

(Ex 1)
  a. $h - 14 = 2$ for $h = 12$

  b. $-11 = j - 4$ for $j = -7$

Solve. Then check the solution.

(Ex 2)
  c. $x - 5 = 17$

  d. $-30 = m - 12$

Solve.

  e. $p + 3 = 37$
(Ex 3)
  f. $-14 = y + 8$
(Ex 3)
  g. $d + 4\frac{1}{2} = 3\frac{1}{6}$.
(Ex 4)

  h. Jagdeesh took the same test twice. On the second test he scored 87, which was 13 points higher than on the first test. What was his first test score?
(Ex 5)

1. Simplify $-3x^2ym + 7x - 5ymx^2 + 16x$.
(18)

Solve each equation.

*2. $x + 5 = 7$
(19)

*3. $x + 5 = -8$
(19)

*4. $x - 6 = 4$
(19)

5. Write the algebraic expression for the phrase "seven times the sum of a number
(17) and -5."

6. Expand the expression $-3(-x - 4)$ by using the Distributive Property.
(15)

7. Simplify $xm^2xm^3x^3m$.
(3)

8. Identify the property illustrated by $3 + 8 = 8 + 3$.
(12)

9. Write True or False: $-5^4 = (-5)^4$. Explain.
(11)

10. Sandra lost 8 points for incorrect answers on her quiz, but gained 5 points for a
(10) bonus question. What is the sum of points Sandra lost and gained?

*11. **Error Analysis** A teacher asked two students to solve the following equation
(19) for x: $x + \frac{1}{3} = \frac{4}{9}$. Which student is correct? Explain the error.

Student A	Student B
$x + \dfrac{1}{3} + \dfrac{1}{3} = \dfrac{4}{9} + \dfrac{1}{3}$	$x + \dfrac{1}{3} - \dfrac{1}{3} = \dfrac{4}{9} - \dfrac{1}{3}$
$x = \dfrac{4}{9} + \dfrac{3}{9}$	$x = \dfrac{4}{9} - \dfrac{3}{9}$
$x = \dfrac{7}{9}$	$x = \dfrac{1}{9}$

*12. **Multiple Choice** A swimming pool is $\frac{4}{5}$ full. A maintenance man removes some of
(19) the water so that the pool is $\frac{1}{3}$ full. As a fraction of the pool's total capacity, how
much water did the maintenance man remove?

A $\dfrac{1}{5}$ **B** $\dfrac{3}{2}$ **C** $\dfrac{7}{15}$ **D** $\dfrac{17}{15}$

*13. (**Chemistry**) Many chemists use kelvins to describe temperatures. To convert from
(19) a temperature in degrees Celsius to kelvins, a chemist will use the equation
$T_{Celsius} + 273.15 = T_{kelvin}$. If a gas cools to a temperature of 325.20K, what is its
temperature in degrees Celsius?

*14. (**Business**) A movie theater needs to sell 3500 tickets over a single weekend to cover
(19) its operating expenses before it starts making a profit. If it sells 1278 tickets on
Friday, what is the minimum number of tickets it needs to sell over the rest of the
weekend in order to make a profit? Write an equation and then solve it.

*15. Write Jeremy is solving the equation $x - 2.5 = 7.0$. What must he do to both side
(19) of the equation in order to isolate x?

*16. Multiple Choice Given the information in the table, which equation best relates
(19) a and b?

a	b
-5	0
0	-5
5	-10
-10	5

A $a - b = 5$ **B** $a - b = -5$ **C** $-5 - b = a$ **D** $a - 5 = b$

17. Error Analysis Two students simplify the expression $6x + 8 - 4x - 2$. Which student
(18) is correct? Explain the error.

Student A	Student B
$2x + 6$ $= 8x$	$2x + 6$

18. Geometry Write an expression to represent the sum of the degrees in
(18) the triangle.

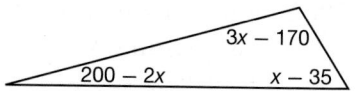

$3x - 170$

$200 - 2x$ $x - 35$

19. Multi-Step At a family camp, the big race is on the final day. Each
(18) family member runs for t hours and the family that runs the farthest
wins. The rate each person ran is shown in the chart. To find how far
they ran, multiply their rate by the amount of time they ran.
a. Write an expression to represent how far each person ran.

b. Write an expression to represent how far the family ran.

c. How far did they run if each person ran $\frac{1}{6}$ hour?

Family Member	Rate (mph)
Julio	4
Jorge	5
Sam	3

20. Error Analysis Two students translate the phrase "five more than the product of a
(17) number and three" into an algebraic expression. Which student is correct?
Explain the error.

Student A	Student B
$\frac{x}{3} + 5$	$3x + 5$

*21. When $x = 1.5$ and $y = -2$, what is the value of $\left| x^2 + y^3 \right|$?
(16)

22. Multiple Choice *(16)* A store owner makes a pyramid-shaped display using a stack of soup cans. She arranges the cans so that the highest level of the stack has one can. The second-highest level has four cans arranged in a square supporting the top can. The third-highest level has nine cans arranged in a square that supports the second-highest level. Which of the following expressions best represents the number of cans in the lowest level of a display that is *l* levels high?

A $3l$ **B** $4l$ **C** l^2 **D** l^3

23. Write *(5, 16)* **a.** What is the sign of the result when a negative value is cubed?

b. What is the sign of the result when the absolute value of an expression is taken?

24. (**Sites**) Use the table to answer the questions. *(14)*
a. If a building is randomly chosen, what is the probability that it is exactly 1250 feet tall?

b. What is the probability that a building exactly 1046 feet tall is chosen?

c. What is the probability that a building that was built between 1960 and 1980 is chosen?

Building	Height (ft)	Year Built
Sears Tower	1451	1974
Empire State Building	1250	1931
Aon Center	1136	1973
John Hancock Center	1127	1969
Chrysler Building	1046	1930
New York Times Building	1046	2007
Bank of America Plaza	1023	1992

25. Write *(13)* What is a perfect square?

26. (**Personal Finance**) The expression $P(1 + i)^2$ can be used to find the value of *(9)* an investment P after 2 years at an interest rate of i. What is the value of an investment of $500 deposited in an account with a 3% interest rate after 2 years? (Hint: Remember to convert the percent to a decimal before calculating.)

27. (**Racing**) The formula for the cylindrical volume of an engine on a dragster is *(4)* $\left(\frac{\pi}{4}\right)b^2s$, where b is the inside diameter (the bore) and s is the distance that the piston moves from its highest position to its lowest position (the stroke). Following the order of operations, describe the steps you would take to simplify the formula.

28. Justify *(6)* What is the additive inverse of 12? Justify your answer.

29. Multi-Step *(15)* Theater tickets cost $14 dollars for adults, a, and $8 for children, c. Additionally, each person who went to the theater on Thursday made a $5 contribution to charity. Write an expression using the Distributive Property to show the amount of money that the theater received on Thursday. Simplify the expression.

30. Probability *(14)* What is the probability that an ace will be chosen from a full deck of 52 playing cards? What is the probability of another ace being drawn if the first ace drawn is not returned to the deck?

Graphing on a Coordinate Plane

Warm Up

1. Vocabulary The distance from a number to 0 on the number line is
(5) the _____.

Simplify.

2. $\left|3 + (-5) - (-7)\right|$
(7)

3. $\left|3 + (-5) + (-7)\right|$
(7)

4. $4(8 + c) + 5$
(15)

5. $5y^2 + 3x^4 - 5y^2 - 5x^4$
(18)

New Concepts

A **coordinate plane** is made of two perpendicular number lines, one horizontal and one vertical. The horizontal line is called the **x-axis,** and the vertical line is called the **y-axis.** The number lines divide the plane into four **quadrants,** numbered and named as shown. The intersection of the x- and y-axis is called the **origin.**

Math Language

Perpendicular lines intersect at right angles. The sides of a book are perpendicular. They intersect and form a right angle at the corner of the book.

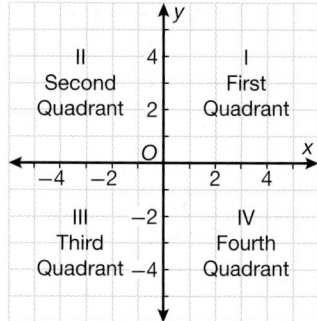

Each point on the coordinate plane is identified by an **ordered pair,** or two numbers in parentheses, separated by a comma. An ordered pair is written as follows: (x, y). The ordered pair that represents the origin is $(0, 0)$.

The first number in an ordered pair is called the **x-coordinate** and indicates the distance to the right or left of the origin. The second number, the **y-coordinate,** is the distance above or below the horizontal axis. A **coordinate** is a number that helps locate a point on a graph.

To find or graph a point, always start at the origin. Then use the sign of the coordinate to determine the location of the point.

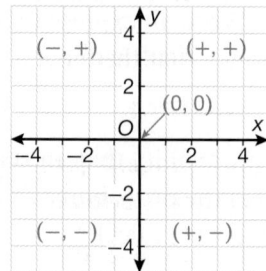

Online Connection
www.SaxonMathResources.com

Example 1 — Graphing Ordered Pairs on a Coordinate Plane

Graph each ordered pair on a coordinate plane. Label each point.

a. $(4, 2)$

SOLUTION

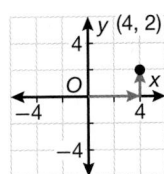

Point $(4, 2)$ is located in the first quadrant, 4 units to the right of the origin and 2 units above the horizontal axis.

b. $(-3, 0)$

SOLUTION

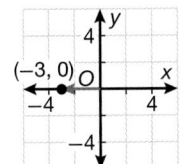

Point $(-3, 0)$ is on the x-axis. It is located 3 units to the left of the origin.

Hint

When graphing a point, always move left or right first.

When there is a relationship between two variable quantities, one variable is the independent variable and the other is the dependent variable.

Reading Math

In an ordered pair (x, y), x is the independent variable and y is the dependent variable.

Variables
Independent variable: The variable whose value can be chosen. Also called the input variable.
Dependent variable: The variable whose value is determined by the input value of another variable. Also called the output value.

The dependent variable always depends on what value is chosen for the independent variable.

Math Reasoning

Analyze The total charge on a bill is usually a dependent variable. Explain.

Example 2 — Identifying Independent and Dependent Variables

For each pair of variables, identify the independent variable and the dependent variables.

a. number of traffic violations, cost of auto insurance

SOLUTION

independent variable: number of traffic violations; dependent variable: cost of auto insurance

The cost of auto insurance depends upon the number of traffic violations.

b. electric bill total, kilowatts of electricity used

SOLUTION

independent variable: kilowatts of electricity used; dependent variable: electric bill total

Electric bills are based, or dependent, on the electricity usage. The kilowatts of electricity determine the electric bill total.

A solution to an equation with two variables is an ordered pair that makes the equation true. There are infinite solutions to the equation $y = 4x + 2$. Solutions can be found by substituting values for the independent variable, x, to find the corresponding value of the dependent variable, y.

Example 3 Determining the Dependent Variable

Complete the table for the equation $y = 4x + 2$.

x	y
-2	
0	
2	
$\frac{3}{4}$	

SOLUTION

Substitute the x-values into the equation to determine the y-values.

First substitute -2 for x in the equation.

$y = 4x + 2$	Write the equation.
$y = 4(-2) + 2$	Substitute -2 for x.
$y = -8 + 2$	Evaluate.
$y = -6$	

One solution to the equation is the ordered pair $(-2, -6)$.

Then substitute the other values to complete the table.

$x = 0$
$y = 4x + 2$
$y = 4(0) + 2$
$y = 0 + 2$
$y = 2$

$x = 2$
$y = 4x + 2$
$y = 4(2) + 2$
$y = 8 + 2$
$y = 10$

$x = \dfrac{3}{4}$
$y = 4x + 2$
$y = 4\left(\dfrac{3}{4}\right) + 2$
$y = 5$

The completed table shows the ordered pairs for the given values of x.

x	y
-2	-6
0	2
2	10
$\frac{3}{4}$	5

Values are assigned to the variable x. The value of the variable y is dependent on the value chosen for the variable x.

Example 4 Application: Wages

The federal minimum wage is about $5 per hour. The total on a minimum-wage worker's paycheck is dependent on the number of hours worked. The paycheck total can be calculated using the equation $y = 5x$.

Find the pay for 1, 3, 5, and 8 hours of. Make a graph to represent the equation $y = 5x$.

SOLUTION

Understand Since a worker makes $5 per hour, a worker's pay is calculated by multiplying the number of hours worked by 5.

Plan Find the amount of pay, y, when x is equal to 1, 3, 5, and 8 hours. Then graph the ordered pairs.

Solve Substitute 1, 3, 5, and 8 for x.

$y = 5x$	$y = 5x$	$y = 5x$	$y = 5x$
$y = 5(1)$	$y = 5(3)$	$y = 5(5)$	$y = 5(8)$
$y = 5$	$y = 15$	$y = 25$	$y = 40$

The pay for 1, 3, 5, and 8 hours is $5, $15, $25, and $40 respectively.

The ordered pairs are $(1, 5)$, $(3, 15)$, $(5, 25)$, and $(8, 40)$.

Graph the ordered pairs. Connect the points with a smooth line.

Check As the number of hours increases; so does the pay. The pay should increase steadily, which is shown by the straight line on the graph.

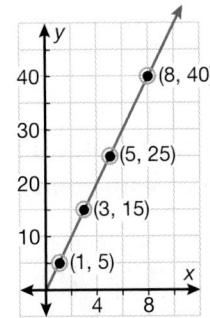

Math Reasoning

Predict How many hours would someone have worked if they are paid $122.50?

Lesson Practice

Graph each ordered pair on a coordinate plane. Label each point.
(Ex 1)

  a. $(0, 5)$ **b.** $(-1, -6)$

  c. $(-2, 0)$ **d.** $(-3, 4)$

  e. $(5, -1)$ **f.** $(2, -4)$

For each pair of variables, identify the independent variable and the dependent variable.
(Ex 2)

  g. the amount paid, the number of toys purchased

  h. the number of hours worked, the number of yards mowed

  i. Complete the table for the equation $y = 2x - 1$.
(Ex 3)

x	-3	-2	-1
y			

j. (**Fundraising**) The prom committee raises money for the prom by selling
(Ex 4) flowers. The money earned for the prom is dependent on the number of
flowers sold. Money earned is represented by the equation $y = 3x - 75$.

Find the amount of money raised when 25, 50, 75, and 100 flowers
are sold. Make a graph to represent the equation $y = 3x - 75$.

Practice   Distributed and Integrated

Simplify.

1. $(+3) + (-14)$
(5)

2. $4xyz - 3yz + zxy$
(18)

3. $3xyz - 3xyz + zxy$
(18)

Solve.

4. $x - 4 = 10$
(19)

5. $x + \dfrac{1}{5} = -\dfrac{1}{10}$
(19)

*6. Graph the ordered pair $(3, -4)$ on a coordinate plane.
(20)

*7. Graph the ordered pair $(0, 5)$ on a coordinate plane.
(20)

*8. Multiple Choice Which ordered pair is associated
(20) with point Z?

   A $(3, 0)$ **B** $(0, 3)$

   C $(-3, 0)$ **D** $(0, -3)$

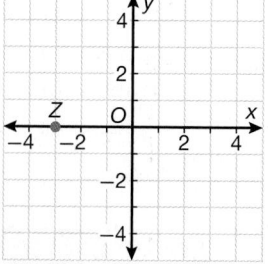

*9. (**Babysitting**) Ellen charges \$3 plus \$1 per child for an hour of
(20) babysitting. To determine her hourly rate, she uses the formula
$r = 3 + c$, where r is the rate and c is the number of children
Complete the table and graph the solutions.

c	r
1	
2	
3	
4	

*10. (**Reading**) Thomas read 10 pages in a book before starting his
(20) speed-reading lessons. After his lessons, he could read 3 pages
per minute. The equation $y = 3x + 10$ calculates the total
number of pages read after x minutes. Complete the table.

x	y
15	
20	
30	
50	

*11. **Error Analysis** Two students completed an x/y chart for the equation $y = 3 + 2x$ to
(20) find a solution to the equation. Which student is correct? Explain the error.

Student A	Student B
<table><tr><td>x</td><td>y</td></tr><tr><td>2</td><td>10</td></tr></table> $y = 3 + 2(2)$ $y = 5(2)$ $y = 10$ $(2, 10)$ is a solution.	<table><tr><td>x</td><td>y</td></tr><tr><td>2</td><td>7</td></tr></table> $y = 3 + 2(2)$ $y = 3 + 4$ $y = 7$ $(2, 7)$ is a solution.

*12. **Multi-Step** For a lemonade stand, profit depends on
(20) the number of cups sold. Profit is represented by
the equation $y = x - 5$, where x is the number of
cups sold and y is the profit in dollars.

x	5	10	20	50
y				

   a. Complete the table and graph the solutions.

   b. How would you find the profit if 30 cups were sold?

13. **Geometry** The triangle has a perimeter of 24 centimeters. Find the value for x.
(19)

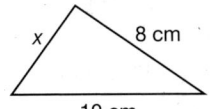

*14. **Multi-Step** To climb to the highest observation deck in the Empire State Building,
(19) you have to walk up 1860 steps. Starting at the lowest step, a security guard walks
up $\frac{1}{4}$ the total number of steps during his morning rounds. At the end of his
afternoon rounds, he stands on the 310th step. How many steps did he walk down
during the afternoon rounds?

*15. **Error Analysis** Two students simplify the expression $5x^2 + 7x^2$. Which student is
(18) correct? Explain the error.

Student A	Student B
$12x^2$	$12x^4$

16. **Write** Why do mathematicians use symbols rather than words?
(17)

17. **Multiple Choice** Which equation demonstrates the Associative Property of
(12) Addition?

   A $6 - 3c = 3c - 6$ **B** $c^3 - 6 = c^3 + 6$

   C $(6 - c)^3 = (c - 6)^3$ **D** $(6 + c^3) - 4 = 6 + (c^3 - 4)$

18. Evaluate each of the following expressions when $a = 2$.
(16)   **a.** a^2 **b.** $-a^2$ **c.** $-a^3$ **d.** $(-a)^3$ **e.** $|(-a)^2|$

19. **Analyze** A school is holding a blood drive. If 3 students out of the 50 who give
(14) blood are Type A, what is the probability that a randomly selected student is
Type A? Write the probability as a decimal.

20. Evaluate $\sqrt{441} + \sqrt{1089}$.
(13)

21. **Analyze** Use an example to show that the Associative Property holds true for multiplication.
(12)

22. **Statistics** Use the data in the table to find the average yearly change in the deer population during a five-year period.
(11)

Deer Population

Year	Decrease in Number of Deer
2000	10
2001	7
2002	9
2003	10
2004	12

23. (Stocks) A Stock Market Report shows the value of stocks in points. The value of the stock is determined by the number of points. If a stock is at $79\frac{5}{7}$ points and it drops 3 points, what is the value of stock?
(10)

24. (Nutrition) One hundred grams of honey contains about 0.3 grams of protein. How many milligrams is 0.3 grams of protein?
(8)

25. (Tiling) A contractor lays patterned tile floors. He often begins with a polygon and makes diagonal lines that pass from corner to corner of the polygon. He uses the following expression $\frac{n^2 - 3n}{2}$, where n equals the number of sides of the polygon to find the number of diagonal lines for any given polygon.
(7)
a. Find the number of diagonals for a hexagon.

b. **Model** Check your work by drawing the diagonals in a hexagon.

26. Write and simplify a mathematical expression that shows "fourteen minus the quotient of three squared and the sum of three plus six."
(4)

27. **Verify** Indicate whether each statement is true or false. If the statement is false, explain why.
(2)
a. The coefficient of x in the expression $x + 3$ is 3.

b. The factors of the expression $\frac{2mn}{5}$ are $\frac{2}{5}$, m, and n.

28. Name the coefficient(s), variables, and number of terms in the expression $b^2 - 4ac$.
(2)

29. **Multi-Step** Pencils cost ten cents and erasers cost five cents.
(17)
a. Write an expression to represent the total number of school supplies purchased.

b. Write an expression to represent how much the supplies cost in cents.

*30. **Analyze** A person runs 5 miles per hour. The equation $d = 5t$ tells how far the person has run in t hours. Make a table when $t = 0, 1, 2$, and 4 hours. Graph the ordered pairs in a graph and connect all the points. What do you notice?
(20)

Graphing a Relationship

A graph is a visual representation of how data change and relate to each other. A graph can convey the numeric relationship between data like time and distance.

Beach Trip Maria takes a trip to the beach. She stays at the beach all day before driving back home. As Maria drives to the beach, her distance from home increases. While she is at the beach, there is no change in her distance from home. As she returns home, her distance from home decreases.

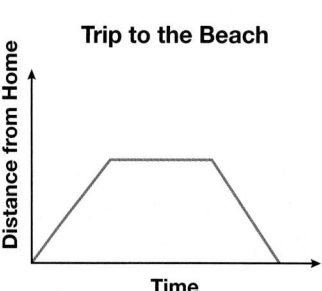

Trip to the Beach

Horse's Speed The graph shows the various speeds at which a horse travels.

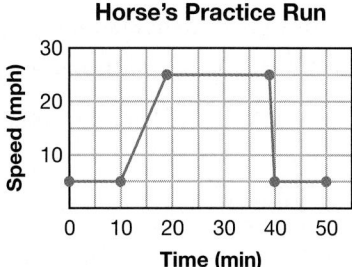

Horse's Practice Run

Online Connection
www.SaxonMathResources.com

1. **Analyze** Use the graph to complete the table. Describe the horse's speed in each of the time intervals as increasing, no change, or decreasing.

Interval	Description
0 to 10 minutes	
10 to 18 minutes	
18 to 38 minutes	
38 to 40 minutes	
40 to 50 minutes	

Math Reasoning

Analyze How does the increase in the horse's speed compare to the decrease in its speed? Explain.

You can use a graph to show how data change. When drawing a graph to represent a real-world situation,

- choose appropriate intervals for the units on the axes;
- be sure to space the intervals equally;
- only use values that make sense, such as positive numbers of books or whole numbers of people.

(Cost of Pecans) Customers at a local grocery store pay \$3.00 per pound for pecans. They can purchase the pecans in fractions of a pound.

2. Justify Should the graph representing this situation display negative values for pounds of pecans? Explain.

3. Estimate What is a reasonable maximum number of pounds to graph?

4. What is the cost of purchasing 1 pound of pecans? 4.5 pounds?

5. Draw a graph to represent the situation.

The cost-per-pound data modeled in the graph are continuous. Continuous data are data where numbers between any two data values have meaning. A graph of this data is drawn with a solid line. A **continuous graph** is a graph that has no gaps, jumps, or asymptotes.

Data that involve a count of items, such as a number of people, are called **discrete data**. A **discrete graph** is made up of separate, disconnected points determined by a set of discrete data.

(Photography) A sheet of photos at an automatic photo booth costs \$5. Patrons may purchase only full sheets of photos. The photo booth can print up to 10 sheets per patron.

6. Predict What will the graph look like?

7. What is the least number of photo sheets for purchase? The greatest number of sheets?

8. Draw a graph that represents the situation.

9. Write Use the graph to describe Maura's hike on Windy Hill. In the description, use the phrases increasing, no change, and decreasing.

Windy Hill Hike

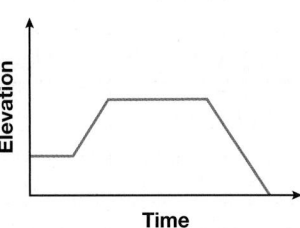

A graph represents the relationship between two quantities. The "Windy Hill Hike" graph shows the relationship between a hiker's time and altitude.

10. Analyze Describe another set of data that could be related to the hiker's time.

Many quantities can be measured and compared, such as a plane's traveling speed and its altitude.

(Air Travel) A commercial airplane travels at 600 miles per hour and typically flies at a height of about 6 miles. The graph shows the flight time and the altitude of an airplane.

11. What is the plane's altitude at the beginning and end of its 6-hour trip? Explain.

Plane's Altitude

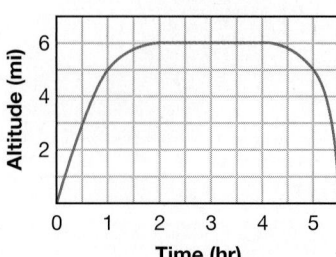

12. **Write** Describe the plane's flight in the first and last hour of the trip.

13. **Write** Explain why the graph of the plane's flight is relatively flat between 2 and 4 hours of the flight.

Investigation Practice

Graph each situation. Indicate whether the graph is continuous or discrete. Then describe the graph as increasing, no change, and/or decreasing.

a. Boxes of greeting cards sell for $5 a box. Income is calculated based on the number of boxes sold.

b. A scuba diver dives to a depth of 100 feet below sea level, then spends some time exploring the aquatic life at that level. The diver then descends to 250 feet below sea level for the remainder of the dive. (Hint: Assume the diver descends about 100 ft per 5 minutes.)

c. A driver brakes as she approaches an intersection. She stops to watch for traffic and pedestrians. The driver continues when the way is clear.

d. **Multiple Choice** The temperature of an ice cube increases until it starts to melt. While it melts, its temperature stays constant. Which graph best represents the situation?

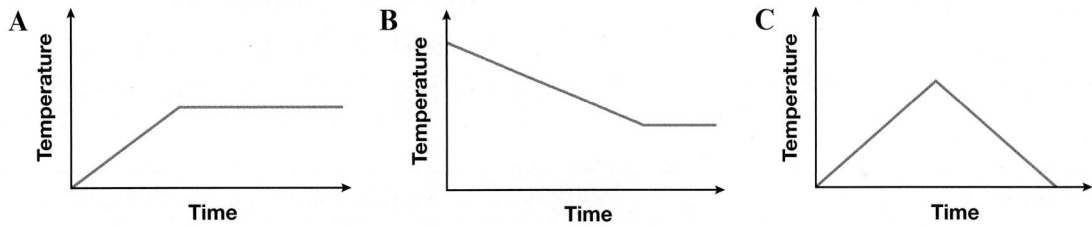

Describe the shape of the graph representing each situation.

e. **Write** A rocket is launched into orbit and, in time, returns to Earth. The graph relates time to the rocket's distance from Earth.

f. **Write** The ink in a printer is used until the ink cartridge is empty. The graph relates time used to the amount of ink in the cartridge.

g. **Write** An employee of a delivery service earns $3 for every package she delivers. The graph shows the employee's total earnings based on the number of packages delivered.

Solving One-Step Equations by Multiplying or Dividing

Warm Up

1. **Vocabulary** In the equation $5x = 10$, x is the _____. (*variable*,
(2) *coefficient*)

2. Multiply $\frac{4}{5}$ and $\frac{1}{2}$. Give the answer in simplest form.
(11)

3. Divide $\frac{3}{4}$ by $\frac{1}{2}$. Give the answer in simplest form.
(11)

4. Evaluate $8n + 2$ for $n = 0.5$.
(9)

5. **Multiple Choice** Which is the solution?
(19)

$5 + x = 7$

A 12　　　　　　　　　　　　**B** 7

C 5　　　　　　　　　　　　**D** 2

New Concepts

To find the solution of an equation, isolate the variable by using inverse operations. You must use the same inverse operation on each side of the equation.

Inverse Operations

Add ⟷ Subtract

Multiply ⟷ Divide

Multiplication and Division Properties of Equality
Multiplication Property of Equality
Both sides of an equation can be multiplied by the same number, and the statement will still be true.

Examples
$$2 = 2 \qquad\qquad a = b$$
$$3 \cdot 2 = 3 \cdot 2 \qquad\qquad a \cdot c = b \cdot c$$
$$6 = 6 \qquad\qquad ac = bc$$

Division Property of Equality

Both sides of an equation can be divided by the same number, and the statement will still be true.

Examples
$$10 = 10 \qquad\qquad a = b$$
$$\frac{10}{2} = \frac{10}{2} \qquad\qquad \frac{a}{c} = \frac{b}{c} (c \neq 0)$$
$$5 = 5$$

Online Connection
www.SaxonMathResources.com

Using Inverse Operations

Copy and complete each table. Find the value of x by using the given values for the expression. Then explain how you found the values in the first column.

a.

x	$\dfrac{60}{x}$
	1
	2
	3
	4
	5
	6

b.

x	$4x$
	8
	20
	32
	36
	48
	60

c. **Justify** Is 20 a solution of the equation $\dfrac{60}{x} = 3$? Explain.

d. **Justify** Is 7 a solution of the equation $4x = 54$? Explain.

Example 1 **Solving Equations by Multiplying**

Solve each equation. Then check the solution.

a. $\dfrac{x}{6} = 8$

b. $-11 = \dfrac{1}{4}w$

Hint

Inverse operations "undo" each other. Multiplying by 6 "undoes" dividing by 6.

Math Reasoning

Verify Show that dividing both sides of the equation by 5 or multiplying both sides of the equation by $\frac{1}{5}$, will result in the same solution.

SOLUTION

$\dfrac{x}{6} = 8$

$6 \cdot \dfrac{x}{6} = 8 \cdot 6$ Multiplication Property of Equality

$x = 48$

Check Substitute 6 for x.

$\dfrac{48}{6} \overset{?}{=} 8$

$8 = 8$ ✓

SOLUTION

$\dfrac{4}{1} \cdot -11 = \dfrac{4}{1} \cdot \dfrac{1}{4}w$ Multiplication Property of Equality

$-44 = w$ Simplify.

Check Substitute -44 for w.

$-11 = \dfrac{1}{4}w$

$-11 \overset{?}{=} \dfrac{1}{4}(-44)$

$-11 = -11$ ✓

Example 2 Solving Equations by Dividing

Solve each equation. Then check the solution.

a. $5x = 20$

SOLUTION

$$5x = 20$$

$$\frac{5x}{5} = \frac{20}{5} \qquad \text{Division Property of Equality}$$

$$x = 4 \qquad \text{Simplify.}$$

Check Substitute 4 for x.

$$5x = 20$$

$$5(4) \stackrel{?}{=} 20$$

$$20 = 20 \ \checkmark$$

b. $-12 = 3n$

SOLUTION

$$-12 = 3n$$

$$-\frac{12}{3} = \frac{3n}{3} \qquad \text{Division Property of Equality}$$

$$-4 = n \qquad \text{Simplify.}$$

Check Substitute -4 for n.

$$-12 = 3n$$

$$-12 \stackrel{?}{=} 3(-4)$$

$$-12 = -12 \ \checkmark$$

c. $\frac{2}{5}p = 7$

SOLUTION

$$\frac{2}{5}p = 7$$

$$\left(\frac{2}{5} \div \frac{2}{5}\right)p = \left(7 \div \frac{2}{5}\right) \qquad \text{Divide both sides by } \frac{2}{5}.$$

$$\left(\frac{\cancel{2}^{1}}{\cancel{5}^{1}} \cdot \frac{\cancel{5}^{1}}{\cancel{2}^{1}}\right)p = \left(7 \cdot \frac{5}{2}\right) \qquad \text{Divide by multiplying by the reciprocal of } \frac{2}{5}, \text{ which is } \frac{5}{2}.$$

$$p = \frac{35}{2}$$

Check Substitute $\frac{35}{2}$ for p.

$$\left(\frac{\cancel{2}^{1}}{\cancel{5}}\right)\left(\frac{\cancel{35}^{7}}{\cancel{2}}\right) \stackrel{?}{=} 7$$

$$7 = 7 \ \checkmark$$

<aside>

Reading Math

$\frac{2}{5}p$ can be written as $\frac{2p}{5}$, $\left(\frac{2}{5}\right)p$, $\frac{2}{5} \cdot p$, or $\frac{2}{5} \times p$.

</aside>

Write equations to solve real-world problems.

Example 3 Application: Architecture

Anita is an architect. She is designing a rectangular room that has an area of 126 square feet. If the length of the room is 12 feet, what is its width?

Understand

The answer will be the width of the room in feet.

List the important information:

- The room is a rectangle.
- The area is 126 square feet.
- The length is 12 feet.

Plan

To find the area of a rectangle, multiply the length by the width.

Solve

$$A = lw \qquad \text{Write the formula.}$$

$$126 = 12w \qquad \text{Substitute 126 for } A \text{ and 12 for } l.$$

$$\frac{126}{12} = \frac{12w}{12} \qquad \text{Division Property of Equality}$$

$$10\frac{6}{12} = w \qquad \text{Simplify.}$$

The width will be $10\frac{1}{2}$ feet.

Check

Area of a rectangle = length × width

$$126 \overset{?}{=} 12 \times 10\frac{1}{2}$$

$$126 = 126 \quad \checkmark$$

Lesson Practice

Solve each equation. Then check the solution.

a. $\frac{k}{9} = 3$
(Ex 1)

b. $-20 = \frac{1}{5}m$
(Ex 1)

c. $8y = 24$
(Ex 2)

d. $-15 = 3x$
(Ex 2)

e. $\frac{3}{4}y = 11$
(Ex 2)

f. $8 = -\frac{5}{12}n$
(Ex 2)

g. A rectangular pond has an area of 140 square feet. If the length of the pool is 16 feet, what is its width?
(Ex 3)

*1. (Safety) For every 4 feet a ladder rises, the base of the ladder should be placed
(21) 1 foot away from the bottom of a building. If the base of the ladder is 7 feet from
the bottom of a building, find the height the ladder rises up the building?

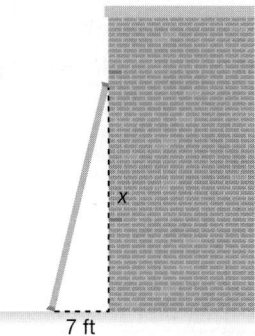

7 ft

2. What is a term of an algebraic expression?
(2)

*3. **Write** Explain how to use inverse operations to solve $\frac{2}{3}x = 8$.
(21)

*4. (Physics) In physics equations, a change in a quantity is represented by the delta
(19) symbol, Δ. A change in velocity, Δv, is calculated using the equation $\Delta v = v_f - v_i$,
where v_i is the initial velocity and v_f is the final velocity. If a cart has an initial
velocity of 5 miles per second and experiences a change in velocity of 2 miles
per second, what is the final velocity of the cart?

5. Graph the ordered pair $(-2, 6)$ on a coordinate plane.
(20)

6. **Geometry** The length of a rectangular picture frame is 3 times the width.
(3) **a.** Draw a picture of the picture frame and label the dimensions.

b. Write an expression for the area of the frame.

7. Complete the table for $y = 2x + 7$.
(20)

x	-5	1	4
y			

*8. Solve $\frac{x}{3} = 5$.
(21)

*9. **Multiple-Choice** Which step can you use first to solve $-\frac{x}{9} = -52$?
(21) **A** Multiply both sides by $\frac{1}{9}$.

B Multiply both sides by -9.

C Divide both sides by -52.

D Divide both sides by 52.

*10. **Estimate** Alan makes \$1 for each snow cone he sells. Alan calculates his profit
(19) by subtracting the daily cost of \$195 to run the stand from the total amount he
makes on the snow cones that he sells each day. How many snow cones does Alan
need to sell to make a profit of \$200 a day?

11. Write Explain which terms in $3z^2y + 2yz - 4y^2z - z^2y + 8yz$ can be combined.
(18)

12. (Astronomy) The relative weight of an object on the surface of Jupiter can be found
(9) using $2.364w$, where w is the weight of the object on Earth. The space shuttle
weighs about 4,500,000 pounds on earth. What would be the weight of the space
shuttle on Jupiter?

13. Geometry The length of a frame is 8 inches. Let w be the width of the frame.
(20) The formula $A = 8w$ calculates the area of backing needed for a framed picture.
Complete the table and graph the solutions.

w	A
2	
4	
6	
8	

14. Simplify $-4 - 3 + 2 - 4 - 3 - 8$.
(6)

15. Multiple Choice Simplify $5p + 7 - 8p + 2$.
(18)
   A $9 - 3p$ **B** $3p - 9$ **C** $13p + 5$ **D** $13p - 9$

16. Verify Evaluate $\frac{2}{3}\left(4 + \frac{3}{4}\right)$ using two different methods. Verify the solution of each
(15) method.

17. Probability A letter of the alphabet is randomly chosen. What is the probability
(14) that the letter is a vowel?

18. Justify The area of a square is 100 square feet, what is the length of each side?
(13) Explain.

19. Measurement A picture framer calculates the amount of materials needed
(12) using $2l + 2w$. If the framer used $2w + 2l$, would the results be the same? Explain.

*20. Multi-Step Alda's school is 1200 yards from her house. She walks 150 yards
(20) per minute. The equation $y = 1200 - 150x$ represents how far she will be
from the school after x minutes.
  a. Complete the table and graph the solutions.

x	y
1	
4	
6	
8	

  b. What does it mean to say that after 8 minutes, she is 0 yards from the school?

*21. Analyze A student says that to solve $-\frac{3}{4}x = 12$ you should divide each side
(21) by $-\frac{3}{4}$. Another student says that to solve the equation you should multiply
each side by $-\frac{4}{3}$. Will both methods result in the correct solution? Explain.

22. Multi-Step Determine whether $4^3 \cdot \left(\frac{1}{4}\right)^3 = 1$.
(3)

    a. Simplify the expressions 4^3 and $\left(\frac{1}{4}\right)^3$.

    b. Write an expression for the multiplication of 4^3 and $\left(\frac{1}{4}\right)^3$ without using exponents. Then check to see if the product of the expressions is 1.

23. Write Will dividing two integers ever produce an irrational number? Explain.
(1)

24. Analyze If a student is converting from 225 square units to 22,500 square units, what units of measure is he or she most likely converting?
(8)

25. (Golf) A round of golf takes 4.5 hours and each hole takes 0.25 hours. In the equation $y = 4.5 - 0.25x$, x is the number of holes played and y is the remaining time to finish the round. Make a table for 4, 8, 12, and 16 holes and then graph the ordered pairs in your table.
(20)

26. Simplify $-|15 - 5|$.
(5)

*27. (Pricing) One fruit stand has s strawberries and k kiwis to sell. Another stand has twice as many strawberries and four times as many kiwis to sell.
(18)

    a. Write expressions representing the number of strawberries and kiwis each stand has to sell.

    b. Write an expression for the total number of pieces of fruit.

*28. Sketch a graph to represent the following situation: A tomato plant grows at a slow rate, and then grows rapidly with more sun and water.
(Inv 2)

29. Write an algebraic expression for "0.21 of what number is 7.98?"
(17)

30. Error Analysis Two students solve $x - 5 = 11$. Which student is correct? Explain the error.
(19)

Student A	Student B
$x - 5 = 11$	$x - 5 = 11$
$\underline{+5 = +5}$	$\underline{-5 = -5}$
$x \quad = 16$	$x \quad = 6$

Analyzing and Comparing Statistical Graphs

Warm Up

1. Vocabulary The set of real numbers includes all _____ numbers and
(1) all _____ numbers.

Name the point on the number line that corresponds to each given value.
(SB 1)

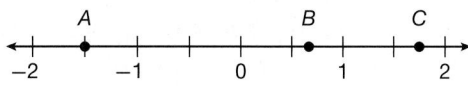

2. -1.5 **3.** 1.75 **4.** $\dfrac{2}{3}$

5. Find the difference between 12.3 million and 20,000.
(7)

New Concepts

Numerical data can be displayed in different ways. **Bar graphs** use vertical and horizontal bars to represent data.

> **Exploration** **Analyzing Bar Graphs**
>
> A sample survey asked students to name their favorite type of pet. The results are shown in the bar graph.

Math Reasoning

Predict If 1000 students are surveyed, how many are likely to pick dogs as their favorite pets?

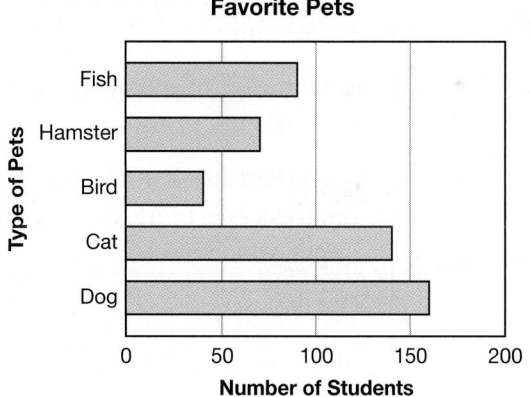

a. What information is shown on the vertical axis? the horizontal axis?

b. Use the graph to complete the table.

Pet	Dog	Cat	Bird	Hamster	Fish
Number of Students					

c. How many students were surveyed?

d. **Analyze** Which pet did students choose twice as often as the hamster? Explain.

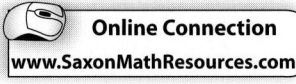
Online Connection
www.SaxonMathResources.com

A **double-bar graph** shows groups of two bars side by side. This allows easier comparison of two related sets of data.

Example 1 Interpreting Double-Bar Graphs

Sal and Harry both own sandwich shops. The double-bar graph shows the number of shops they owned at the end of each year. What conclusions can be made from the graph?

Sandwich Shops

SOLUTION

- Harry always had more shops open than Sal, except in 2004, when they both had the same number of shops open.

- The number of shops Harry owned increased from the years 2001 to 2006.

- The number of shops Sal owned increased from the years 2001 to 2004, but decreased from the years 2004 to 2006.

A **stem-and-leaf plot** is a data display that uses some digits as "stems" and others as "leaves." The "stems" have a greater place value than the "leaves." Stem-and-leaf plots are useful for organizing and ordering data.

Example 2 Interpreting Stem-and-Leaf Plots

The stem-and-leaf plot shows the ages of members of a hiking club.

Find the age of members at the hiking club that occurs most often.

SOLUTION Look at the key. The stems represent tens and the leaves represent ones. So 3|2 represents 3 tens 2 ones, which is 32.

Age of Hiking Club Members

Stem	Leaf
1	0 0 7
2	4 6
3	2 3 4
4	1 1 1 3
5	3 6 6 9

Key: 1|0 means 10

The data set:

10, 10, 17, 24, 26, 32, 33, 34, 41, 41, 41, 43, 53, 56, 56, 59

41 is the data value that occurs most often.

The age that occurs most often is 41 years.

In a **line graph**, a line is drawn through points on a grid to show trends and changes in data over time. As with bar graphs, two related data sets can be compared in a **double-line graph.**

Example 3 · Interpreting Line and Double-line Graphs

The double-line graph shows the same data as the double-bar graph in Example 1.

Sandwich Shop

Key
—●— Sal's Deli
—□— Harry's Deli

What conclusions can you make from each graph?

SOLUTION

- Sal had fewer sandwich shops than Harry in 2001, but in 2004 they both had the same number of sandwich shops.

- The graph of Harry's shops is a straight line that shows a steady increase in the number of shops each year.

- Harry had 6 more shops than Sal in 2001, they both had 14 shops in 2004, and Harry had 11 more shops than Sal in 2006.

Math Reasoning

Predict If the number of shops Harry owns increases at the same yearly rate, how many shops will he own in 2010?

Example 4 · Comparing Data using Double-Bar Graphs

The table shows Andre's bank account transactions.

Month	January	February	March	April	May	June
Deposits	$475	$200	$350	$425	$500	$150
Withdrawals	$100	$275	$350	$400	$200	$225

Make a graph to compare the deposits and withdrawals.

SOLUTION Use a double-bar graph to compare the deposits and withdrawals.

- The graph shows that the deposits were greater than the withdrawals in January, April, and May.

- The withdrawals were greater than the deposits in February and June.

- Andre deposited and withdrew the same amount of money in March.

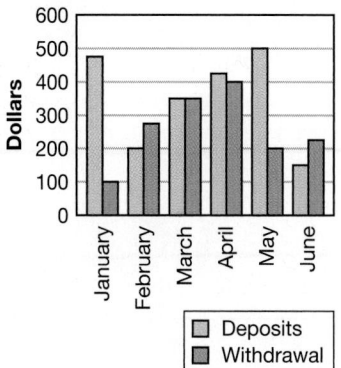

A **circle graph** uses sections of a circle to compare parts of the circle to the whole circle. The whole circle represents the entire set of data.

Example 5 Application: Yearly Sales

The circle graph shows Art Online's total yearly sales by quarter. The total amount of sales for the year was $20 million. Find the sales for each quarter.

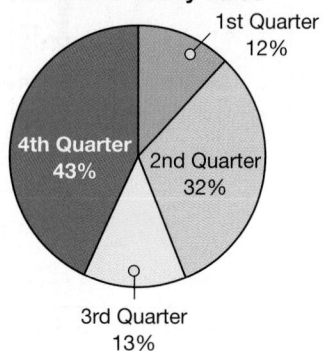

Art Online Yearly Sales

1st Quarter 12%
2nd Quarter 32%
3rd Quarter 13%
4th Quarter 43%

SOLUTION

Multiply the percent of sales for each quarter by the total amount for the year.

1st Quarter: $12\% \times 20$ million $= 0.12 \times 20$ million $= 2.4$ million
2nd Quarter: $32\% \times 20$ million $= 0.32 \times 20$ million $= 6.4$ million
3rd Quarter: $13\% \times 20$ million $= 0.13 \times 20$ million $= 2.6$ million
4th Quarter: $43\% \times 20$ million $= 0.43 \times 20$ million $= 8.6$ million

Check Find the sum of the amounts calculated for each quarter.

$2,400,000 + 6,400,000 + 2,600,000 + 8,600,000 = 20,000,000$

Caution

Circle graphs are sometimes labeled with actual data values instead of percents. Always check the labels and keys of a graph.

Lesson Practice

a. Use the double-bar graph in Example 1. What year shows the greatest difference between the number of shops Sal and Harry owned?
(Ex 1)

b. Use the double-line graph in Example 3. What was the greatest number of shops Sal opened in one year?
(Ex 3)

c. Make a stem-and-leaf plot of the data showing the height in inches of grandchildren in the Jackson family: 56, 52, 68, 49, 49, 40, 72, 71, 43, 54. What height occurs most often?
(Ex 2)

d. Use the data in Example 4. Which month shows the greatest difference between deposits and withdrawals?
(Ex 4)

e. **Predict** Use the circle graph from Example 5. If first quarter sales the next year are $3,000,000, predict the total sales for the year.
(Ex 5)

*1. True or False: A stem-and-leaf plot can help analyze change over time. If false, explain why.
(22)

2. Complete the table for $y = -3x - 9$.
(20)

x	-1	0	1
y			

3. Simplify $2p(xy - 3k)$.
(15)

4. Solve $y - 3 = 2$.
(19)

*5. Solve $x - \dfrac{1}{4} = \dfrac{7}{8}$.
(19)

6. Solve $4x = 2\dfrac{2}{3}$.
(21)

7. Solve $7x = 49$.
(21)

*8. Choose an appropriate graph to display the change in profit of a company over several years. Explain your choice.
(22)

9. Verify Determine whether each statement below is true or false. If false, provide a counterexample.
(1)

   a. The set of integers is closed under division.

   b. The set of irrational numbers is closed under division.

   c. The set of integers is closed under addition.

*10. (Racing) The table shows the Indianapolis 500 fastest lap times to the nearest second, every 5 years since 1960. Make an appropriate graph to display the data. Then make a conclusion about the data.
(22)

Fastest Lap Times in the Indianapolis 500

Year	1960	1965	1970	1975	1980	1985	1990	1995	2000	2005
Time (seconds)	62	57	54	48	47	44	40	40	41	39

11. Graph the ordered pair $(-4, -1)$ on a coordinate plane.
(20)

12. Error Analysis Two students plotted the point $(-4, 3)$. Which student is correct? Explain the error.
(20)

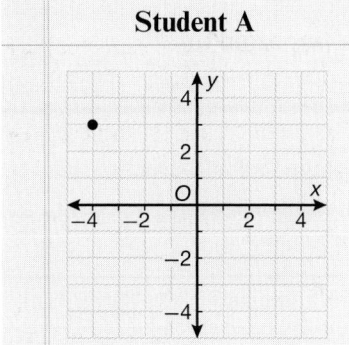

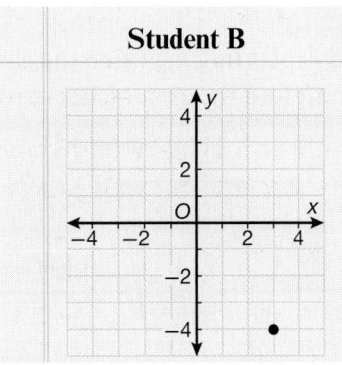

13. Multiple Choice A baker needs 25 eggs for all the cakes she plans to bake. She only
(19) has 12 eggs. If x is the number of eggs she will buy to complete her ingredients list,
which of the following equations best represents how she can find x?

A $12 - x = 25$ **B** $12 + x = 25$ **C** $25 + x = 12$ **D** $x - 12 = 25$

*14. Analyze For the equation $x = 14 - y$, what must be true of each value of x if y is
(19) **a.** greater than 14?

b. equal to 14?

c. less than 14?

*15. Multiple Choice Which graph would best compare the ages of people living in
(22) two different cities?

A circle graph **B** stem-and-leaf plot

C double-line graph **D** double-bar graph

16. (Travel) A man travels 25 miles to work. On his way home, he stops to fill up
(17) with gas after going d miles. Write an expression to represent his distance
from home.

17. Verify Show that each equation is true for the given values of x and y.
(16) **a.** $x\left(\dfrac{y}{y-x}\right)^2 = -\dfrac{4}{9}$; $x = -4$ and $y = 2$ **b.** $\left|(x-y)^3\right| = 27$; $x = -1$ and $y = 2$

18. Write What is a sample space?
(14)

*19. (Endangered Animals) The table shows the number of threatened or endangered
(22) animal species as of July 22, 2007. Make an appropriate graph to display the data.
Then make a conclusion about the data.

Number of Threatened or Endangered Species in the U.S. and Foreign Countries

	Mammals	Birds	Reptiles	Amphibians	Fish	Clams	Snails	Insects	Arachnids	Crustaceans
U.S.	81	89	37	23	139	70	76	57	12	22
Foreign	276	182	81	9	12	2	1	4	0	0

20. Generalize Use the pairs of equations. What can be concluded about the Commutative
(12) Property?

$9 - 5 = 4$ and $5 - 9 = -4$

$12 - 6 = 6$ and $6 - 12 = -6$

$7 - 3 = 4$ and $3 - 7 = -4$

21. (Landscape Design) Wanchen is planting a garden the shape of a trapezoid in
(4) her yard. Use the diagram to find the area of her garden.

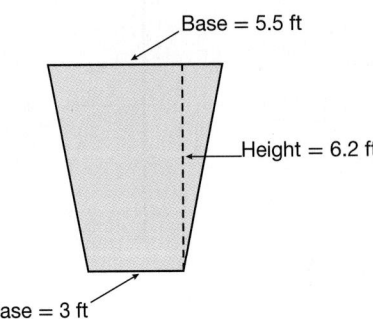

Base = 5.5 ft

Height = 6.2 ft

Base = 3 ft

22. Simplify $-7 + (-3) + 4 - 3 + (-2)$.
(6)

 *23. **Geometry** An arc of a circle is a segment of the circumference of a circle. If
(21) an arc measures 16 inches and is $\frac{4}{9}$ the circumference of a circle, what is the
circumference of the circle?

24. **Multi-Step** A house has an area of 1200 square feet. The owners add on a new
(4) room that is 15 feet long and 20 feet wide. What is the area of the house now?

  a. Write an expression to represent the area of the new room.

  b. Write an expression to represent the total area of the house now.

  c. Find the area of the house now.

25. **Write** Describe a situation that could be represented by the expression $2d - w$.
(9)

26. Simplify $3ab^2 - 2ab + 5b^2a - ba$.
(18)

 *27. The circle graph shows the result of a poll on the sleeping habits of children ages
(22) 9–12. What portion of the children said they slept the recommended $9\frac{1}{2}$ to $10\frac{1}{2}$
hours for their age group? Express the answer as a decimal rounded to the nearest
hundredth.

Sleeping Habits

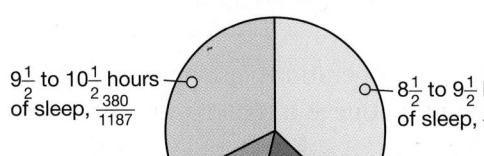

28. Simplify x^2yyyx^3yx.
(3)

*29. **Multi-Step** Enrique pays $31.92 (not including tax) for 6 books that are on sale. Each
(21) book costs the same amount. Enrique pays $\frac{4}{5}$ of the original cost of the books.

  a. What is the sale price of each book?

  b. What was the original cost of each book?

30. **Probability** In a standard deck of cards, there are 13 cards in each
(Inv 1) of four suits: hearts, diamonds, clubs, and spades. Jose randomly
draws a card from a deck and replaces it after each draw. His
results are recorded in the table. Find the experimental probability
of each event.

  a. drawing a heart

  b. not drawing a club

Outcome	Frequency
Hearts	8
Diamonds	8
Clubs	6
Spades	4

Solving Two-Step Equations

1. **Vocabulary** In the equation $-5x = 20$, -5 is the _____
(2) (*variable, coefficient*).

Simplify.

2. $3(x - 4)$
(15)

3. $-2(x - 3) + 4(x + 1)$
(18)

4. Evaluate $\dfrac{3}{4}n + \dfrac{5}{6}$ for $n = \dfrac{2}{9}$.
(9)

5. **Multiple Choice** What is the solution of $-7 + x = 14$?
(19) **A** -2

B 2

C 7

D 21

New Concepts If an equation has two operations, use inverse operations and work backward to undo each operation one at a time.

To reverse the order of operations:

- First add or subtract.

- Then multiply or divide.

> **Example** **1** **Evaluating Expressions and Solving Equations**
>
> **a.** Evaluate $3x - 2$ for $x = 4$.
>
> **SOLUTION** Substitute 4 for x and use the order of operations.
>
> $3(4) - 2$ Multiply first.
>
> $12 - 2 = 10$ Then subtract.
>
> **b.** Solve $3x - 2 = 10$.
>
> **SOLUTION** Reverse the order of operations.
>
> $3x - 2 = 10$
>
> $\underline{+\, 2 = +\, 2}$ Undo the subtraction by adding.
>
> $3x = 12$
>
> $\dfrac{3x}{3} = \dfrac{12}{3}$ Undo the multiplication by dividing.
>
> $x = 4$

Example 2   Solving Two-Step Equations with Positive Coefficients

Solve the equation. Then check the solution.

$$4x + 5 = 17$$

SOLUTION To isolate x, first eliminate 5 and then eliminate the 4.

$$4x + 5 = 17$$

$$\underline{-5 = -5} \qquad \text{Subtraction Property of Equality}$$

$$4x = 12 \qquad \text{Simplify.}$$

$$\frac{4x}{4} = \frac{12}{4} \qquad \text{Division Property of Equality}$$

$$x = 3$$

Check Substitute 3 for x in the original equation.

$$4(3) + 5 \overset{?}{=} 17$$

$$12 + 5 \overset{?}{=} 17$$

$$17 = 17 \quad \checkmark$$

Math Reasoning

Write Explain why the first step in checking the solution is to multiply by 4 and the last step in solving the equation is to divide by 4.

Example 3   Solving Two-Step Equations with Negative Coefficients

Solve the equation. Then check the solution.

$$8 = -5m + 6$$

SOLUTION To isolate m, first eliminate the 6 and then eliminate the -5.

$$8 = -5m + 6$$

$$\underline{-6 = \qquad -6} \qquad \text{Subtraction Property of Equality}$$

$$2 = -5m \qquad \text{Simplify.}$$

$$\frac{2}{-5} = \frac{-5}{-5}m \qquad \text{Division Property of Equality}$$

$$-\frac{2}{5} = m \qquad \text{Simplify.}$$

Check Substitute $-\frac{2}{5}$ for m.

$$8 \overset{?}{=} -5\left(-\frac{2}{5}\right) + 6$$

$$8 \overset{?}{=} 2 + 6$$

$$8 = 8 \quad \checkmark$$

Example 4 | Solving Two-Step Equations with Fractions

Math Language

When you multiply a number by its **reciprocal**, the product is 1.

$$\frac{2}{1} \cdot \frac{1}{2} = 1$$

Solve the equation. Then check the solution to see if it is reasonable.

$$\frac{1}{2}n - \frac{1}{3} = \frac{3}{4}$$

SOLUTION

To isolate n, first eliminate the $\frac{1}{3}$ and then eliminate the $\frac{1}{2}$.

$$\frac{1}{2}n - \frac{1}{3} = \frac{3}{4}$$

$$\underline{+\frac{1}{3} = +\frac{1}{3}} \qquad \text{Addition Property of Equality}$$

$$\frac{1}{2}n = \frac{13}{12} \qquad \text{Simplify.}$$

$$\frac{2}{1} \cdot \frac{1}{2}n = \frac{13}{12} \cdot \frac{2}{1} \qquad \text{Multiplication Property of Equality}$$

$$n = \frac{13}{6} \qquad \text{Simplify.}$$

Estimate to verify that the solution is reasonable.

$\frac{13}{6}$ is about 2. Substitute 2 for n. $\frac{1}{2}$ of 2 is 1.

$\frac{1}{3}$ subtracted from 1 is $\frac{2}{3}$, which is close to $\frac{3}{4}$.

So, the solution $\frac{13}{6}$ is reasonable.

Example 5 | Application: Fitness

Caution

Read the problem carefully. The number of months is unknown, but the question asks for the number of years.

A gym charges a $90 fee plus $30 per month. Another gym charges a fee of $1500. How many years will it take for the charges at the first gym to reach $1500?

SOLUTION Write an expression to represent the total cost at the first gym.

monthly cost	times	the number of months	plus	the membership fee
30	·	x	+	90

Use the expression to write an equation equal to the total cost of $1500.

$$30x + 90 = 1500$$

$$\underline{-90 = -90} \qquad \text{Subtraction Property of Equality}$$

$$30x = 1410 \qquad \text{Simplify.}$$

$$\frac{30}{30}x = \frac{1410}{30} \qquad \text{Division Property of Equality}$$

$$x = 47 \qquad \text{Simplify.}$$

47 months is about 4 years. It will take about 4 years for the total charges at the first gym to reach $1500.

a. Justify Which step would you use first to evaluate $9y + 6$ for $y = 2$? Explain.
(Ex 1)

b. Justify Which step would you use first to solve $9y + 6 = 24$? Explain.
(Ex 1)

Solve each equation. Then check the solution.

c. $8w - 4 = 28$
(Ex 2)

d. $-10 = -2x + 12$
(Ex 3)

e. Solve $\frac{1}{8}m + \frac{3}{4} = \frac{7}{12}$. Then check the solution to see if it is reasonable.
(Ex 4)

f. (**Energy Conservation**) The Green family conserves energy by using energy-efficient bulbs. They pay \$125 for energy-efficient bulbs. If the family saves \$7 per month on their electricity bill, and the power company gives them a rebate of \$25, in about how many months will they have paid for the bulbs?
(Ex 5)

Practice   Distributed and Integrated

1. Evaluate $(x - y) - (x - y)$ for $x = 3.5$ and $y = 2.5$.
(9)

2. Write Explain how to graph the point $(-2, 4)$.
(20)

*3. Multiple Choice What is the value of x in the equation $3x + 5 = 32$?
(23)
   A 24   **B** 9   **C** 81   **D** $12\frac{1}{3}$

4. Error Analysis Two students solve $-12x = -72$. Which student is correct? Explain the error.
(21)

Student A	Student B
$-12x = -72$	$-12x = -72$
$-\dfrac{12x}{12} = -\dfrac{72}{12}$	$\dfrac{-12x}{-12} = \dfrac{-72}{-12}$
$x = -6$	$x = 6$

*5. (**Altitude**) A plane increases altitude by 350 meters every minute. If the plane started at an altitude of 750 meters above sea level, what is the plane's altitude after 6 minutes?
(17)

6. Verify Is $x = 9$ the solution for $3x - 8 = 22$? Explain. If false, provide a correct solution and check.
(23)

7. Justify Find a counterexample to the following statement: A rational number that is not an integer, such as $\frac{3}{5}$, multiplied by any integer will produce a rational number that is not an integer.
(1)

*8. **Multi-Step** Three hundred people were surveyed as they left a movie theater.
(22) They were asked which type of movie they like best. The circle graph shows
the survey results.

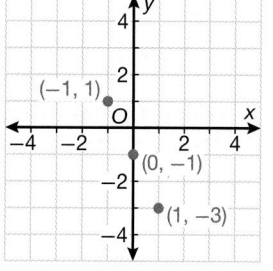

a. Which type of movie was most popular?

b. How many people liked horror movies the best?

c. How many more people liked action movies than dramas?

*9. Choose an appropriate graph to display the number of different types of DVDs
(22) sold at two video stores. Explain your answer.

*10. A class of 20 students answered a survey about their favorite places to go on
(22) vacation. Use the data in the table to make a bar graph.

Beach	Amusement Park	Mountains	Museums
5	8	3	4

*11. **Geometry** A circle has a circumference of $\frac{8}{9}\pi$ meters. What is the radius of
(21) the circle?

12. **Multiple Choice** Which equation has solutions that are represented by the
(21) graphed points?

A $y = 2x + 1$

B $y = 2x + 3$

C $y = -2x$

D $y = -2x - 1$

13. (Coins) Jenny and Sam took the coins out of their pockets. Jenny has x quarters
(7) and y dimes. Sam has h half dollars and z nickels.

a. Write expressions representing the value of the coins, in cents, in each person's
pocket.

b. Write an expression for the total number of cents they have.

14. **Verify** "12 more than the product of x and 3" can be written as $3x + 12$ or
(17) $12 + 3x$. Substitute 2 for x and show that the expressions are equivalent.

15. Use $>$, $<$, or $=$ to compare the expressions.
(7)

$$24 + \frac{16}{4} - (4 + 3^2) \cdot 2 \bigcirc 24 + \left(\frac{16}{4} - 4\right) + 3^2 \cdot 2$$

Solve.

16. $y - \frac{1}{2} = -2\frac{1}{2}$
(19)

*17. $2x + 3 = 11$
(23)

*18. $3x - 4 = 10$
(23)

*19. Solve $2.2x + 2 = 8.6$
(23)

*20. **Statistics** A basketball player attempted 1789 free throws. He made 801 of them.
(Inv 1) What is the probability that the player will make the next shot he attempts? Write
the probability as a decimal rounded to the nearest hundredth.

21. (Presidential Facts) Many of our first 43 U.S. Presidents had the same
(14) first name. Use the table.

Names	Number of Presidents
James	6
John	4
William	4
George	3

  a. If a U.S President is chosen at random, what is the theoretical
  probability of choosing one whose name is George?

  b. What is the probability of choosing one whose name is William
  or John?

  c. What is the probability of choosing a president whose name is not
  shown in the table?

22. (Carpentry) Alice wants to add a square porch to the back of her house. The area of
(13) the porch is 361 square feet. What is the length of each side of the porch?

23. (Meteorology) The highest temperature ever recorded at the South Pole is $-13.6°C$.
(11) The lowest temperature is about 6 times lower than the highest temperature
recorded. Approximately what is the lowest temperature recorded?

24. Model On Monday the low temperature was $-4°F$. The temperature rose $21°F$ to
(5) the high temperature for that day. What was the high temperature on Monday?
Use a number line or thermometer to model the addition.

25. Multi-Step Paula's bank statement showed the following transactions for last month.
(5) The beginning balance was \$138.24. There was a withdrawal of \$46.59, then a
deposit of \$29.83, plus \$1.87 in interest added. What was the balance after these
transactions?

26. Simplify $4 \div 2 + 6^2 - 22$.
(4)

27. Write Explain how to simplify $a^3b^2ac^5a^4b$.
(3)

28. Convert 332 meters per second to centimeters per second.
(8)

29. Multiple Choice In 2000, the U.S. economy gained \$111,349 million from the sale of
(10) goods exported to Mexico. However, the U.S. economy lost \$135,926 million from
the sale of goods imported from Mexico. What was the U.S. balance of trade with
Mexico in the year 2000?

  A \$247,275 million

  B \$24,926 million

  C \$1.2 million

  D $-$\$24,577 million

30. Probability Describe each of the following events as impossible, unlikely, as likely
(Inv 1) as not, likely, or certain.

  a. Tanisha buys a new pair of shoes and the first shoe she pulls out of the box is
  for the left foot.

  b. Ralph rolls a number less than 7 on a standard number cube.

  c. November will have 31 days.

Solving Decimal Equations

New Concepts

To write decimals as integers, multiply by a power of 10.

> **Example** **1**   **Solving by Multiplying by a Power of 10**

Solve.

a. $8 + 0.5x = 10.5$

SOLUTION

$8 + 0.5x = 10.5$	
$10(8) + 10(0.5)x = 10(10.5)$	Multiply each term by 10.
$80 + 5x = 105$	Multiply.
$\underline{-80 \qquad\quad -80}$	Subtraction Property of Equality
$5x = 25$	Simplify.
$\dfrac{5x}{5} = \dfrac{25}{5}$	Division Property of Equality
$x = 5$	Simplify.

b. $0.006a + 0.02 = 0.2$

SOLUTION

$0.006a + 0.02 = 0.2$	
$1000(0.006a) + 1000(0.02) = 1000(0.2)$	Multiply each term by 1,000.
$6a + 20 = 200$	Multiply.
$\underline{-20 \quad -20}$	Subtraction Property of Equality
$6a = 180$	Simplify.
$\dfrac{6a}{6} = \dfrac{180}{6}$	Division Property of Equality
$x = 30$	Simplify.

Hint

If the decimals are in the thousandths, hundredths, and tenths places, multiply by a power of 10 that will make the decimal with the least value an integer.
$0.006 \times 1000 = 6$

Online Connection
www.SaxonMathResources.com

A decimal equation can also be solved by using inverse operations without multiplying by a power of 10 first.

Example 2 Solving Two-Step Decimal Equations

Solve.

a. $0.2m + 0.8 = 1.8$

SOLUTION

$$0.2m + 0.8 = 1.8$$

$$\underline{-0.8 = -0.8} \qquad \text{Subtraction Property of Equality}$$

$$0.2m = 1 \qquad \text{Simplify.}$$

$$\frac{0.2m}{0.2} = \frac{1}{0.2} \qquad \text{Division Property of Equality}$$

$$m = 5 \qquad \text{Simplify.}$$

b. $-0.03n - 1.2 = -1.44$

SOLUTION

$$-0.03n - 1.2 = -1.44$$

$$\underline{+1.2 = +1.2} \qquad \text{Addition Property of Equality}$$

$$-0.03n = -0.24 \qquad \text{Simplify.}$$

$$\frac{-0.03n}{-0.03} = \frac{-0.24}{-0.03} \qquad \text{Division Property of Equality}$$

$$n = 8 \qquad \text{Simplify.}$$

Finding a decimal part of a number is the same as finding a fraction or percent of a number.

Example 3 Finding Decimal Parts of Numbers

0.48 of 86 is what number?

SOLUTION

decimal number	of	given number	is	what number
0.48	$\cdot$	86	$=$	n

$$0.48 \cdot 86 = n \qquad \text{Multiply.}$$

$$41.28 = n$$

Estimate the answer to see if it is reasonable.

0.48 is less than 0.50 or $\frac{1}{2}$.

$\frac{1}{2}$ of 86 is 43.

41.28 is close to 43, so the answer is reasonable.

┌─ **Example 4** **Application: Zoology**

The height of an average mandrill (a large species of baboon) is 2.54 cm more than 12 times the length of its tail. If the height of a mandrill is 78.74 centimeters, then what is the length of its tail?

SOLUTION

height of mandrill = (12 times the tail length) plus 2.54 cm

Write and solve an equation to find the length of the mandrill's tail.

$12t + 2.54 = 78.74$

$\underline{-2.54 = -2.54}$ Subtraction Property of Equality

$12t = 76.20$ Simplify.

$\dfrac{12t}{12} = \dfrac{76.20}{12}$ Division Property of Equality

$t = 6.35$ cm   Simplify.

Check

$12t + 2.54 = 78.74$

$12(6.35) + 2.54 \overset{?}{=} 78.74$ Substitute 6.35 for t.

$76.20 + 2.54 \overset{?}{=} 78.74$ Multiply.

$78.74 = 78.74$ ✓   Add.

The mandrill's tail is 6.35 cm long.

Hint

Draw a diagram to help visualize the problem.

Lesson Practice

Solve each equation.

a. $0.25 + 0.18y = 0.97$
(Ex 1)

b. $0.05 = 0.5 - 0.15q$
(Ex 1)

c. $-0.5n + 1.4 = 8.9$
(Ex 2)

d. 0.6 of 24 is what number?
(Ex 3)

e. (**Highway Mileages**) Use the diagram. The distance from Town A to Town
(Ex 4) C is 52.8 kilometers. What is the distance from Town B to Town C?

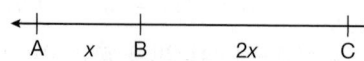

A   x   B   2x   C

Practice   Distributed and Integrated

1. **Multiple Choice** What is the solution of $\frac{4}{5}x = -24$ for x?
(21)

     A -30 **B** $-\dfrac{96}{5}$ **C** $\dfrac{96}{5}$ **D** 30

2. Simplify $3(2x + 5x)$ using the two different methods shown below.
(18)
    a. Combine like terms, and then multiply.

    b. Distribute, and then combine like terms.

*3. Solve $0.45x - 0.002 = 8.098$.
(24)

*4. Justify If you multiply both sides of an equation by a constant c, what happens
(21) to the solution? Explain your answer.

*5. (Stock Market) An investor buys some stock at $6.57 a share. She spends $846.25
(24) which includes a transaction fee of $25. How many shares of stock did she buy?

*6. Multiple Choice 0.8 is 0.32 of what number?
(24)
    A 2.5   **B** 0.25   **C** 0.4   **D** 4

*7. Verify Solve $0.45x + 0.9 = 1.008$. Will both methods shown below result in the
(24) same solution? Verify by using both methods to solve.

    Method I: Multiply both sides of the equation by 1000 first.

    Method II: Subtract 0.9 from both sides first.

8. Identify the coefficient, the variable(s), and the number of terms in the
(2) expression $\frac{9}{5}C + 32$.

*9. Verify Solve $0.25x + \frac{1}{2} = 0.075$. Will both methods shown below result in the same
(24) solution? Explain.

    Method I: First write the fraction as a decimal.

    Method II: First write the decimals as fractions.

*10. Error Analysis Two students use the circle graph to find the total percent
(22) of students who have fewer than two siblings. Which student is correct?
Explain the error.

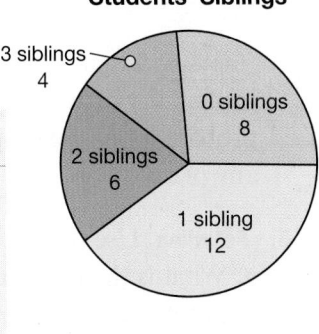

Students' Siblings

Student A	Student B
0 siblings or 1 sibling = 20 20% of the students	Total students: $8 + 12 + 6 + 4 = 30$ 0 siblings or 1 sibling = 20 $\frac{20}{30} \approx 67\%$ of the students

*11. Measurement The graph shows an estimation of the changes
(22) in the diameter of a tree, in inches, every 20 years. What
was the approximate circumference of the tree when the
tree was 100 years old? Use 3.14 for π. Round the answer
to the nearest tenth.

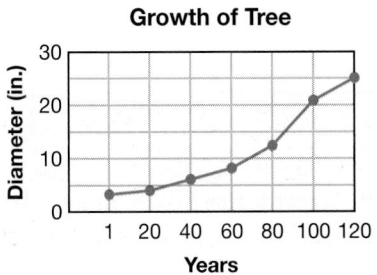

Growth of Tree

*12. The circle graph shows the amount of money Will spent on different snacks at
₍₂₂₎ a store. If Will spent $12, how much money did he spend on each item?

Will's Spendings

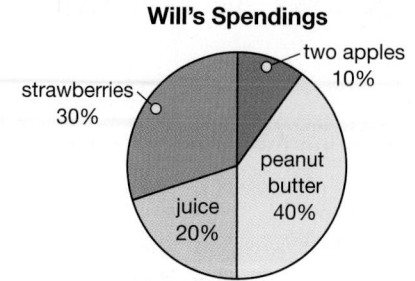

13. Graph the ordered pair on a coordinate plane (2, 1).
₍₂₀₎

14. Probability A spinner is divided in equal sections and labeled as shown in
₍₁₆₎ the diagram.

    a. If x is an even number, what is the probability the spinner will land on an
    even number?

    b. If x is an odd number, what is the probability the spinner will land on an
    odd number?

    c. If $x = 20$, what is the probability the spinner will land on a number less
    than 20?

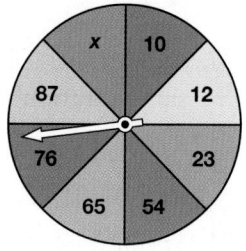

15. Multi-Step Each camp counselor at Camp Wallaby walked 6 miles for a health and
₍₁₅₎ fitness activity. Each camper walked 2 miles. The camp leader paid $0.50 into a
Fun Day account for every mile walked. Write an expression to represent the total
amount of money earned from walking by counselors and campers.

16. Verify Are the expressions below equivalent? Explain.
₍₉₎ $(11w^4 \cdot 3z^9)(2w^7z^2) \overset{?}{=} 66w^{11}z^{11}$

17. $\boxed{\textbf{Contests}}$ Miguel entered a contest offering prizes to the top 3 finishers. The
₍₁₄₎ probability of winning 1st is 12%, the probability of winning 2nd is 18%, and the
probability of winning 3rd is 20%. What is the probability that Miguel will not win
any prize?

18. $\boxed{\textbf{Retailing}}$ Use the circle graph.
₍₁₄₎
    a. What is the probability that a randomly chosen person who
    purchased a shirt paid $40.00 or more?

    b. What is the probability that a randomly chosen person who
    purchased a shirt paid $30 or less?

Shirt Sales

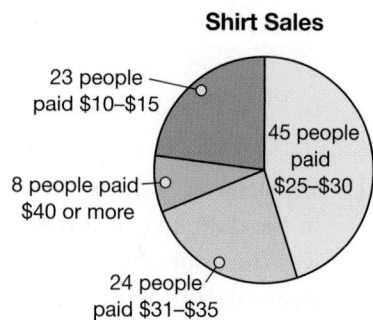

19. $\boxed{\textbf{Construction}}$ To calculate the amount of fencing for a rectangular area, Kelvin
₍₁₂₎ uses the formula $P = 2(l + w)$. Bonnie uses the formula $P = 2(w + l)$. Will their
calculations of the perimeter be the same? Explain.

20. Write Explain how to simplify $\dfrac{4}{7} \div \left[\left(-\dfrac{3}{8} \right) \cdot \left(-\dfrac{8}{3} \right) \right]$.
₍₁₁₎

21. Simplify $\frac{2}{5} \div \left(-\frac{7}{2}\right) \cdot \left(-\frac{5}{2}\right)$.
(4)

22. Write Explain why $k^2 \cdot m \cdot b^4 \cdot c^3$ cannot be simplified using the Product Rule
(3) of Exponents.

23. Justify Write the expression so there are no parentheses. Justify your change
(15) with a property. $6(ab + ef)$

24. Generalize Some real numbers can contain patterns within them, such as
(1) 21.12122122212222…

    a. Find a pattern in the number above. Is the pattern you found a repeating
    pattern?

    b. Is this number a rational number or an irrational number? Explain.

25. Convert 630 cubic centimeters to cubic inches. (Hint: 1 in. = 2.54 cm)
(8)

26. Multi-Step The temperature at 6 a.m. was 30°C. If the temperature increases by
(10) 2 degrees every half hour, what will the temperature be by 9 a.m.? What time will
it be when the temperature is 50°C?

27. Simplify $-|10 - 7|$.
(5)

*28. (**Internet Usage**) The circle graph shows
(22) approximate total Internet usage in the world.

    a. The estimated number of Internet users
    worldwide is 1,154,358,778. About how
    many people in North America use the
    Internet?

    b. About how many more people use the Internet
    in Asia than in North America?

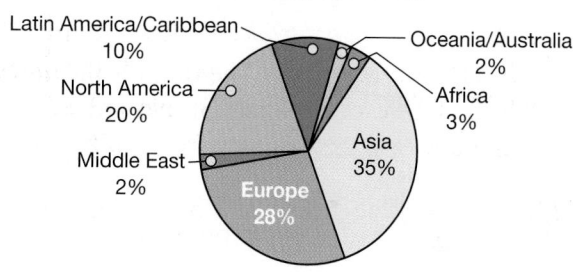

Internet Usage per Region

Latin America/Caribbean 10%
Oceania/Australia 2%
North America 20%
Africa 3%
Middle East 2%
Asia 35%
Europe 28%

29. Geometry A small square park is 784 square yards. A row of trees was planted
(13) on one side of the park. One tree was planted at each corner. Then one tree was
planted every seven yards between the corner trees. How many trees were planted
in the row?

30. (**Quality Control**) Elite Style inspects 500 hair dryers manufactured and finds 495 to
(Inv 1) have no defects. There are 20,000 hair dryers in their warehouse.

    a. What is the experimental probability that a hair dryer will have no defects?

    b. Predict the number of hair dryers that will have no defects in the warehouse.

Differentiating Between Relations and Functions

1. **Vocabulary** In the _____ $(-5, 2)$, -5 is the _____ and 2 is
(20)   the _____.

2. Simplify $(-4)^2 + 3^2 - 2^3$.
(3)

3. Find the value of y when $x = 8$.
(20)

$5y = -3x - 6$

4. Find the value of x when $y = -0.4$.
(24)

$x - 8y = 1.6$

5. **Multiple Choice** Jenny has n dollars in her savings account. If she deposits
(17) d dollars in her savings account each week, which expression represents
the amount she will have in her savings account at the end of a year?

   A $n + 52d$ **B** $52d - n$ **C** $n + d$ **D** $52n + d$

New Concepts

The **domain** is the set of possible values for the independent variable (input values) of a set of ordered pairs.

The **range** is the set of values for the dependent variable (output values) of a set of ordered pairs.

A **relation** is a set of ordered pairs where each number in the domain is matched to one or more numbers in the range. Relations can also be represented using set notation, tables, diagrams, or equations.

> **Math Language**
>
> In an ordered pair (x, y), x is the **independent variable** and y is the **dependent variable.**

Example 1   Determining the Domain and Range of a Relation

Give the domain and range of the relation.

$\{(2, 6), (2, 10), (8, 6), (5, 1), (4, 6), (3, 9)\}$

SOLUTION

Use a mapping diagram. Place the x-values in the oval on the left, and the y-values in the oval on the right.

The domain is all the x-values.

The range is all the y-values.

Domain: $\{2, 3, 4, 5, 8\}$

Range: $\{1, 6, 9, 10\}$

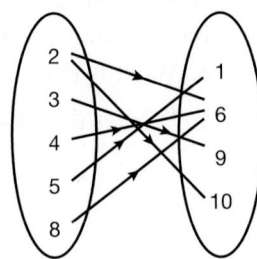

Online Connection
www.SaxonMathResources.com

A **function** is a mathematical relationship pairing each value in the domain with exactly one value in the range.

Example 2 **Identifying a Set of Ordered Pairs as a Function**

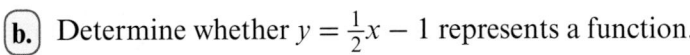

a. Determine whether $\{(3, 3), (10, 1), (0, 3), (8, 9), (4, 4), (10, 2)\}$ represents a function.

SOLUTION

Hint

When you write the domain and range, only write 10 and 3 once.

Domain: $\{0, 3, 4, 8, 10\}$

Range: $\{1, 2, 3, 4, 9\}$

Each domain value must map with exactly one range value.

The diagram shows that the domain value of 10 maps to the range values 1 and 2.

The relation is not a function. Each domain value does not have exactly one range value.

b. Determine whether $y = \frac{1}{2}x - 1$ represents a function.

SOLUTION

No matter what value is substituted for the independent variable x, the equation outputs exactly one value for the dependent variable y.

Domain (x)	-6	0	2	5	7	10
Range (y)	-4	-1	0	$\frac{3}{2}$	$\frac{5}{2}$	4

The equation represents a function.

If a relation is graphed on a coordinate grid, the **vertical-line test** can be used to determine if the relation is a function.

Vertical-Line Test
A graph on the coordinate plane represents a function if any vertical line intersects the graph in exactly one point.

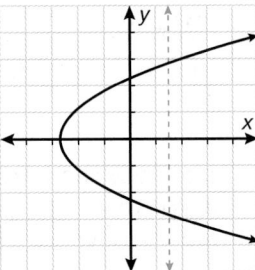

The relation is not a function. The vertical-line cuts the graph in more than one place.

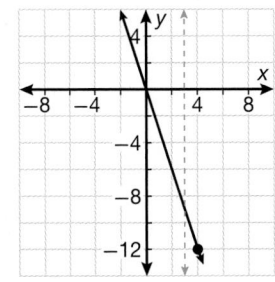

The relation is a function. The vertical-line cuts the graph in exactly one place.

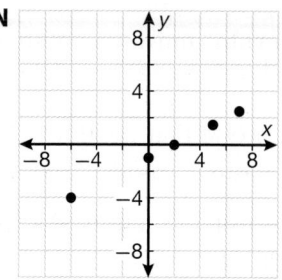

Example 3 | Identifying a Graph as a Function

Use the table. Graph the ordered pairs on a coordinate grid and determine whether the ordered pairs represent a function.

Domain (x)	Range (y)
-6	-4
0	-1
2	0
5	$\frac{3}{2}$
7	$\frac{5}{2}$

SOLUTION

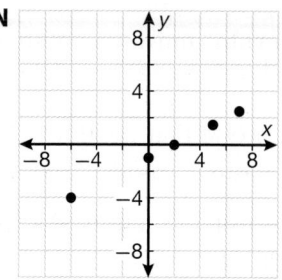

No matter what vertical line is drawn, the graph is intersected at only one point by each line. The ordered pairs represent a function.

In a function, the independent variable determines the value of the dependent variable. This means the dependent variable y is a function of the independent variable x. In terms of the variables, y is a function of x and can be written like the following example:

$$y = f(x)$$
$$y = 6x + 3$$
$$f(x) = 6x + 3$$

Example 4 | Writing a Function

a. Write $x + 2y = 5$ in function form.

SOLUTION

$x + 2y = 5$

$y = -\dfrac{x}{2} + \dfrac{5}{2}$ Solve for *y*.

$f(x) = -\dfrac{x}{2} + \dfrac{5}{2}$

b. Food labels list the grams of fats, carbohydrates, and proteins in a single serving. Proteins convert to 4 calories per gram. Write a rule in function notation to represent the number of calories from protein.

SOLUTION

The number of calories depends on the number of grams of protein eaten.

dependent variable: number of calories

independent variable: number of grams of protein

Let p represent the number of grams of protein.

$y = 4p$

$f(p) = 4p$ Use function notation.

Example 5 Application: Reading

A student reads an average of 25 pages per day while reading a 544-page novel. Write a rule in function notation to find the number of pages she has left to read at the end of any given day.

SOLUTION

Let d represent the days spent reading.

$25d$	number of pages read
$544 - 25d$	number of pages that have not been read

The number of pages left to read depends on the number of days the student has been reading.

$$y = 544 - 25d$$
$$f(d) = 544 - 25d \qquad \text{Use function notation.}$$

Math Reasoning

Write Does it make sense for d to be greater than 21? Explain.

Lesson Practice

a. Give the domain and range of the relation: (1, 2); (2, 1); (4, 6); (8, 5);
(Ex 1) (7, 7); (3, 10)

b. Using a diagram, determine whether the ordered pairs represent a
(Ex 2) function. {(11, 12); (12, 1); (5, 5); (14, 10); (13, 7)}

c. Determine whether $y = 3x - 1$ represents a function.

d. Use the table. Graph the ordered pairs on a coordinate plane and
(Ex 3) determine whether the ordered pairs represent a function.

x	−1	0	1	−2	0
y	3	0	3	6	6

e. (**Printing**) A brochure costs $0.07 per page to print. Write a rule in
(Ex 4) function notation to represent the cost of printing c copies of the
brochure.

f. (**Novelist**) An author writes 30 pages per day. Write a function rule that
(Ex 5) the author can use to find how many pages she has left to write before
reaching page 400.

Practice Distributed and Integrated

1. Solve $0.3 + 0.05y = 0.65$.
(24)

2. Verify Verify that the following solutions are correct for each equation given.
(19)
  a. $103 + x = 99$ when $x = -4$

  b. $\dfrac{1}{2} - x = \dfrac{3}{4}$ when $x = -\dfrac{1}{4}$

*3. Make a table to determine whether $y = x + 2$ represents a function.
(25)

*4. (Hiking) A hiker can average 15 minutes per mile. Write a rule in function notation
(25)   to describe the time it takes the hiker to walk m miles.

5. Subtract $3.16 - 1.01 - 0.11$.
(10)

*6. Multiple Choice Which set of ordered pairs represents a function?
(25)   **A** $\{(1, 1); (2, 2); (3, 3); (4, 4)\}$

   B $\{(1, 0); (2, 1); (1, 3); (2, 4)\}$

   C $\{(1, 1); (1, 2); (1, 3); (1, 4)\}$

   D $\{(10, 1); (10, 2); (12, 3); (12, 4)\}$

*7. A square has a side length of s. Write a rule in function notation to represent the
(25)   perimeter.

*8. Generalize If a set of ordered pairs is a function, are the ordered pairs also a relation?
(25)   Explain.

*9. Analyze A student draws a circle on a coordinate plane. The center of the circle is
(25)   at the origin. Is this circle a function or a relation? Explain.

*10. (Photography) A student is making a pinhole camera. What is the circumference of
(24)   the pinhole in the box? Use 3.14 for π and round to the nearest hundredth.

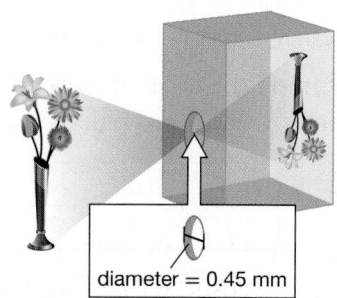

diameter = 0.45 mm

*11. (Astronomical Unit) An astronomical unit is the average distance from the Sun to
(8)   the Earth. 1 AU (astronomical unit) is approximately equal to 93 million miles.
   If Jupiter is about 5.2 AU from the Sun, about how many miles is it from
   the Sun?

12. Write Describe a possible situation for the discrete graph.
(Inv 2)

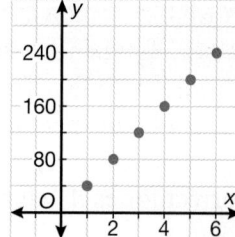

*13. (Movie Club) Stephen belongs to a movie club in which he pays an annual fee of
(23) $39.95 and then rents DVDs for $0.99 each. In one year, Stephen spent $55.79.
   Write and solve an equation to find how many DVDs he rented.

14. Error Analysis Two students solve $5a + 4 = 34$. Which student is correct? Explain
(23) the error.

Student A	Student B
$5a + 4 = 34$	$5a + 4 = 34$
$\dfrac{5a + 4}{5} = \dfrac{34}{5}$	$\underline{+4 \quad +4}$
$a + \dfrac{4}{5} = \dfrac{34}{5}$	$5a = 38$
$a = \dfrac{34}{5} - \dfrac{4}{5}$	$a = \dfrac{38}{5}$
$a = \dfrac{30}{5}$	
$a = 6$	

15. Multiple Choice The graph shows the points scored by Michaela
(22) and Jessie during the first five basketball games of the season.
What conclusion can you make from the graph?

A Michaela is the best player on the team.

B Michaela usually scores more points than Jessie.

C Neither player will score more than 18 points
   in the next game.

D Jessie does not play as much as Michaela.

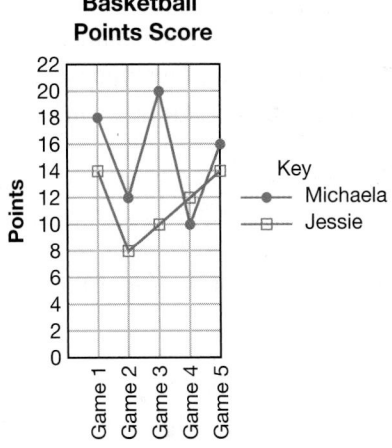

Basketball Points Score

Key
— Michaela
— Jessie

*16. Write Two sets of data represent the number of bottles of water and the number
(22) of bottles of juice a store sells each month. Give reasons why the following types
of graphs would be appropriate to represent the data: a double-bar graph, a
double-line graph, and two stem-and-leaf plots.

17. Choose an appropriate graph to display the portion of students in a class who
(22) have birthdays in each month. Explain your choice.

18. Find the value of $3z - 2(z - 1)^2 + 2$ for $z = 4$.
(9)

19. (Cooking) A recipe calls for 2.5 cups of orange juice for a batch of fruit drink.
(20) In the equation, $y = 2.5x$, y represents the number of cups of orange juice and
x represents number of batches of fruit drink. Make a table when $x = 1, 2, 3,$
and 4 batches of fruit drink. Then graph the ordered pair in your table.

20. Analyze "Three more than x" can be written as $x + 3$ or $3 + x$. Can "three less
(17) than x" be written as $x - 3$ or $3 - x$? Explain.

21. Multi-Step Population growth for a certain type of animal is determined by the
(16) formula $N_n = N_i 2^n$, where N_i is the initial population size and N_n is the population
size after n generations. If the initial population is 45, what is the difference
between the population size after the fourth generation and the population size
after the sixth generation?

22. (Architecture) An architect is designing a very large square mall. Estimate the total area of the mall, if each side length is approximately 4890 feet.
(13)

23. Write True or False. The expression $12 - 8 - 2$ could be simplified using the Associative Property. Explain.
(12)

24. Solve $1\frac{1}{2}y = 6\frac{3}{4}$.
(21)

25. Solve $\frac{1}{8}m - \frac{1}{4} = \frac{3}{4}$.
(23)

26. Verify Determine if each statement below is true or false. If false, explain why.
(9)

　　a. $\dfrac{(5-x)^3 + 12}{(4x)} = \dfrac{41-x}{x^3}$ for $x = 2$.

　　b. $\dfrac{(5-x)^3 + 12}{(4x)} = \dfrac{41-x}{x^3}$ for $x = 3$.

27. Measurement The distance between City A and City C is 312.78 miles. City B lies on a point on a direct line between Cities A and C. If the distance between City C and City B is 191.9 miles, what is the distance between Cities A and B?
(6)

28. (Computer Engineering) Eight bits, or 2^3 bits, equal one byte. How many bits are in 64, or 2^6, bytes?
(3)

29. Geometry The measure of the length of a rectangle is $4x - y$ feet and the width is xy. What expression would show the area of the rectangle? Explain.
(15)

30. Simplify $|-2 - 3| - 4 + (-8)$.
(6)

Solving Multi-Step Equations

Warm Up

1. **Vocabulary** The product of a number and its _____ is 1.
(11)

2. Simplify $2x + 5y + 3x - 2y$ by adding like terms.
(18)

3. Solve $2x + 5 = 12$. Check your solution.
(23)

4. **Multiple Choice** Which is the solution of $3x + 6 = 33$?
(23)

   A 13   **B** 9

   C 7   **D** 8

New Concepts

Equations that are more complex may have to be simplified before they can be solved. More than two steps may be required to solve them. If there are like terms on one side of an equation, combine them first. Then apply inverse operations and the properties of equality to continue solving the equation.

Example 1   Combining Like Terms

Solve $5x + 8 - 3x + 2 = 20$. Justify each step. Check the solution.

SOLUTION

$5x + 8 - 3x + 2 = 20$	
$5x - 3x + 8 + 2 = 20$	Commutative Property of Addition
$2x + 10 = 20$	Combine like terms.
$-10 = -10$	Subtraction Property of Equality
$2x = 10$	Simplify.
$\dfrac{2x}{2} = \dfrac{10}{2}$	Division Property of Equality
$x = 5$	Simplify.

Check Substitute 5 for x.

$$5x + 8 - 3x + 2 = 20$$
$$5(5) + 8 - 3(5) + 2 \stackrel{?}{=} 20$$
$$25 + 8 - 15 + 2 \stackrel{?}{=} 20$$
$$20 = 20 \checkmark$$

> **Math Language**
>
> **Like terms** have the same variable(s) raised to the same power(s).

Complex equations can contain symbols of inclusion such as parentheses and brackets. Eliminate the symbols of inclusion first. Use the Distributive Property if multiplication is indicated by the symbols of inclusion. Then combine like terms on each side of the equation. Continue to solve the equation by applying inverse operations and the properties of equality.

Online Connection
www.SaxonMathResources.com

Example 2 Using Distributive Property

Solve $x + 3(2x + 4) = 47$. Justify each step. Check the solution.

SOLUTION

$$x + 3(2x + 4) = 47$$

$$\begin{aligned}
x + 6x + 12 &= 47 && \text{Distributive Property} \\
7x + 12 &= 47 && \text{Combine like terms.} \\
\underline{-12} &= \underline{-12} && \text{Subtraction Property of Equality} \\
7x &= 35 && \text{Simplify.} \\
\frac{7x}{7} &= \frac{35}{7} && \text{Division Property of Equality} \\
x &= 5 && \text{Simplify.}
\end{aligned}$$

Check Substitute 5 for x.

$$\begin{aligned}
x + 3(2x + 4) &= 47 \\
5 + 3[2(5) + 4] &\stackrel{?}{=} 47 \\
5 + 3[10 + 4] &\stackrel{?}{=} 47 \\
5 + 3[14] &\stackrel{?}{=} 47 \\
47 &= 47 \quad \checkmark
\end{aligned}$$

<aside>
Math Reasoning

Write What is another way to eliminate the coefficient 7 from $7x$?
</aside>

When equations contain symbols of inclusion and like terms, first apply the Distributive Property. Next, add like terms. Then apply inverse operations and the properties of equality to solve the equation.

Example 3 Simplifying before Solving

Solve $5x - (x - 3) - 1 = 18$. Justify each step. Check the solution.

SOLUTION

$$5x - (x - 3) - 1 = 18$$

$$\begin{aligned}
5x - x + 3 - 1 &= 18 && \text{Distributive Property} \\
4x + 2 &= 18 && \text{Combine like terms.} \\
\underline{-2} &= \underline{-2} && \text{Subtraction Property of Equality} \\
4x &= 16 && \text{Simplify.} \\
\frac{1}{4} \cdot 4x &= 16 \cdot \frac{1}{4} && \text{Multiplication Property of Equality} \\
x &= 4 && \text{Simplify.}
\end{aligned}$$

Check Substitute 4 for x.

$$\begin{aligned}
5x - (x - 3) - 1 &= 18 \\
5(4) - (4 - 3) - 1 &\stackrel{?}{=} 18 \\
20 - 1 - 1 &\stackrel{?}{=} 18 \\
18 &= 18 \quad \checkmark
\end{aligned}$$

<aside>
Caution

Remember to multiply by -1 when distributing a negative across parentheses.
</aside>

Example 4 Application: Landscaping

Jim is building a right triangular flower bed. One of the acute angles will measure twice the other acute angle. What are the measures of the two acute angles?

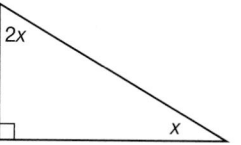

Hint

The sum of the measures of the angles of a triangle is 180°.

SOLUTION

$x + 2x + 90 = 180$	Sum of the angle measures
$3x + 90 = 180$	Combine like terms.
$\underline{-90 = -90}$	Subtraction Property of Equality
$3x = 90$	Simplify.
$\dfrac{3x}{3} = \dfrac{90}{3}$	Division Property of Equality
$x = 30$	Simplify.

The measures of the angles are 30° and 60°.

Lesson Practice

Solve. Justify each step. Check the solution.

a. $3x + 2 - x + 7 = 16$
(Ex 1)

b. $6(x - 1) = 36$
(Ex 2)

c. $5x - 3(x - 4) = 22$
(Ex 3)

 d. **Geometry** Juan is building a triangular shelf. He wants one angle to be a right angle and the other two angles to have the same measure. What are the measures of the angles?
(Ex 4)

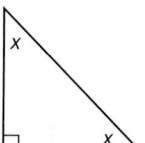

Practice Distributed and Integrated

*1. Solve for x in the equation $\frac{3}{4} + \frac{1}{2}x + 2 = 0$.
(26)

*2. Multiple Choice A vending machine will only accept quarters in change. What are the independent and dependent variables that describe the amount of money in change held by the vending machine?
(25)

A Independent variable: value of 1 quarter; dependent variable: number of quarters

B Independent variable: value of 1 quarter; dependent variable: value of the quarters

C Independent variable: value of the quarters; dependent variable: number of quarters

D Independent variable: number of quarters; dependent variable: value of the quarters

*3. Multiple Choice Which one of the expressions below can be simplified by combining
(18) like terms?

A $6(5x + 1)$ **B** $2x(3 + 8)$

C $7x + 5$ **D** $9x - 6y + 4$

4. A table shows temperature changes over a period of a week.
(22) **a.** Why would a circle graph inaccurately display the data?

b. Which type of graph would best display the data?

*5. (Digital Technology) The average size for the memory storage of an mp3 player is
(26) 2 gigabytes (GB). The average size of an mp3 song is 5.5 megabytes (MB). About
how many songs can you store on a 2-gigabyte player if the player requires
16 megabytes for its own use? (Hint: 1gigabyte = 1024 megabytes)

*6. Write Describe two different methods for solving $12(x + 7) = 96$.
(26)

*7. Justify Solve $-5(3x - 7) + 11 = 1$. Justify each step with an operation or property.
(26)

*8. Verify Draw the graph of a function. Check to see if your graph is truly a function.
(25)

*9. Use the graph. Determine whether the relation is a function.
(25)

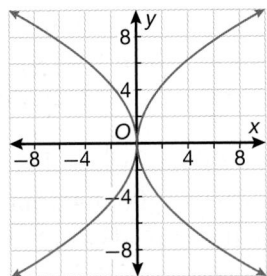

10. Solve $0.4m + 2.05 = 10.45$.
(24)

11. Error Analysis Two students solved $0.4x - 0.08 = 6.32$. Which student is correct?
(24) Explain the error.

Student A	Student B
$0.4x - 0.08 = 6.32$	$0.4x - 0.08 = 6.32$
$10(0.4x) - 100(0.08) = 100(6.32)$	$100(0.4x) - 100(0.08) = 100(6.32)$
$4x - 8 = 632$	$40x - 8 = 632$
$\underline{+8 \quad +8}$	$\underline{+8 \quad +8}$
$4x = 640$	$40x = 640$
$\dfrac{4x}{4} = \dfrac{640}{4}$	$\dfrac{40x}{40} = \dfrac{640}{40}$
$x = 160$	$x = 16$

12. Verify Is $x = 8$ a solution for $7x - 12 = 44$? Explain. If false, provide a correct
(23) solution and check.

*13. Multi-Step Emil cooks 64 hot dogs. He uses 5 packages of hot dogs plus 4 hot dogs
   (23)   left over from a meal earlier in the week. How many hot dogs are in each package?

   a. Write an equation to find the number of hot dogs in a package.

   b. Solve the equation, and then check the solution.

*14. (Kangaroos) A large kangaroo can travel 15 feet in each hop. Write and solve an
   (21)   equation to find how many hops it takes for the kangaroo to travel one mile.
   (Hint: 5,280 feet = 1 mile)

15. Verify Show that the graphed point is a solution to the equation $y = 2x + 9$.
   (12)

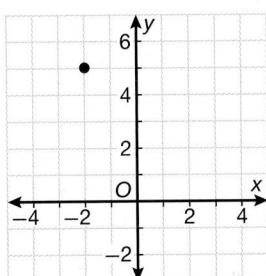

16. Analyze Determine whether $3p^2qd^3$ and $(2qdp \cdot -5d^2p)$ are terms that can be
   (18)   combined. Explain your reasoning.

17. Probability The probability of rain on Monday is a. It is twice as likely to
   (17)   rain on Tuesday. Write an expression to represent the probability of rain on
   Tuesday.

18. (Biology) A biologist wants to calculate the volume of a spherical cell. She uses the
   (16)   equation for the volume of a sphere, which is $V = \frac{4}{3}\pi r^3$. If the cell has a radius of
   2 micrometers, what is its volume? Use 3.14 for π and round to the nearest tenth.

19. (Employment) Jim manages a restaurant that is currently hiring employees. On
   (14)   Tuesday, he interviewed 2 waiters, 2 line cooks, 3 dishwashers, and 1 chef. On
   Thursday, he interviewed 2 waiters, 1 line cook, 2 dishwashers, and 3 chefs. What
   is the probability that a randomly selected person interviewed applied to be a
   waiter?

20. Verify Compare the following expression using $<, >, =$. Verify your answer.
   (13)
   $$\sqrt{324} - \sqrt{144} \bigcirc \sqrt{400} - \sqrt{289}$$

21. Evaluate.
   (7)
   $$\frac{6}{2}[5(3 + 4)]$$

22. Model Use a number line to model $-8 - (-4) - (-6)$. Then simplify the
   (6)   expression.

23. Simplify.
   (4)
   $$2 \cdot (3 + 4)^2 + 15$$

24. Subtract $\frac{1}{4} - \frac{1}{3}$.
(10)

 25. Probability The probability of rolling a 4 on a six-sided number cube is $\frac{1}{6}$. To find
(3) the probability of rolling a 6-sided number cube and getting a 4 five times in a
row, multiply the probability $\frac{1}{6}$ by itself five times. Write the answer using an
exponent.

26. (Investing) To find the amount of money earned on a bank deposit that earns
(2) quarterly compounded interest, the formula $A = P\left(1 + \frac{r}{4}\right)^{4t}$ is used.

P = principal, (the amount originally deposited)

r = the interest rate

t = time in years.
a. How many terms are in $P\left(1 + \frac{r}{4}\right)^{4t}$?

b. How many variables are in $P\left(1 + \frac{r}{4}\right)^{4t}$?

c. What is the coefficient of t?

 27. Identify the coefficient, the variable(s), and the number of terms in $\frac{1}{3}Bh$.
(2)

28. Multi-Step The Noatak National Preserve in Alaska covers 6,574,481 acres. One
(8) acre is equal to 4840 square yards. What is the area of the preserve in square miles?
a. Find the area of the preserve in square yards.

b. Convert square yards to square miles. (Hint: 1 mile = 1760 yards)

29. Geometry To find the volume of a rectangular-prism shaped–
(12) sunscreen bottle, Jagdeesh uses the formula $V = lwh$. Betty uses
the formula $V = wlh$. Will the volume of the bottle be the same?
Explain.

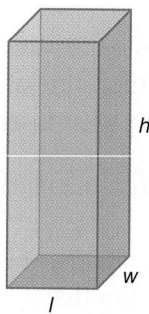

30. The spinner in a board game is divided into four equal sections colored blue, red,
(Inv 1) green, and yellow. Conduct a simulation using random numbers to determine the
number of times the spinner lands on blue in 30 spins. Use the random number
generator in a graphing calculator to simulate the spins.

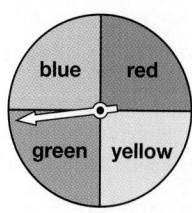

Identifying Misleading Representations of Data

Warm Up

1. (22) **Vocabulary** A bar graph uses _____ to represent data.

2. (22) True or False: A circle graph shows how data change.

3. (Inv 2) Draw a graph that represents a flag being raised up a flagpole slowly at the beginning and quickly at the end.

4. (26) Solve $2(2x + 3) = 24$.

New Concepts

When displaying data, components such as the scale or labels can make a graph misleading.

> **Example 1** Identifying Misleading Line Graphs
>
> The line graph shows the number of members of a health club each month since it opened. Explain why the graph may be misleading.

Hint

When there is a large gap between data values, a graph may use a broken axis. In the graph showing memberships, the vertical axis has a broken scale.

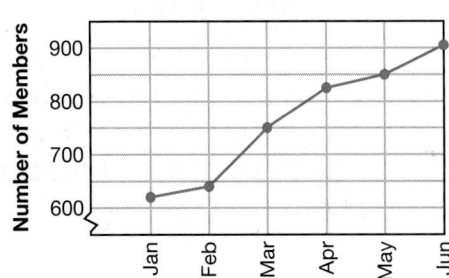

Number of Members at Renaldo's Health Club

SOLUTION Because the scale does not start at zero, the membership appears to have increased much more than it actually did.

Another characteristic that may create a misleading graph is the size of the increments in the scale.

> **Example 2** Identifying Misleading Bar Graphs
>
> A radio station conducted a survey of music preferences of listeners. The bar graph shows the results. Explain why the graph may be misleading.

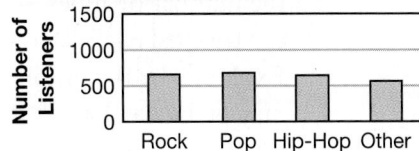

Listener Music Preferences

SOLUTION

The large increments of the scale make the data values appear to be closer than they actually are.

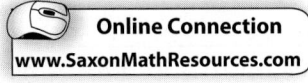

Online Connection
www.SaxonMathResources.com

Example 3 **Identifying Misleading Circle Graphs**

The circle graph shows the number of some types of sandwiches a deli sells in one day. Explain why the graph may be misleading.

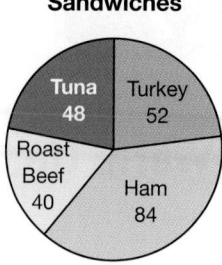

Sandwiches

SOLUTION The title does not specify that these were the only sandwiches the deli sold, and it may not represent all categories. The deli may also have served a chicken salad or other type of sandwich, making the graph misleading.

Example 4 **Application: Television Prices**

An electronics store created the graph to show the average selling price of a television each year.

a. Explain why the graph may be misleading.

SOLUTION The large increments make the data values appear to be closer than they actually are.

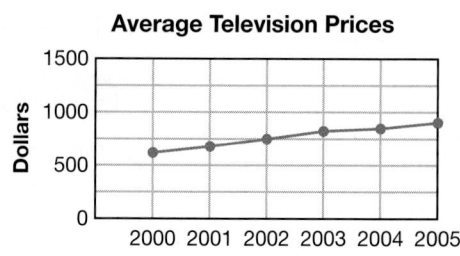

Math Reasoning

Analyze What increments could be used for the vertical axis of the graph in Example **4a** so that the graph is not misleading?

b. What conclusion might be made from the graph? Why might the store have created this graph?

SOLUTION The graph seems to show that the prices have not increased much over the past five years. The store may want it to appear as though prices have not increased significantly; when in reality they have actually increased by almost 50 percent.

c. Make a graph of the sales data that is not misleading.

SOLUTION Use a broken axis and smaller increments.

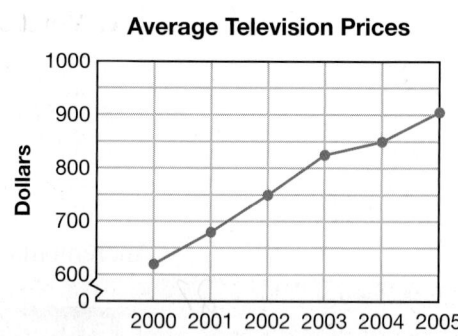

Lesson Practice

a. The graph at right shows the number of miles a car traveled each year. Explain why the graph may be misleading.
(Ex 1)

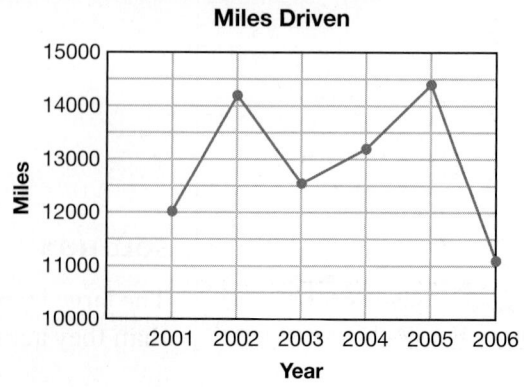

b. The graph below shows baking temperatures of various foods. Explain
(Ex 2) why the graph may be misleading.

Cooking Temperatures

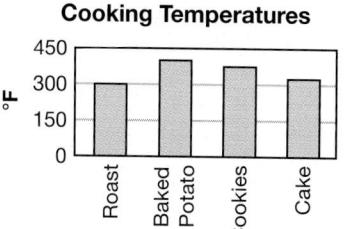

c. The circle graph below shows the number of some kinds of dogs that
(Ex 3) were sold by the pet store. Explain why the graph may be misleading.

Types of Dogs Sold

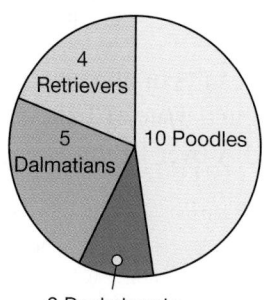

A salesperson created the graph at right to display the number of products he sold each month.
(Ex 4)

Sales

d. Explain why the graph may be misleading.

e. What conclusion might be made from the graph? Why might the salesman have created this graph?

f. Make a graph of the sales data that is not misleading.

Practice   Distributed and Integrated

1. Simplify $(-2 + 3) \div (4 - 5 + 3)$.
(11)

Solve.

2. $0.5x - 0.2 = 0.15$
(23)

3. $\dfrac{1}{4} + \dfrac{2}{5}x + 1 = 2\dfrac{1}{4}$
(26)

4. Multiple Choice Which is the solution to the equation below?
(24)

$-0.4n + 0.305 = 0.295$

A 0.025   **B** −0.025   **C** 0.0004   **D** −0.7375

5. Analyze On a coordinate plane, a student draws a graph of two parallel lines perpendicular to the *y*-axis. Does the graph represent a function?
(25)

6. Identify the property illustrated by $3 \cdot (9 \cdot 5) = (3 \cdot 9) \cdot 5$.
(12)

*7. (Automotive Safety) The stopping distance *d* required by a moving vehicle is dependent on the square of its speed *s*. Write a rule in function notation to represent this information.
(25)

*8. A petting zoo contains 10 species of animals. The graph shows percentages of the 5 most numerous types of animals at the zoo. Give reasons why the circle graph may be misleading.
(27)

Petting Zoo

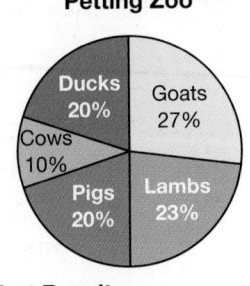

*9. Justify Is 4 a solution to the equation $5x + 8 - 3x + 4 = 20$? Justify your answer.
(26)

*10. The bar graph shows results of a taste test of four different brands of yogurt. True or False. Twice as many people preferred Brand A over Brand D.
(27)

Taste Test Results

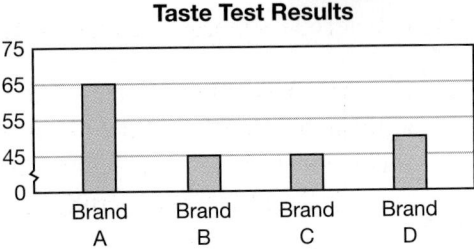

*11. Analyze Using the set of data values 125,000, 105,000, 162,000, 112,000, and 148,000 without using a broken axis or very large intervals, how could a student make a reasonably sized graph of the data?
(27)

*12. (Production) A company has 6 machines to produce parts for its product. A manager uses the bar graph showing the number of parts produced by each machine each day. What incorrect conclusions might the manager make about the efficiency of the machines?
(27)

Machine Production

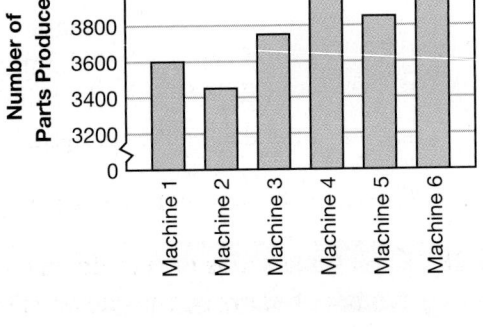

*13. True or False: Large intervals on a scale can make changes in data appear less than they actually are. If false, explain why.
(27)

*14. Multi-Step Three friends rented a kayak. It cost $4 per hour per person to rent the kayak, plus $2 for each life jacket, and $3 to park the car. It cost $57 in all. How many hours did they spend kayaking?
(26)

*15. Geometry The formula for the surface area of a square pyramid is $S = \left(4 \cdot \frac{1}{2}bh\right) + b^2$. If the measure of *b* is 5 m, what is the largest slant height possible for the total surface area to be no more than 150 m²?
(26)

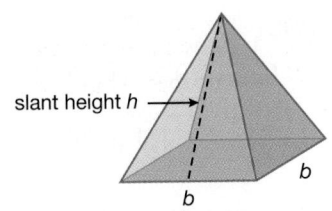

slant height *h*

16. Justify What is the first step in solving $0.35 + 0.22x = 1.67$?
(24)

*17. (**Phone Charges**) The length of the first ten calls Tyrese made one month were 13, 28,
(22) 6, 10, 13, 22, 31, 12, 2, and 9 minutes. In a stem-and-leaf plot of the data which
digit would appear the most in the leaves column?

18. Verify Show that $-\frac{3}{4}x = 12$ and $\frac{5}{32}x = -2\frac{1}{2}$ have the same solution.
(21)

19. Graph the ordered pair $(-1, 0)$ on a coordinate plane.
(20)

20. Measurement To measure the length of a steel rod, an engineer uses a reference
(19) point a few millimeters from the end of the ruler. She then subtracts this
reference point from her final measurement of 325 mm. If the rod's length is
318 mm, what reference point did she use?

21. Convert 37 American dollars to Indian rupees. (Hint: 1 rupee = $0.025)
(8)

22. Statistics Absolute deviation is the absolute value of the difference between a
(5) value in a data set and the mean of the data set. For the data set $\{8, 9, 11, 12, 15\}$,
the mean is 11, so the absolute deviation for the value 15 is $|15 - 11| = |4| = 4$.
What is the absolute deviation for each of the other numbers in the above data set?

23. (**Fundraising**) The cheerleaders made $3 profit on each item sold in a fundraiser.
(15) They sold x calendars and y candles in total. Write and simplify an algebraic
expression to find the total profit.

24. Write A coin is tossed 8 times. What is the probability that the next time the coin
(14) is tossed the result will be heads? Explain.

25. Simplify $11 \cdot 3 + 7$.
(4)

26. Multi-Step A vending machine has q quarters and d dimes.
(9) **a.** Write an expression with variables to represent the value of the money.

b. Find the value of the change in the machine if there are 21 quarters and 13 dimes.

27. Use $<$, $>$, or $=$ to compare the expressions. $\frac{1}{3} + \frac{1}{5} \cdot \frac{2}{15}$ $\bigcirc$ $\left(\frac{1}{3} + \frac{1}{5}\right) \cdot \frac{2}{15}$
(7)

28. Write A man runs up and down stairs. If the number of stairs he runs up plus the
(6) number of stairs he runs down is the total number of stairs, describe his position
at the end of his run.

29. Write Show the steps for simplifying $10 \cdot 4^2 + 72 \div 2^3$.
(4)

30. (**Accounting**) Accountants prepare financial reports for businesses. Identify the set
(1) of numbers that best describes the numbers in a financial report. Explain your
choice.

Solving Equations with Variables on Both Sides

Warm Up

1. **Vocabulary** In the expression $-5x + 2 + 3x$, $-5x$ and $3x$ are
$_{(2)}$ _____ terms.

2. Simplify $10 - 4(5 + 3) + 2^3$.
$_{(7)}$

Solve.

3. $2(3 - x) = 10$
$_{(26)}$

4. $-3(1 + 2x) + x = 32$
$_{(26)}$

5. **Multiple Choice** Which value is a solution to the equation
$3(x - 4) - x = 30$?

    A 14   **B** 9   **C** 6   **D** 21

New Concepts

To solve an equation with variables on both sides, use inverse operations to bring the variables together on one side of the equation.

Materials

• algebra tiles

Exploration **Modeling Variables on Both Sides of an Equation**

Use algebra tiles to model and solve $4x + 5 = 2x + 11$.

$4x + 5$	$2x + 11$	
		Model each side of the equation.
		Add 2 $-x$-tiles to both sides. Remove pairs that equal zero.
		Add 5 -1-tiles to both sides. Remove the zero pairs.
		Arrange into 2 equal groups. What is the value of x?

a. Model $x + 3 = 2x - 4$. Then find the value of x.

b. Model $3x - 1 = x - 3$. Then find the value of x.

Online Connection
www.SaxonMathResources.com

Math Language

Inverse operations undo each other. Addition and subtraction are inverse operations. Multiplication and division are inverse operations.

Example 1 Using Inverse Operations

Solve $6x = 4x - 10$. Justify each step. Check the solution.

SOLUTION

$$6x = 4x - 10$$

$$\underline{-4x = -4x} \qquad \text{Subtraction Property of Equality}$$

$$2x = -10 \qquad \text{Combine like terms.}$$

$$\frac{2x}{2} = \frac{-10}{2} \qquad \text{Division Property of Equality}$$

$$x = -5$$

Check Substitute -5 for x in the original equation.

$$6x = 4x - 10$$

$$6(-5) \stackrel{?}{=} 4(-5) - 10$$

$$-30 \stackrel{?}{=} -20 - 10$$

$$-30 = -30 \quad \checkmark$$

Equations with variables on both sides might also contain symbols of inclusion and like terms. The first step is to apply the Distributive Property. The second step is to add like terms. Then apply inverse operations and the properties of equality to solve the equation.

Example 2 Simplifying Before Solving

Solve $5(2x + 4) - 2x = 6 + 2(3x + 12)$. Justify each step.

SOLUTION

$$5(2x + 4) - 2x = 6 + 2(3x + 12)$$

$$10x + 20 - 2x = 6 + 6x + 24 \qquad \text{Distributive Property}$$

$$10x - 2x + 20 = 6x + 6 + 24 \qquad \text{Commutative Property}$$

$$8x + 20 = 6x + 30 \qquad \text{Combine like terms.}$$

$$\underline{-6x \qquad = -6x} \qquad \text{Subtraction Property of Equality}$$

$$2x + 20 = 30 \qquad \text{Simplify.}$$

$$\underline{-20 = -20} \qquad \text{Subtraction Property of Equality}$$

$$2x = 10 \qquad \text{Simplify.}$$

$$\frac{1}{2} \cdot 2x = 10 \cdot \frac{1}{2} \qquad \text{Multiplication Property of Equality}$$

$$x = 5 \qquad \text{Simplify.}$$

Math Reasoning

Write What is another way to eliminate the coefficient 2 from $2x$?

An **identity** is an equation that is always true. It has infinitely many solutions. If no value of the variable makes an equation true, then the equation has no solution.

Example 3 No Solutions or Infinitely Many Solutions

Solve each equation. Justify each step.

a. $10 - 6x = -2(3x - 5)$

SOLUTION

$$10 - 6x = -2(3x - 5)$$

$10 - 6x = -6x + 10$	Distributive Property
$\underline{+6x = +6x}$	Addition Property of Equality
$10 = 10$	Simplify. Always true.

Since $10 = 10$ is always true, the equation is an identity.

b. $7x - 2 = 9x - 5 - 2x$

SOLUTION

$$7x - 2 = 9x - 5 - 2x$$

$7x - 2 = 7x - 5$	Combine like terms.
$\underline{-7x = -7x}$	Addition Property of Equality
$-2 = -5$	Simplify. Never true.

Since $-2 = -5$ is never true, the equation has no solutions.

Math Reasoning

Analyze When the simplified equation is an identity, what values of the variable will satisfy the original equation?

Math Reasoning

Analyze When all variables are eliminated in an equation, resulting in a false statement, what values of the variable satisfy the original equation?

Example 4 Application: Telephone Rates

Telephone Company A charges $18.95 per month for local calls and $0.04 per minute for long-distance calls. Telephone Company B charges $21.95 per month for local calls and $0.02 per minute for long-distance calls. For what number of minutes of long-distance calls per month is the cost of the plans the same?

SOLUTION

Let $m =$ the number of minutes of long distance calls.

Company A's monthly charge $= \$18.95 + \$0.04m$

Company B's monthly charge $= \$21.95 + \$0.02m$

$18.95 + 0.04m = 21.95 + 0.02m$	Write an equation.
$\underline{-0.02m = \qquad -0.02m}$	Subtraction Property of Equality
$18.95 + 0.02m = 21.95$	Simplify.
$\underline{-18.95 \qquad = -18.95}$	Subtraction Property of Equality
$0.02m = 3.00$	Simplify.
$\dfrac{0.02m}{0.02m} = \dfrac{3.00}{0.02}$	Division Property of Equality
$m = 150$	Simplify.

The costs will be same for 150 minutes.

Solve each equation. Justify each step. Check the solution.

a. $6x = 3x + 27$
(Ex 1)

b. $2 + 3(3x - 6) = 5(x - 3) + 15$
(Ex 2)

Solve each equation. Justify each step. If the equation is an identity, write identity. If the equation has no solution, write no solution.
(Ex 3)

c. $2(x + 3) = 3(2x + 2) - 4x$

d. $3(x + 4) = 2(x + 5) + x$

e. (**Membership Rates**) A fitness center has a membership fee of \$125.
(Ex 4) Members only pay \$5 per day to work out at the center. A nonmember pays \$10 per day to work out. After how many work-out days is the total cost for members, including the membership fee, the same as the total cost for nonmembers?

Practice   Distributed and Integrated

1. Solve for y: $\frac{3}{4}y = 4\frac{7}{8}$.
(21)

*2. Solve for p: $3p - 4 - 6 = 2(p - 5)$.
(28)

*3. Formulate You have \$3 in bills and a certain number of nickels in one pocket. In
(28) the other pocket you have \$2 in bills and a certain number of dimes. You have the same number of dimes as nickels and the same amount of money in each pocket. Write an equation to find the number of dimes and nickels you have.

4. Error Analysis Two students used the Distributive Property to solve the same
(26) multi-step equation. Which student is correct? Explain the error.

Student A	Student B
$4x - 2(12 - x) = 18$	$4x - 2(12 - x) = 18$
$4x - 24 - x = 18$	$4x - 24 + 2x = 18$
$3x - 24 = 18$	$6x - 24 = 18$
$3x = 42$	$6x = 42$
$x = 14$	$x = 7$

*5. (**Wages**) A worker at one farm is paid \$486 for the week, plus \$0.03 for every pound
(28) of apples she picks. At another farm, a worker is paid \$490 for the week, plus \$0.02 for every pound of apples. For how many pounds of apples are the workers paid the same amount?

*6. Multiple Choice What is the value of x when $(x + 15)\frac{1}{3} = 2x - 1$?
(28)

A $\frac{18}{5}$ **B** $\frac{5}{18}$ **C** $\frac{18}{7}$ **D** $\frac{7}{18}$

*7. Error Analysis Two students solved the same multi-step equation. Which student
(28) is correct? Explain the error.

Student A	Student B
$3x - 4 = 2x - (4 + x)$	$3x - 4 = 2x - (4 + x)$
$3x - 4 = 2x - 4 + x$	$3x - 4 = 2x - 4 - x$
$3x - 4 = 3x - 4$	$3x - 4 = x - 4$
$0 = 0$	$2x = 0$
All real numbers.	$x = 0$

*8. Generalize If the equation $yx = zx$ is true, when yx is positive, $x \neq 0$, and z is
(26) a negative integer. Will x be positive or negative?

 9. Geometry The graph shows areas of several square
(27) sheets of paper.

Area of Paper Squares

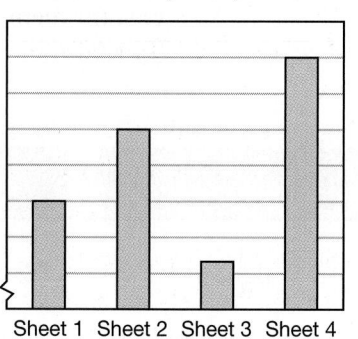

  a. About how many times greater does the
  area of Sheet 4 appear to be than that of
  Sheet 3?

  b. The squares have side lengths of 9, 10, 8, and
  11 inches. About how many times greater is the
  area of Sheet 4 than the area of Sheet 3?

10. True or False: A broken scale can make changes in data appear less than they
(27) actually are. If false, explain why.

11. Multi-Step Average home prices in several cities are shown in the table.
(27)

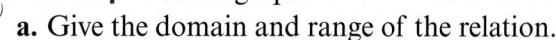

City	Woodside	Reefville	Boynton	Dunston	York
Average Home Price (in thousands)	$265	$210	$320	$375	$350

  a. Make a bar graph with a scale from 200 to 400. Use intervals of 40.

  b. Without looking at the scale, what conclusions might the graph lead to?

  c. Why might a real estate agent who sells houses only in Reefville want to show
  potential clients a graph like this?

*12. Multi-Step Use the graph.
(25)
  a. Give the domain and range of the relation.

  b. Determine whether the relation is a function. Explain.

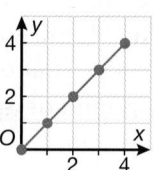

*13. Multiple Choice Use the graph shown. A conservation group
(25) has been working to increase the population of a herd of
Asian elephants. The graph shows the results of their
efforts. Which relations represent the data in the graph?

  A $\{(1, 4.5), (2, 6), (3, 10), (4, 14.5)\}$

  B $\{(1, 5), (2, 6), (3, 10), (4, 15)\}$

  C $\{(4.5, 1), (6, 2), (10, 3), (14.5, 4)\}$

  D $\{(5, 1), (6, 2), (10, 3), (15, 4)\}$

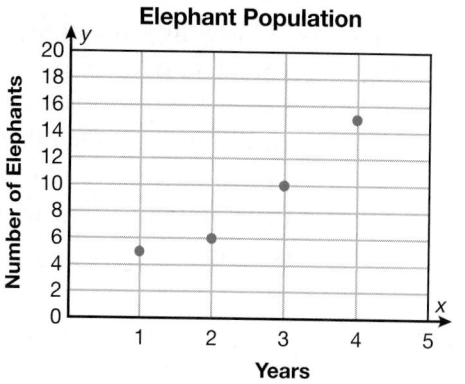

14. 0.28 of what number is 18.2?
(24)

15. ⎛Internet Access⎞ At a local diner, customers can enjoy wireless
(23) Internet access.

  a. Write an equation that can be used to find the cost of being online
for m minutes.

  b. Estimate You know it will require $1\frac{1}{2}$ to 2 hours to get your research
done online. About how much will it cost to do your work
at the diner?

16. Determine whether the statement is true or false. If false, explain why.
(22) A line graph can help analyze change over time.

17. Use the coordinate grid.
(20) Find the coordinates of point K.

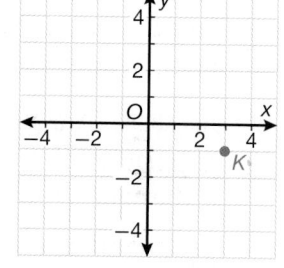

*18. Silvia had \$247 in her savings account. She made a deposit into her savings
(19) account. Now, her account has \$472. Write an equation that shows the amount
of money that is currently in her account. Determine how much money was
deposited.

19. ⎛Cooking⎞ George has already sliced 1 carrot and continues to slice 6 carrots per
(18) minute. Frank has already sliced 16 carrots and continues to slice 4 carrots
per minute.

  a. Write expressions representing the number of carrots sliced by each person in
m minutes.

  b. Write an expression for the total number of carrots sliced.

20. ⎛Grades⎞ A student raised her grade by 13 points. Write an expression to represent
(17) her new grade.

*21. **(Astronomy)** The gravitational force between two objects can be approximated
$_{(6)}$ by using $F = \frac{m_1 m_2}{d^2}$, where F is the gravitational force in newtons, m_1 is the mass
in kilograms of the first object, m_2 is the mass in kilograms of the second object,
and d is the distance between them expressed in meters. If the mass of a satellite
is 500 kilograms, the mass of a small asteroid is 1500 kilograms, and the distance
between them is 1000 meters, what is the gravitational force between the satellite
and the asteroid?

22. **Verify** Use two different methods to evaluate $8(10 - 4)$. Verify that each method
$_{(15)}$ gives the same result.

23. Evaluate $\sqrt{49} + 4^2$.
$_{(13)}$

24. True or False: $(b + c) + d = b + (c + d)$. Justify your answer.
$_{(12)}$

25. Evaluate the expression $3n^2 p^5 + 4(n - 8)^2$ for the given values $n = -3$ and $p = 1$.
$_{(9)}$

26. **Write** Give a counterexample for the following statement: The set of irrational
$_{(1)}$ numbers is closed under subtraction.

27. **Measurement** Find the perimeter of the polygon.
$_{(18)}$

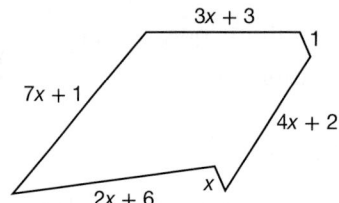

28. **Probability** A coin is tossed 3 times.
$_{(1)}$
    a. What set of numbers could be used to express the different probabilities of how
the coin is tossed?

    b. Could the probability ever be a whole number? Explain.

29. **Write** When a student converts from miles to feet, will the student multiply or
$_{(8)}$ divide? Explain.

*30. **Write** Describe a situation that could be represented by a continuous graph.
$_{(Inv\ 2)}$

Solving Literal Equations

1. Vocabulary A _____ (*constant, variable*) is a letter used to represent an unknown.
(2)

2. Evaluate the expression rt if $r = 4$ and $t = 7$.
(9)

3. Solve the equation $3x - 24 = 6$.
(26)

4. Solve the equation $4x + 14 = 2x + 20$.
(28)

5. Solve the equation $5x + 2 = 2x - 9$.
(28)

New Concepts

Recall when solving an equation with one variable, inverse operations are used to isolate the variable as shown below.

$2x - 6 = 14$

$\underline{+6 = +6}$ Add 6 to undo subtracting 6.

$2x = 20$ Simplify.

$\dfrac{2x}{2} = \dfrac{20}{2}$ Divide by 2 to undo multiplication.

$x = 10$ Simplify.

> **Math Reasoning**
>
> **Connect** Give an example of an equation that would contain more than one variable.

A **literal equation** is an equation with more than one variable. As in an equation with one variable, use inverse operations and properties of equalities to solve for a specific variable in a literal equation. The solution for the specific variable will be in the terms of the other variables and numbers.

Example 1   Solving for a Variable

Solve for y: $2x + 3y = 10$. Justify each step.

SOLUTION

$2x + 3y = 10$ Find y in the equation.

$\underline{-2x \qquad = -2x}$ Subtract $2x$ to eliminate from the y side.

$3y = -2x + 10$ Simplify.

$\dfrac{3y}{3} = \dfrac{-2x}{3} + \dfrac{10}{3}$ Divide by 3 to eliminate the coefficient of y.

$y = \dfrac{-2x}{3} + \dfrac{10}{3}$ Simplify.

> **Online Connection**
> www.SaxonMathResources.com

If the variable being solved for is on both sides of the equation, the first step is to eliminate the variable on one side or the other.

Example 2 Solving for Variables on Both Sides

Solve for p: $4p + 2a - 5 = 6a + p$. Justify each step.

SOLUTION

$$4p + 2a - 5 = 6a + p$$

$$\underline{-p \qquad\qquad = \qquad -p}$$ Eliminate the p on the right side.

$$3p + 2a - 5 = 6a$$ Combine like terms.

$$\underline{-2a + 5 = -2a + 5}$$ Eliminate the $2a$ and -5 from the left side.

$$3p = 4a + 5$$ Combine like terms.

$$\frac{3p}{3} = \frac{4a}{3} + \frac{5}{3}$$ Divide both sides by 3.

$$p = \frac{4a}{3} + \frac{5}{3}$$ Simplify.

A formula is a type of literal equation. Use inverse operations to isolate any variable in the formula.

Example 3 Solving a Formula for a Variable

The formula $C = \frac{5}{9}(F - 32)$ expresses Celsius temperature in terms of Fahrenheit temperature. Find the Fahrenheit temperature when the Celsius temperature is 20°.

SOLUTION

Step 1: Solve for F. Justify each step.

$$C = \frac{5}{9}(F - 32)$$

$$\frac{9}{5} \cdot C = \frac{9}{5} \cdot \frac{5}{9}(F - 32)$$ Multiplication Property of Equality

$$\frac{9}{5}C = F - 32$$ Simplify.

$$\underline{+32 = \qquad +32}$$ Addition Property of Equality

$$\frac{9}{5}C + 32 = F$$ Simplify.

Step 2: Substitute 20 for C.

$$\frac{9}{5}C + 32 = F$$

$$\frac{9}{5}(20) + 32 = F$$

$$36 + 32 = F$$

$$68 = F$$

20°C is equivalent to 68°F.

Hint

Remember that dividing by a fraction is the same as multiplying by the reciprocal.

Example 4 Application: Geometry

The formula for the circumference of a circle is $C = 2\pi r$. If the circle's circumference is 24 inches, what is the radius? Leave the symbol π in the answer.

SOLUTION

Step 1: Since the question asked for the radius, the first step is to solve the formula for r.

$$C = 2\pi r$$

$$\frac{C}{2\pi} = \frac{2\pi r}{2\pi} \qquad \text{Isolate the variable } r.$$

$$\frac{C}{2\pi} = r \qquad \text{Simplify.}$$

Step 2: Substitute 24 for C.

$$\frac{24}{2\pi} = r$$

$$\frac{12}{\pi} = r \qquad \text{Simplify.}$$

The radius of the circle is $\frac{12}{\pi}$ inches.

Example 5 Application: Travel Plans

The Ramirez family is taking a trip to the coast. They live 270 miles from the coast. They want to make the trip in $4\frac{1}{2}$ hours. Use the distance formula $d = rt$ to determine the average speed the family needs to drive.

SOLUTION

Step 1: The answer will be the speed they are driving, so solve the formula for r.

$$d = rt$$

$$\frac{d}{t} = \frac{rt}{t} \qquad \text{Divide both sides by } t.$$

$$\frac{d}{t} = r \qquad \text{Simplify.}$$

Step 2: Substitute 270 for d and 4.5 for t.

$$\frac{d}{t} = r$$

$$\frac{270}{4.5} = r$$

$$60 = r$$

The Ramirez family needs to average a speed of 60 mph to make the trip in $4\frac{1}{2}$ hours.

> **Hint**
>
> In the formula $d = rt$;
>
> d is distance, r is rate or speed, and t is time.

a. Solve for n: $3m + 2n = 8$.
(Ex 1)

b. Solve for x: $3x + 2y = 8 + x$.
(Ex 2)

c. Temperature The formula $F = \frac{9}{5}C + 32$ expresses a Fahrenheit
(Ex 3) temperature in terms of Celsius temperature. Find the Celsius temperature when the Fahrenheit temperature is 86°.

d. Geometry The formula for the volume of a rectangular prism with
(Ex 4) length l, width w, and height h, is $V = lwh$. Find the height in inches of a rectangular prism with volume 6 ft³, width 12 in., and length 24 in.

e. Traveling Costs The fuel economy rating of a vehicle is determined
(Ex 5) by the formula $F = \frac{m}{g}$. In the formula, F is fuel economy, m is miles traveled, and g is gallons of fuel. Felicia's car has a fuel rating of 28 miles per gallon. Her trip is 350 miles. How many gallons of fuel does she need?

> **Hint**
>
> Since the question asks for gallons, the first step is to solve the formula for g.

Practice Distributed and Integrated

*1. Solve $3x + 2y = 5 - y$ for y.
(29)

*2. Solve $-2y + 6y - x - 4 = 0$ for y.
(29)

3. Average Cost Boris uses a coupon for \$35 off any framing order of \$50 or more. He
(24) wants to frame 5 photographs. With the coupon it will cost \$107.50 not including tax. What is the average cost to frame a photograph without the coupon?

*4. Multiple Choice The floor area of recreation center will be a rectangle with a length
(29) of 130 feet and a width of 110 feet. Which formula can be used to find the area of the recreation center?

A $A = s^2$ **B** $A \cdot l = w$

C $A = lw$ **D** $A = \frac{1}{2}ab$

5. Give the domain and range of the relation.
(25)

$\{(9, 3); (8, 1); (8, 2); (8, 3); (7, 0); (7, 4); (6, 2)\}$

*6. Multiple Choice Which operation should be performed first when solving the
(26) multi-step equation $12x + 6(2x - 1) + 7 = 37$?

A Divide both sides of the equation by 12.

B Multiply $(2x - 1)$ by 6.

C Add 1 to both sides of the equation.

D Subtract 37 from both sides of the equation.

*7. Write Explain how to solve $5x + 4z = 10z - 2x$ for x.
(29)

*8. Basketball Lee's basketball team played 22 games this season. Lee scored an
(17) average of t three-pointers and s two-pointers per game during the season. Write an expression to show how many total points he scored during the season.

9. Analyze The measures of the angles in the two triangles can be found
(26) using the equations $x + x + 90 = 180$ and $3y + y + 90 = 180$.
Which triangle will contain the smallest angle?

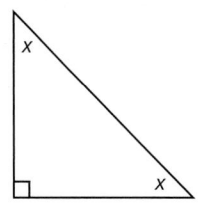

Triangle A   Triangle B

*10. Error Analysis Two students are making a bar graph of test scores ranging from
(27) 85 through 100. They want to emphasize the difference in the range of scores.
Which student is correct? Explain the error.

Student A	Student B
Use a vertical scale from 75 to 100 in increments of 5.	Use a vertical scale from 0 through 100 in increments of 10.

11. Analyze The expression xy^3 has a positive value. What must be true of the value
(16) of x if y is negative?

*12. What should you watch for when analyzing a circle graph?
(27)

13. Round $\sqrt{26}$ to the nearest integer.
(13)

*14. Geometry A triangle and a rectangle have the same area. Use the diagrams to find
(28) the area.

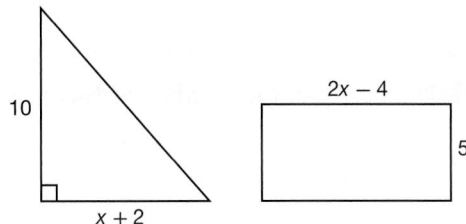

*15. Multi-Step A gym charges for attending exercise classes. Raquel pays $10 to attend
(28) each class because she is a non-member. Since Viola is a member, she pays $15 per
month for a membership fee, but only $5 for each class.

  a. Write an expression to show how much it cost Raquel per month for c exercise
  classes.

  b. Write an expression to show how much it cost Viola per month for membership
  and c exercise classes.

  c. Set the two expressions equal to each other. Solve this equation to determine how
  many classes they would each have to attend to have the same cost.

16. Verify Is $x = 11$ a solution for $6x + 8 = 74$? Explain. If false, provide a correct
(23) solution and check.

17. Choose an appropriate graph to display the average grade received by students
(22) on a science test. Explain your choice.

18. Measurement To convert between feet and inches, use the equation $i = 12f$ where i
(20) is the number of inches and f is the number of feet. Complete the table and graph
the solutions.

f	i
3	
5	
8	
10	

19. Verify True or False. A repeating decimal multiplied by a variable is an irrational
(2) number. If the statement is false, give a counterexample.

20. (**Astronomy**) The temperature on the surface of Mars varies by 148°F. The highest
(6) temperature is about 23°F. What is that lowest temperature on the surface of Mars?

21. (**Consumer Economics**) A strawberry container costs $1 and the strawberries cost
(17) $2 per pound. Write an expression to represent the total cost for a container
with s pounds of strawberries.

22. Simplify $x^2 - 3yx + 2yx^2 - 2xy + yx$.
(18)

23. Solve $-3y + \dfrac{1}{2} = \dfrac{5}{7}$.
(23)

24. Solve $k + 4 - 5(k + 2) = 3k - 2$.
(28)

25. Generalize The value of $z + 2$ is an odd integer. What generalizations can be made
(9) about z using this information?

26. Which expression is greater: $\dfrac{1}{3} - 1$ or $\dfrac{1}{2} - 1$.
(10)

27. Justify Simplify $(3 + 5) - 2^3$. Justify each step using the order of operations or
(7) mathematical properties.

28. Analyze Find the value of y when $x = 2$.
(6)

$$-x - (-2) = y$$

29. (**Population Growth**) The expression $303{,}000{,}000 \times (1.015)^t$, where t stands for years,
(3) represents the population growth of the U.S.A. Based on this expression, about
how many people will live in the U.S.A. eight years from now?

30. Probability On the first street in Hidden Oaks subdivision, 5 out of 20 families
(Inv 1) own trucks.

  a. What is the probability that a randomly selected family in the subdivision
  owns a truck?

  b. Predict the number of truck-owning families you can expect among the
  140 families living in the subdivision.

Creating a Table

Graphing Calculator Lab (*Use with Lesson 30*)

An equation describes a relationship between two quantities. Sometimes it is inconvenient to calculate a large quantity of outputs by substituting given values into the equation. Instead, use your graphing calculator to quickly make a table of values.

Find the value of y for the equation $y = 3x + 5$ when $x = 15, 45, 75, 105,$ and 135.

1. To enter the equation into the Y = editor, press the `Y=` key. Then press **3** `X,T,θ,n` `+` **5.**

2. Open the Table Setup menu by pressing `2nd` `WINDOW` (TBLSET). TblStart is the value of x to start the table of values. ΔTbl is the increment by which x-values in the table should increase.

   Since the smallest value of x is 15, press **1 5** `ENTER`. Consecutive x-values increase by 30, so for ΔTbl, press **3 0** `ENTER`.

Online Connection
www.SaxonMathResources.com

```
TABLE SETUP
 TblStart=15
 ΔTbl=30
Indpnt: AUTO Ask
Depend: AUTO Ask
```

3. Press `2nd` `GRAPH` (TABLE) to view the table of values.

   From this screen's table of values, you can see that $y = 50$ when $x = 15$, $y = 140$ when $x = 45$, $y = 230$ when $x = 75$, $y = 320$ when $x = 105$, and $y = 410$ when $x = 135$.

```
 X    │ Y1
 15   │ 50
 45   │ 140
 75   │ 230
 105  │ 320
 135  │ 410
 165  │ 500
 195  │ 590
X=15
```

4. Press the ▼ key repeatedly to see larger values of x and y,

   For $x = 405$, $y = 1220$.

```
 X    │ Y1
 225  │ 680
 255  │ 770
 285  │ 860
 315  │ 950
 345  │ 1040
 375  │ 1130
 405  │ 1220
X=405
```

You can compare y-values for more than one equation for a given set of x-values. Enter equations into the [Y=] editor for Y_1, Y_2, and so on, for as many equations as you have. Then set TblStart and ΔTbl values in the Table Setup menu and press [2nd] [GRAPH] (TABLE) to view the table of values. Use the ◀ and ▶ keys to navigate across the equations and the ▲ and ▼ keys to scroll through values of x in the table.

Lab Practice

Use a table to find y for the equation for the given values of x. Indicate the TblStart and ΔTbl values you use.

a. $y = 2x - 2$ for $x = 2, 5, 8,$ and 11

b. $y = 4x$ for $x = 1, 8, 15,$ and 22

Stephanie is growing two varieties of flowers for a show taking place in three months. The height y in inches of Flower A after x months can be modeled by the equation $y = 2x + 1$. Flower B grows according to the equation $y = 3x - 2$. Stephanie will plant the flowers at the same time and monitor their height at the end of each month. If Flower A and Flower B are the same height, she will use them to make an arrangement to present at the flower show.

c. How would Stephanie simulate the growth of each flower?

d. What would Stephanie enter into the calculator to simultaneously model the growth of Flower A and Flower B?

e. What TblStart value should Stephanie use?

f. What ΔTbl value should she use?

g. How tall are Flower A and Flower B at the end of each month?

h. Will Stephanie be able to create an arrangement of Flowers A and B for the flower show? Explain.

LESSON
30

Graphing Functions

For help with creating tables, refer to Graphing Calculator Lab 2, p. 177.

Warm Up

1. Vocabulary A _____ (*relation, function*) is a set of ordered pairs where each number in the domain is matched to one or more numbers in the range.
(25)

Determine the coordinates of each point labeled on the coordinate grid.

2. Point A
(20)

3. Point B
(20)

4. Point C
(20)

5. Evaluate $2x + 3$ for $x = 4$.
(9)

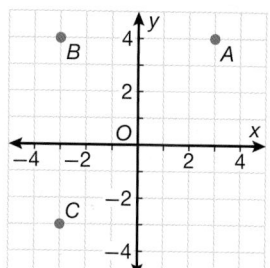

New Concepts

A **linear equation** is an equation whose graph is a line. You can use a table of ordered pairs to graph an equation. To determine if the graph represents a function, use the vertical line test. If a vertical line intersects the graph at more than one point, then the graph is not a function. A **linear function** is a function whose graph is a line. A linear function can be written in the form $f(x) = mx + b$, where m and b are real numbers.

Graphing Calculator

For help with creating tables, refer to Graphing Calculator Lab 2, p. 177.

> **Example 1** Using Tables to Graph Functions
>
> Graph each equation using a table of values. Use a graphing calculator to check your table. Decide whether the graph represents a function and whether it is linear or nonlinear.
>
> **a.** $y = x$
>
> **SOLUTION**

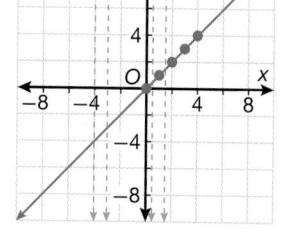

x	0	1	2	3	4
y	0	1	2	3	4

Any vertical line intersects this graph at only one point, so the graph is a function. The graph is a line, so it is a linear function.

b. $y = x^2$

SOLUTION

x	-2	-1	0	1	2
y	4	1	0	1	4

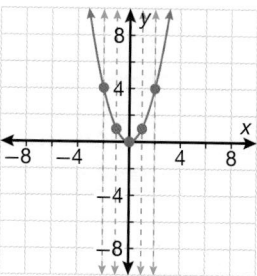

According to the vertical line test, the graph is a function. The graph is not a line, so it is a nonlinear function.

Math Reasoning

Generalize How can values in a table be used to tell whether data are linear?

Example **2** Matching a Graph to a Table

Use the coordinates in each table to match each
graph with one of the tables.

Table 1 Rule: $f(x) = \frac{1}{3}x + 4$

x	−3	0	3	6	9
$f(x)$	3	4	5	6	7

Table 2 Rule: $f(x) = 5x - 1$

x	−2	−1	0	1	2
$f(x)$	−11	−6	−1	4	9

Table 3 Rule: $f(x) = -\frac{1}{2}x + 2$

x	−4	−2	0	2	4
$f(x)$	4	3	2	1	0

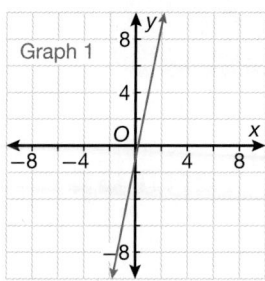

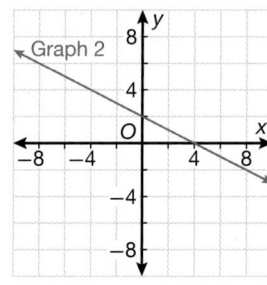

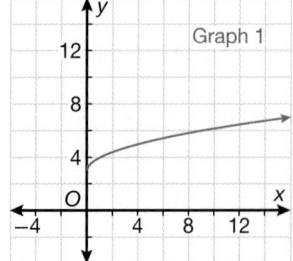

Math Reasoning

Analyze To match an
equation to a graph,
what characteristic(s) of
the graph can often be
most easily identified in
the equation?

SOLUTION

Table 1 has the ordered pair (0, 4). The graph in
Graph 3 is the only graph that includes this point.
The ordered pairs (3, 5) and (6, 6) also are on the
graph. Graph 3 matches the values in Table 1.

For Table 2, look at the ordered pair (0, −1). This
ordered pair only occurs in Graph 1. The ordered pairs (−1, −6)
and (1, 4) also are on the graph. Graph 1 matches the values in Table 2.

Graph 2 matches Table 3. The ordered pairs (−4, 4), (0, 2), and (4, 0) are
on Graph 2.

Example **3** Matching an Equation to a Graph

Match the three equations below to the three graphs shown.

Equation A: $y = x + 3$

Equation B: $y = |x| + 3$

Equation C: $y = \sqrt{x} + 3$

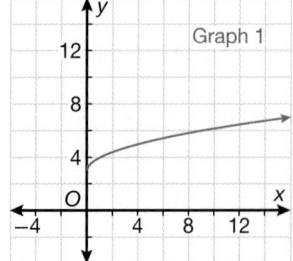

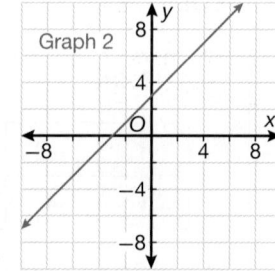

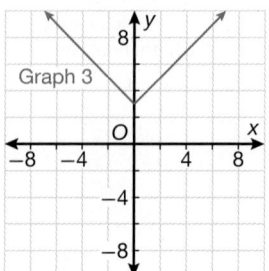

SOLUTION

Find three ordered pairs for each equation. Check to see which graph includes the ordered pairs.

Equation A: Substituting different values of x into $y = x + 3$ results in the following ordered pairs: $(0, 3)$, $(1, 4)$ and $(2, 5)$. Only Graph 2 includes these ordered pairs, so Equation A matches Graph 2.

Equation B: For $y = |x| + 3$, any value for x will have a positive y-value. Equation B matches Graph 3.

Equation C: For $y = \sqrt{x} + 3$, there cannot be x-values that are negative. Equation C matches Graph 1.

Example 4 · Identifying the Domain and Range

Use the graphs to identify the domain and range of each function.

 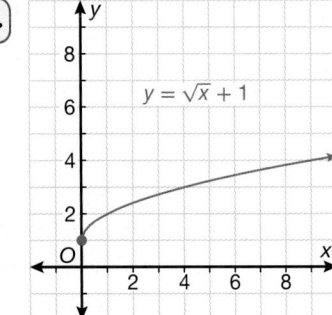

$y = \sqrt{x} + 1$

SOLUTION

The domain is $x \geq 0$ because you cannot take the square root of a negative number. By inspection of the graph, the range is $y \geq 1$.

 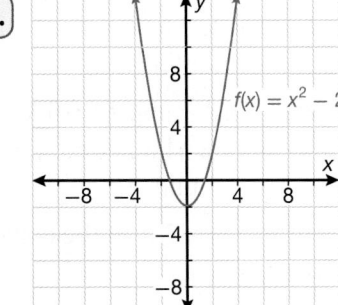

$f(x) = x^2 - 2$

SOLUTION

By inspection of the graph, the domain is all real numbers and the range is $y \geq -2$.

Example 5 Application: Car Wash Fundraiser

The soccer team raises money by washing cars. They charge $5 per car and spend a total of $4 on soap. The table shows the money they raise. Make a graph and use it to find the amount they raise by washing 7 cars. Write the rule in functional notation and use it to check the answer.

Math Reasoning

Verify Why is the money raised for 0 cars −$4.00?

Number of Cars Washed, x	0	1	2	3	4	5
Money Raised, $f(x)$	−4	1	6	11	16	21

SOLUTION

Use the ordered pairs to make a graph. Extend the line beyond $x = 7$. The y-value on the line is 31 when $x = 7$, so the soccer team raises $31 by washing 7 cars.

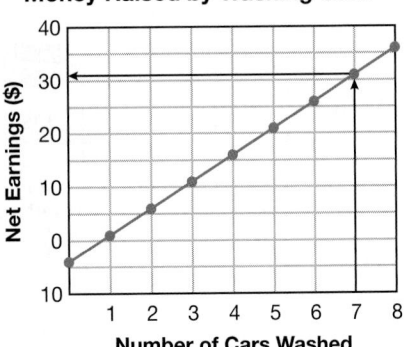

Money Raised by Washing Cars

Check the answer by evaluating the function for $x = 7$. The rule is $5 times the number of cars x minus $4, or

$f(x) = 5x - 4$.

$f(x) = 5x - 4$

$f(7) = 5(7) - 4$

$\quad = 35 - 4$

$\quad = 31$

Lesson Practice

a. Graph $y = 2x + 5$ using a table of values. Use a graphing calculator to
(Ex 1) check your table. Decide whether the graph represents a function and whether it is linear or nonlinear.

b. Graph $y = x^2 + 1$ using a table of values. Use a graphing calculator to
(Ex 1) check your table. Decide whether the graph represents a function and whether it is linear or nonlinear.

c. Match the equation $y = -2x^2$ to the correct graph.
(Ex 3)

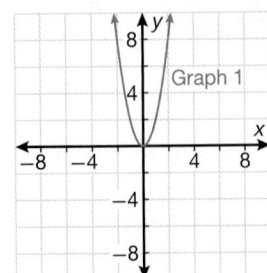

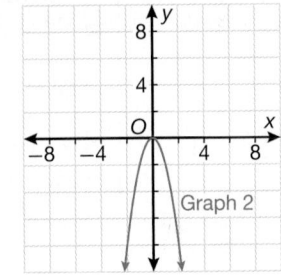

Use the coordinates in the tables to match the graph with each table.

(Ex 2)

d. $y = \frac{1}{3}x + 1$

x	-6	-3	0	3	6
y	-1	0	1	2	3

e. $y = 3x + 1$

x	-3	-2	0	1	2
y	-8	-5	1	4	7

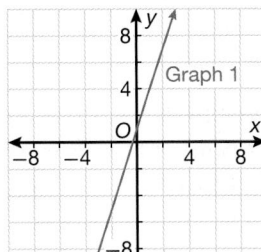 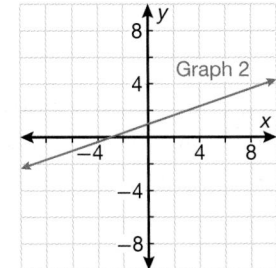

Identify the domain and range of the function shown in each graph.

(Ex 4)

f. 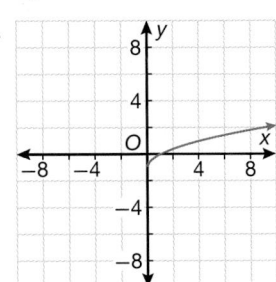   **g.**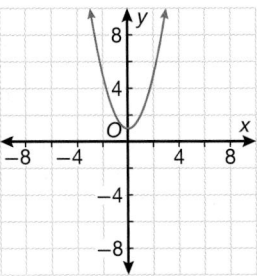

h. (**Emails to Congress**) The table shows the number of emails history classes
(Ex 5) send to their senators. Make a graph and use it to find how many emails
were sent from 8 classes. Write the rule in function notation and use it to
check your answer.

Number of Classes, x	1	2	3	4
Emails Sent, $f(x)$	30	60	90	120

Practice   Distributed and Integrated

Solve.

1. $x + \frac{1}{2} = 2\frac{1}{5}$
(19)

2. $0.4x - 0.3 = -0.14$
(23)

3. $\frac{1}{3} + \frac{5}{12}x - 2 = 6\frac{2}{3}$
(26)

4. $\frac{2}{3} - \frac{4}{9}x + 1 = 2\frac{7}{9}$
(26)

*5. Solve and check $x - 4(x - 3) + 7 = 6 - (x - 4)$.
(28)

*6. Verify Is the statement below true or false? Explain.
(25)

The graph of a circle shows that the equation of the circle, $x^2 + y^2 = 1$, is a function.

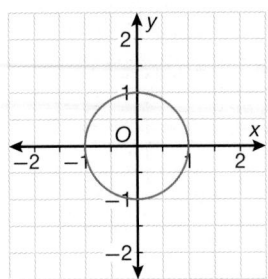

*7. (Savings) For every dollar Mirand deposits into her checking account, she deposits
(30) 1.5 times as much into her savings account, which started with \$50. So, $s = 1.5c + 50$, where s is the amount in savings and c is the amount deposited in checking. Which graph represents this equation?

Graph 1   **Graph 2**

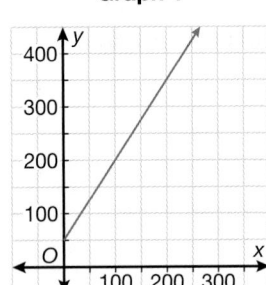   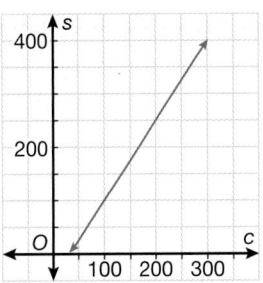

*8. Multiple Choice Which equation represents the line on the graph?
(30)

A $y = x + 10$

B $y - x = 10$

C $-x = 10 + y$

D $y = -x + 10$

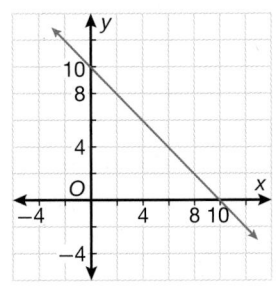

*9. Multi-Step The table shows the total number of shrubs a gardener plants after each
(30) half hour.

Time (hours)	0.5	1	1.5	2
Number of Shrubs	1	3	7	8

a. Plot these data on a coordinate grid.

b. Is the graph a function? Explain.

c. Predict Can you predict the number of shrubs the gardener will plant in 3 hours? Why or why not?

*10. Use the table to make a graph. Is the graph linear? Explain.
(30)

x	0	1	2	3
y	4	7	10	13

11. **Error Analysis** Two students solved $2x - y = 6$ for y. Which student is correct?
(29) Explain the error.

Student A	Student B
$2x - y = 6$	$2x - y = 6$
$2x = y + 6$	$2x = y + 6$
$2x - 6 = y$	$2x + 6 = y$

12. **Geometry** What is the area of the shaded part of the rectangle?
(29)

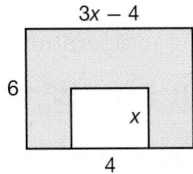

*13. **Multi-Step** Solve $\frac{x}{2} + \frac{y}{3} = 2$ for y. Find y when $x = 3$.
(29)

*14. **Consumer Math** Joel deposited money in an account that has a certain annual
(29) interest rate. Using the formula $i = prt,$ or interest = principal • rate • time,
how could he compute for the rate if the numeric value of the other items
was given?

15. Simplify $\dfrac{3 + 7(-3)}{-7 - 2(-3)}.$
(11)

16. **Error Analysis** Two students solved the same multi-step equation. Which student
(28) is correct? Explain the error.

Student A	Student B
$2x - 4(3x + 6) = -6(2x + 1) - 4$	$2x - 4(3x + 6) = -6(2x + 1) - 4$
$2x - 12x + 6 = -12x + 1 - 4$	$2x - 12x - 24 = -12x - 6 - 4$
$-10x + 6 = -12x - 3$	$-10x - 24 = -12x - 10$
$2x = -9$	$2x = 14$
$x = -4\frac{1}{2}$	$x = 7$

17. **Measurement** On a map, 1 centimeter represents 50 kilometers. The actual distance
(21) between two cities is 675 kilometers. Find the distance between the two cities on
the map.

*18. **Multiple Choice** What would make the graph of basketball scores less
(27) misleading?

   A Using a broken scale on the horizontal axis

   B Using a broken scale on the vertical axis

   C Using larger intervals

   D Using smaller intervals

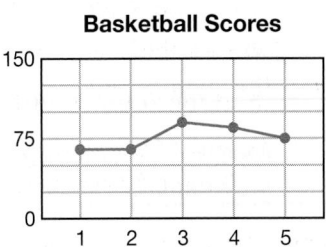

19. **Generalize** What effect do large intervals have on the appearance of a graph?
(27)

*20. (Sales) The circle graph shows the amounts of orange juice and fruit
(27) punch sold each month. Explain why this graph is misleading and
determine what may be a more appropriate graph to compare
the sales of the two beverages.

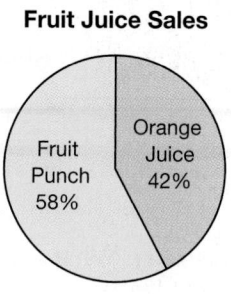

Fruit Juice Sales

21. **Model** Make a stem-and-leaf plot of the following temperatures in Woodmont:
(22)

72°F, 74°F, 63°F, 62°F, 63°F, 78°F, 65°F, 51°F, 53°F, 53°F, 61°F, 80°F.

22. (Hair Growth) Hair grows approximately half an inch each month.
(12) John's hair is 2 inches long. Let m be the number of months. The
formula $h = 2 + 0.5m$ calculates the length John's hair will be in
m months if he does not cut it. Complete the table and graph the
solutions.

m	h
4	
6	
10	
20	

23. A television remote has a key for each of the channels 0 through 9. If one key is
(14) chosen at random, what is the chance that channel 5 is chosen? Write your answer
as a percent.

24. **Multi-Step** Todd has 18 boxes of cards with x cards in each box. He divides the cards
(12) equally with 5 friends. The expression $18x \div 6$ represents the number of cards each
person has. Simplify the expression and justify each step.

25. **Justify** Evaluate $5.2 - 1.6 + 4.08 + 8$. Justify each step.
(10)

26. **Generalize** In unit analysis, you often need to apply unit ratios multiple times to
(8) convert to the desired units. For example, $4518 \text{ cm}^2 \cdot \frac{1 \text{ m}}{100 \text{ cm}} \cdot \frac{1 \text{ m}}{100 \text{ cm}} = 0.4518 \text{ m}^2$
converts from square centimeters to square meters. State a general rule for
applying a unit ratio the correct number of times to perform a unit conversion.

27. **Justify** Evaluate $3 + \left(\frac{5-2}{4} + 2^2 \right)$. Justify each step.
(7)

28. (Consumer Economics) A gym charges \$2 a visit for the first 15 visits in a month.
(4) After that, the cost is reduced to $\frac{1}{4}$ of the price per visit. Use the expression
$15 \cdot \$2 + (23 - 15) \cdot \frac{1}{4} \cdot \$2$ to show how much someone will pay if they go to
this gym 23 times in a month.

29. **Analyze** Given the equations $a = (1.01)^x$ and $b = (0.99)^x$, which value, a or b,
(3) grows smaller as the exponent x grows larger?

30. **Write** Write a possible situation that could be represented by the graph at the right.
(Inv 2)

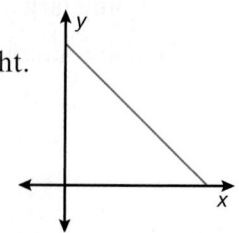

Analyzing the Effects of Bias in Sampling, Surveys, and Bar Graphs

To gather complete and accurate information about a particular population, researchers need to collect data from all of the population's members.

Sampling It is not always practical to survey every individual in the population, so researchers use data from the sample to draw conclusions about the entire population. The table below identifies five sampling methods.

Math Language

A **population** is a group that someone is gathering information about.

A **sample** is part of a population.

A sample is **random** if every member of the population has an equal chance of being chosen.

Online Connection
www.SaxonMathResources.com

	Sampling Method	**Example**
Simple Random	Select a group at random from the larger population.	Draw names of people to survey from a hat.
Stratified Random	Separate a population into smaller groups that have a certain characteristic. Then survey at random within each group.	Separate a herd of cows by breed; then survey a random sample from each breed.
Systematic Random	After calculating the required sample size, survey every nth member.	Choose the number 5 at random. Survey every 5th person.
Convenience	Select individuals from the population based on easy availability and/or accessibility.	Survey the first five people who arrive at a local mall.
Voluntary	Sample individuals who self-select into a survey by responding to a general appeal.	A news program asks viewers to participate in an online poll.

(**Luggage Survey**) A luggage company wants to know the most popular backpack color among high school students. Company representatives record the color of backpacks carried by boys in the cafeteria during lunch. Since the survey excludes high school girls, the sample is biased. It does not include some members of the population.

Analyze Give a reason why the sampling method may be biased.

1. A chef asks the first four customers who order the new cheese sauce if they like it.

2. At a convention of science teachers, attendees are asked to identify what their favorite subject was in high school.

3. A librarian sends questionnaires about library usage to families with children.

(Zoo Survey) Researchers for an advertising campaign survey people to find out why they like to visit the zoo.

4. Give an example of an unbiased sample for this survey.

5. Describe a systematic sampling method.

6. Justify Would it be biased to only survey families with children? Explain.

(Biased Questions) Occasionally, researchers ask biased questions that force the person being questioned to respond with a particular answer. For instance, "Didn't you eat enough?" uses a negative question, which indicates that the person who is being questioned has eaten enough.

Write Create one biased and one non-biased question for each survey.

7. A restaurant owner polls ten patrons on whether they enjoyed the chef's special.

8. A music store questions five customers about their listening habits.

(Marketing) Advertisers may accidentally or intentionally present data in a misleading way. Consider these graphs of the data collected from a survey of pet owners.

Hints

Biased sampling methods exclude certain members of the population.

Biased questions exclude unsatisfactory responses.

Graph A: This could be misleading because of the break in the graph. It appears that the number of people who have dogs is much greater than those who have cats, birds, or fish.

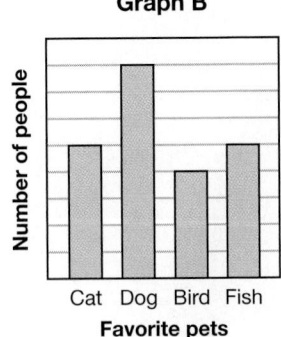

Graph B: This could be misleading because there are no labels on the vertical axis. It is not possible to determine whether each grid represents 1 person or 100 people.

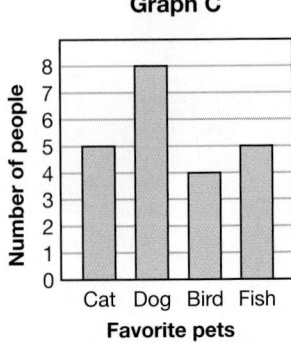

Graph C: This is not misleading. The vertical scale starts at 0 and the intervals are equal.

Your school district is discussing the possibility of requiring students to wear school uniforms. Your class was chosen to select the colors for the uniforms. They will be either blue or white. Each student should indicate a color preference.

Materials
- paper bag
- small squares of blue paper
- large squares of white paper

9. Record the results in a table.

10. Make a bar graph of the data.

11. Draw a set of axes. Label the horizontal axis with the uniform colors. Label the vertical axis with the number of students.

12. Draw two bars, each with a height equal to the number of people who chose the color.

Create a biased bar graph of the data.

13. Draw a set of axes. Label the horizontal axis with the uniform colors.

14. Use the colored squares of paper to create a blue or white column. If 5 students chose blue, then build a bar with 5 blue squares.

15. **Analyze** What is the difference between the two graphs you created?

Investigation Practice

Managers of an apartment complex want to know what visitors to the complex think of the complex and the management office employees. They survey every fifth person who signs a lease.

a. What is the population?

b. Identify the sample.

c. Which of the following is the sampling method used?
   A random   **B** systematic
   C stratified   **D** voluntary

d. What is a possible bias for this survey?

e. The approximate areas of four different oceans are listed below. Create a graph of the data that is misleading. Then redraw your graph so it is not misleading.

Ocean	Approximate area (million mi²)
Arctic	5
Indian	27
Atlantic	30
Pacific	60

Using Rates, Ratios, and Proportions

Online Connection
www.SaxonMathResources.com

Warm Up

1. **Vocabulary** The simplest form of $\frac{3}{6}$ is $\frac{1}{2}$. When you _____ a fraction, you are writing it in simplest form.
   (4)

Simplify.

2. $2.3 - 3.6 \div 4 - 1.7$
   (4)

3. $\dfrac{-0.4 + 1.3 \cdot 4}{0.5 - 5.1 \div 3}$
   (4)

Solve.

4. $8x = 112$
   (21)

5. $2.5y = 62.5$
   (21)

New Concepts

A **ratio** is a comparison of two quantities using division.

Examples: 2 boys to 3 girls   2 to 3, 2:3, $\dfrac{2}{3}$

A **rate** is a ratio that compares quantities measured in different units.

Examples: 5 feet per 30 seconds   15 apples for $6.00   25,000 hits per month

A **unit rate** is a rate whose denominator is 1. A unit price is the cost per unit.

Examples: 55 miles per hour $2.50 per box

Example 1 Finding Unit Rates

Which is the better buy: 5 cans of tuna for $4.95 or 6 cans for $5.75?

SOLUTION

$\dfrac{\text{total cost}}{\text{number of cans}} = \dfrac{\$4.95}{5} = \$0.99$ per can   Find the unit price.

$\dfrac{\text{total cost}}{\text{number of cans}} = \dfrac{\$5.75}{6} = 0.96$ per can   Find the unit price.

$\$0.96 < \$0.99$ Compare the unit prices.

6 cans for $5.75 is the better buy.

Hint

When working with rates, usually you will see the words *per, for,* and *each* indicated by a forward slash (/).

1 mile per 2 minutes

1 mi/2 min

Example 2 Converting Rates

a. A bus driver drives at 30 miles per hour. What is the rate of the bus in miles per minute?

SOLUTION

$\dfrac{30 \text{ miles}}{1 \text{ hour}} \cdot \dfrac{1 \text{ hour}}{60 \text{ minutes}}$ Multiply by a conversion factor.

$\dfrac{^1\cancel{30} \text{ miles}}{1 \cancel{\text{ hour}}} \cdot \dfrac{1 \cancel{\text{ hour}}}{_2\cancel{60} \text{ minutes}}$ Cancel like units of measure.

If the driver drives 1 mi/2 min, then he drives $\frac{1}{2}$ mi/min.

b. An engineer opens a valve that drains 60 gallons of water per minute from a tank. How many quarts were drained per second?

SOLUTION

$$\frac{60 \text{ gallons}}{1 \text{ minute}} = \frac{? \text{ quarts}}{1 \text{ second}}$$

$$\frac{60 \text{ gallons}}{1 \text{ minute}} \cdot \frac{4 \text{ quarts}}{1 \text{ gallon}} = \frac{240 \text{ quarts}}{1 \text{ minute}}$$

Use a conversion factor to change gallons to quarts. Then simplify.

$$\frac{240 \text{ quarts}}{1 \text{ minute}} \cdot \frac{1 \text{ minute}}{60 \text{ seconds}} = \frac{240^{\,4} \text{ quarts}}{60^{\,1} \text{ seconds}}$$

Use a conversion factor to change minutes to seconds. Then simplify.

The tank drains at a rate of 4 quarts per second.

> **Caution**
>
> Set up the conversion factor so the units of measure cancel.
>
> Use the factor
>
> $\frac{4 \text{ quarts}}{1 \text{ gallon}}$, not $\frac{1 \text{ gallon}}{4 \text{ quarts}}$.

A **proportion** is an equation that shows two ratios are equal. The equation $\frac{3}{5} = \frac{9}{15}$ is a proportion.

Cross Products Property
If $\frac{a}{b} = \frac{c}{d}$ and $b \neq 0$ and $d \neq 0$, then $ad = bc$.
In $\frac{a}{b} \Large\times \normalsize \frac{c}{d}$, ad and bc are the **cross products**.

Example 3   **Solving Proportions Using Cross Products**

Solve each proportion.

a. $\dfrac{x}{15} = \dfrac{2}{3}$

SOLUTION

$$\frac{x}{15} = \frac{2}{3}$$

$3 \cdot x = 15 \cdot 2$	Write the cross products.
$3x = 30$	Simplify.
$x = 10$	Solve.

b. $\dfrac{x-1}{12} = \dfrac{1}{6}$

SOLUTION

$$\frac{x-1}{12} = \frac{1}{6}$$

$6(x-1) = 12(1)$	Write the cross products.
$6x - 6 = 12$	Distribute and multiply.
$6x = 18$	Simplify.
$x = 3$	Solve.

Proportions are used to represent many real-world situations that require finding a missing value. Using the cross products is an efficient method for solving the proportions.

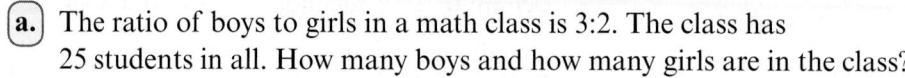

Example 4 **Solving Multi-Step Proportions**

(a.) The ratio of boys to girls in a math class is 3:2. The class has 25 students in all. How many boys and how many girls are in the class?

SOLUTION

The ratio of boys to girls is 3 to 2. There are 3 boys in each group of 5 students.

$$\frac{\text{number of boys}}{\text{total in group}} = \frac{3}{5}$$ Write a ratio.

Write and solve a proportion. Let b represent the number of boys in the class.

$$\frac{3}{5} = \frac{b}{25}$$ There are b boys to 25 students.

$3 \cdot 25 = 5 \cdot b$ Write the cross products.

$5b = 75$ Simplify.

$b = 15$ Solve.

There are 15 boys in the class. So, there are $25 - 15$ or 10 girls in the class.

(b.) On the map, Albany to Jamestown measures 12.6 centimeters, Jamestown to Springfield measures 9 centimeters, and Springfield to Albany measures 4.75 centimeters. What is the actual distance from Albany to Jamestown to Springfield and back to Albany?

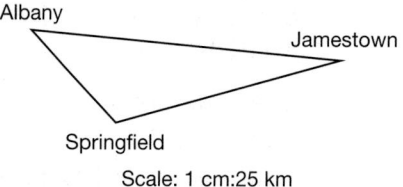

Scale: 1 cm:25 km

SOLUTION

$12.6 + 9 + 4.75 = 26.35$ cm   Find the total distance on the map.

$$\frac{26.35 \text{ cm}}{x \text{ km}} = \frac{1 \text{ cm}}{25 \text{ km}}$$ Set up a proportion using the map scale.

$26.35 \cdot 25 = 1 \cdot x$ Write the cross products.

$658.75 = x$ Solve.

The actual distance is 658.75 kilometers.

Proportions are frequently used to solve problems involving variations of the distance formula $d = rt$.

$$\text{rate} = \frac{\text{distance}}{\text{time}} \quad \text{or} \quad \text{time} = \frac{\text{distance}}{\text{rate}}$$

Math Reasoning

Estimate It takes 5.75 hours to drive about 300 miles. How long will it take to drive about 580 miles at the same rate?

Example 5 Application: Trucking

Mr. Jackson drove a truck 300 miles in 6 hours. If he drives at a constant speed, how long will it take him to drive 450 miles?

SOLUTION

Let x represent the number of hours it will take to drive 450 miles.

$$\text{rate} = \frac{\text{distance}}{\text{time}}$$

$$\frac{300 \text{ miles}}{6 \text{ hours}} = \frac{450 \text{ miles}}{x \text{ hours}} \qquad \text{Set up a proportion.}$$

$$300 \cdot x = 450 \cdot 6 \qquad \text{Write cross products.}$$

$$300x = 2700 \qquad \text{Solve.}$$

$$x = 9$$

Mr. Jackson will drive 450 miles in 9 hours.

Lesson Practice

a. Which is the better buy: 8 boxes for $4.96 or 5 boxes for $3.25?
(Ex 1)

b. A chemist raised the temperature of a liquid 45°F in 1 minute. What is this amount in degrees Fahrenheit per second?
(Ex 2)

c. Jamie typed 20 pages of a document in 2 hours. How many pages did she type in 1 minute?
(Ex 2)

Solve each proportion.
(Ex 3)

d. $\dfrac{c}{7} = \dfrac{3}{21}$ 　　　　　　**e.** $\dfrac{5}{n+2} = \dfrac{10}{16}$

f. The ratio of blue chips to red chips in a bag is 5:7. The bag has 60 chips in all. How many blue chips and how many red chips are in the bag?
(Ex 4)

g. A map shows a 5.5-inch distance between Orange City and Newtown, and a 3.75-inch distance from Newtown to Westville. The scale on the map is 1 inch:100 miles. What is the actual distance, if you drive from Orange City via Newtown to Westville?
(Ex 4)

h. If Jeff walks 4 miles in 48 minutes, how far can he walk in 72 minutes?
(Ex 5)

Practice Distributed and Integrated

Simplify.

1. $7 - 4 - 5 + 12 - 2 - |-2|$
(10)

2. $-6 \cdot 3 + |-3(-4 + 2^3)|$
(11)

Solve.

  3. $-0.05n + 1.8 = 1.74$
  (24)

  4. $-y - 8 + 6y = -9 + 5y + 2$
  (28)

*5. **Multiple Choice** What is the value of x when $2x - 4.5 = \frac{1}{2}(x + 3)$?
(28)
  A 9   **B** 2.4   **C** 2   **D** 4

  6. Solve for y: $4 + 2x + 2y - 3 = 5$.
  (29)

  7. Simplify $4k(2c - a + 3m)$.
  (15)

Evaluate.

  8. $3x^2 + 2y$ when $x = -2$ and $y = 5$
  (16)

  9. $2(a^2 - b)^2 + 3a^3b$ when $a = -3$ and $b = 2$
  (16)

*10. If 10 boxes of cereal sell for \$42.50, what is the unit price?
(31)

*11. **Geometry** In the diagram, $\triangle ABC$ and $\triangle XYZ$ are similar triangles. What is the
(31) value of n?

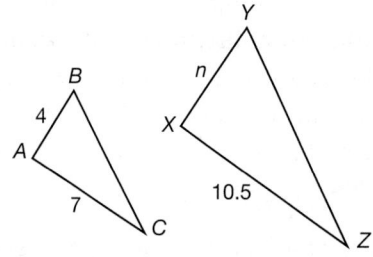

*12. **Predict** An estimate of the number of tagged foxes to the total number of foxes in
(31) a forest is 3:13. A forest warden recorded 21 tagged foxes. About how many foxes
are in the forest?

13. **Multi-Step** A skydiver falls at a rate given by $s = 1.05\sqrt{w}$, where s is the falling
(13) speed in feet per second and w is the weight of the skydiver with gear in pounds.
What is the approximate falling speed of a 170-pound man with 40 pounds of
gear? (Round to the nearest whole number.)

14. Copy and complete the table for $y = x^2 + 2$. Then use the table to graph the
(30) equation.

x	-3	-1	0	1	3
y	11	3	2		

*15. **Shopping** Glenn buys 4 computers for \$2800. How much will
(31) 6 computers cost?

16. Probability A spinner is divided into 5 sections labeled *A* through *E*. The bar graph
(22) shows the results of 50 spins. What is the experimental probability that the next
spin will land on *A* or *D*?

Spin Results

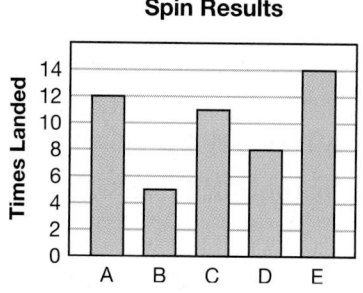

17. (Mileage) The table shows how far a car travels for each gallon of gasoline it uses.
(30)

Number of Gallons, x	1	2	3	4
Miles Traveled, $f(x)$	33	66	99	132

a. Use the table to make a graph.

b. Write a rule for the function.

c. How far will the car travel using 10 gallons of gasoline?

18. Multi-Step Students are paid d dollars per hour for gardening and g dollars per hour
(18) for babysitting and housework. Sally babysat for 6 hours and mowed lawns for 3
hours. Her brother weeded gardens for 5 hours and mopped floors for 1 hour.

a. Write an expression to represent the amount each student earned.

b. Write expressions for the total amount they earned together.

c. If they are paid $5 an hour for gardening and $4 an hour for babysitting and
housework, how much did they earn together?

*19. (Carpentry) A carpenter has propped a board up against a wall. The wall, board,
(26) and ground form a right triangle. What will be the measures of the three angles?

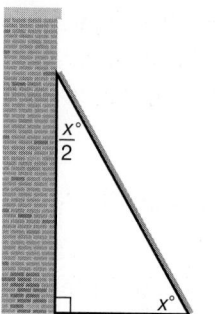

20. Give the domain and range of the relation.
(25)

$$\{(12, 2); (11, 10); (18, 0); (19, 1); (13, 4)\}$$

*21. Use a graphing calculator to make a table of values for $f(x) = x^2 - 1$.
(30) Graph the function and determine the domain and range.

*22. Write Why is there no conclusive value for x in the equation
(28) $\frac{3}{2}x + 5 = 2x - \frac{1}{2}x + 5$? Explain.

23. Multi-Step Amy works in a kitchen appliance store. She earns $65 daily and a
(17) commission worth $10 less than one-fifth of the value of each appliance she sells.
Let m equal the value of an appliance.

a. Write an expression for Amy's daily salary if she sells one appliance every day.

b. Write an expression for Amy's daily salary if she sells n appliances every day.

c. If you know the value of m and n, which part of the expression would you
solve first?

24. Multiple-Choice Which expression is equivalent to $4(x^2 - 4) + 3z^3(4z^7)$?
(15)
   A $4x^2 - 16 + 3z^{10}$ **B** $4x^2 - 16 + 12z^{10}$

   C $4x^2 - 16 + 12z^{21}$ **D** $4x - 16 + 12z^{10}$

*25. Error Analysis Two students solved $\frac{3z}{2} - \frac{4q}{3} = 6$ for z. Which student is correct?
(29) Explain the error.

Student A	Student B
$\dfrac{3z}{2} - \dfrac{4q}{3} = 6$	$\dfrac{3z}{2} - \dfrac{4q}{3} = 6$
$3(3z) - 2(4q) = 6$	$3(3z) - 2(4q) = 6(6)$
$9z - 8q = 6$	$9z - 8q = 36$
$9z = 6 + 8q$	$9z = 36 + 8q$
$z = \dfrac{6 + 8q}{9}$	$z = 4 + \dfrac{8}{9}q$

26. (Finance) Compound interest is calculated using the formula $A = P\left(1 + \frac{r}{1}\right)^t$, where
(16) P = principal (amount originally deposited), r = the interest rate, and t = time in
years. If $1500 is deposited into an account and compounded annually at 5.5%,
how much money will be in the account after 10 years?

*27. Verify Suppose that $\frac{3}{4} = \frac{x}{100}$. Show that x equals 75.
(31)

28. Verify Is $m = \frac{2}{3}$ a solution for $\frac{1}{3}m + \frac{5}{6} = \frac{11}{18}$? Explain. If false, provide a correct
(23) solution and check.

29. Justify Simplify $20 \cdot \$9 + 10 \cdot \$13$. Justify each step.
(4)

30. (The Great Pyramid) The base of the great Pyramid of Giza is almost a perfect
(21) square. The perimeter of the base measures about 916 meters. What is the length
of each side of the pyramid's base?

Simplifying and Evaluating Expressions with Integer and Zero Exponents

Warm Up

1. Vocabulary The _____ of a power is the number used as a factor.
(3)

Simplify.

2. 3^4
(3)

3. $x^5 \cdot x^6$
(3)

4. $26 + (-18)$
(5)

5. $-34 - 19$
(6)

New Concepts

Algebraic expressions may contain exponents that are positive, negative, or zero. The relationship between the different exponents can be understood by looking at successive powers of a positive integer greater than 1. Look at the powers of 2.

> **Math Reasoning**
>
> **Verify** Show why $2^4 = 16$.

Power of 2		Value
2^4	=	16
2^3	=	8
2^2	=	4
2^1	=	2

In the left column, each entry is found by decreasing the exponent in the previous entry by one. In the right column, each entry is found by halving the previous entry, or by dividing it by 2. Use this pattern to find the next three powers.

Power of 2		Value
2^4	=	16
2^3	=	8
2^2	=	4
2^1	=	2
2^0	=	1
2^{-1}	=	$\frac{1}{2}$ or $\frac{1}{2^1}$
2^{-2}	=	$\frac{1}{4}$ or $\frac{1}{2^2}$

The pattern illustrates the properties for negative and zero exponents.

Negative and Zero Exponent Properties
Negative Exponent Property
For every nonzero number x, $x^{-n} = \frac{1}{x^n}$ and $x^n = \frac{1}{x^{-n}}$.
Zero Exponent Property
For every nonzero number x, $x^0 = 1$.

> **Math Language**
>
> **The Product Property of Exponents** states that the exponents of powers with the same base are added.
>
> $x^3 \cdot x^4 = x^{3+4} = x^7$

An algebraic expression is not considered simplified if it contains negative or zero exponents. The Product Property of Exponents applies to negative and zero exponents.

Example 1   Simplifying Expressions with Negative Exponents

Simplify each expression. All variables represent nonzero real numbers.

a. x^{-3}

SOLUTION

$$x^{-3} = \frac{1}{x^3}$$ Write with only positive exponents.

b. $\dfrac{y^{-4}}{x^2}$

SOLUTION

$$\frac{y^{-4}}{x^2} = \frac{1}{x^2 \cdot y^4} = \frac{1}{x^2 y^4}$$ Write with only positive exponents.

c. $\dfrac{1}{w^{-4}}$

SOLUTION

$$\frac{1}{w^{-4}} = w^4$$ Write with only positive exponents.

Example 2   Evaluating Expressions with Negative and Zero Exponents

Evaluate each expression for $a = -2$ and $b = -3$.

a. $a^2 b^0$

SOLUTION

$$a^2 b^0$$
$$= a^2 \cdot 1$$ Simplify using the Zero Exponent Property.
$$= a^2$$ Multiplicative Identity
$$= (-2)^2$$ Substitute -2 for a.
$$= 4$$ Simplify.

b. $3b^{-3} \cdot b$

SOLUTION

$$3b^{-3} \cdot b$$
$$= 3b^{-2}$$ Product Property of Exponents
$$= \frac{3}{b^2}$$ Simplify using the Negative Exponent Property.
$$= \frac{3}{(-3)^2}$$ Substitute -3 for b. Then simplify.
$$= \frac{3}{9} = \frac{1}{3}$$ Simplify.

Caution

When working through problems, you may incorrectly replace b^0 with 0 instead of 1.

Online Connection
www.SaxonMathResources.com

The Quotient Property of Exponents is used when dividing algebraic expressions. This property states that to divide two algebraic expressions with the same base, subtract their exponents.

Quotient Property of Exponents
If m and n are real numbers and $x \neq 0$, then $$\frac{x^m}{x^n} = x^{m-n} = \frac{1}{x^{n-m}}$$ $$\frac{5^4}{5^2} = 5^{4-2} = 5^2 = 25 \qquad\qquad \frac{5^2}{5^4} = \frac{1}{5^{4-2}} = \frac{1}{5^2} = \frac{1}{25}$$

Example 3 Using the Quotient Property of Exponents

Simplify each expression. All variables represent nonzero real numbers.

Math Reasoning

Analyze Why is $\frac{x^5}{x} = x^4$?

a. $\dfrac{x^7}{x^3}$

SOLUTION

$\dfrac{x^7}{x^3}$

$= x^{7-3}$ Quotient Property of Exponents

$= x^4$ Simplify.

b. $\dfrac{x^3}{x^{-7}}$

SOLUTION

$\dfrac{x^3}{x^{-7}}$

$= x^{3-(-7)}$ Quotient Property of Exponents

$= x^{10}$ Simplify.

Math Reasoning

Analyze Use the Quotient Property of Exponents to show another method for simplifying $\frac{x^{-5}}{x}$.

c. $\dfrac{x^{-5}y^6z}{z^{-3}y^2x}$

SOLUTION

$\dfrac{x^{-5}y^6z}{z^{-3}y^2x}$

$= x^{-5-1}y^{6-2}z^{1-(-3)}$ Quotient Property of Exponents

$= x^{-6}y^4z^4$ Simplify.

$= \dfrac{y^4z^4}{x^6}$ Write with only positive exponents.

Example **4** Application: The Intensity of Sound

The intensity of sound can be measured in watts per square meter. The table below lists intensity levels for some common sounds.

Intensity of Sound

Watts/Square Meter	Common Sound
10^3 to 10^7	Rocket Liftoff
10^0 to 10^2	Jet Liftoff
10^{-2} to 10^0	Loud Music
10^{-6} to 10^{-4}	Vacuum Cleaner
10^{-9} to 10^{-6}	Regular Speech
10^{-10} to 10^{-9}	Soft Whisper

How many times more intense is the sound of a rocket liftoff at 10^3 watts per square meter than that of regular speech at 10^{-7} watts per square meter?

Express the answer in exponential and standard form.

SOLUTION

$\dfrac{10^3}{10^{-7}}$ Write a ratio to compare the sound intensities.

$= 10^{3-(-7)}$ Quotient Property of Exponents

$= 10^{10}$ Simplify the exponent.

$= 10,000,000,000$ Simplify.

The sound of a rocket liftoff is 10^{10} or 10,000,000,000 times more intense than that of regular speech.

Math Reasoning

Write Which value is greater, 10^{-2} or 10^1? Explain.

Math Language

10^{10} is in **exponential form.** 10,000,000,000 is in **standard form.**

Lesson Practice

Simplify each expression. All variables represent nonzero real numbers.
(Ex 1)

a. x^{-5} **b.** $\dfrac{p^{-8}}{q^4}$ **c.** $\dfrac{1}{d^{-8}}$

Evaluate each expression for $a = 4$, $b = 6$, and $c = 3$.
(Ex 2)

d. a^0bc^2 **e.** $4a^{-2}$

Simplify each expression. All variables represent nonzero real numbers.
(Ex 3)

f. $\dfrac{x^{10}}{x^4}$ **g.** $\dfrac{x^9}{x^{-2}}$ **h.** $\dfrac{xy^{-3}z^5}{y^2x^2z}$

i. Refer to the table in Example 4. How many times more intense is
(Ex 4)   the sound of a jet liftoff at 10^1 watts per square meter than that of a vacuum cleaner at 10^{-5} watts per square meter? Express the answer in exponential and standard form.

Simplify.

***1.** $y^0 \dfrac{y^6}{y^5}$
(32)

***2.** $\dfrac{m^3 p^2 q^{10}}{m^{-2} p^4 q^{-6}}$
(32)

Solve.

3. $9x - 2 = 2x + 12$
(28)

***4.** $3y - y + 2y - 5 = 7 - 2y + 5$
(28)

5. $2y + 3 = 3(y + 7)$
(28)

6. $5(r - 1) = 2(r - 4) - 6$
(28)

***7. Geometry** Express the ratio of the area of the circle to the area of the square.
(32)

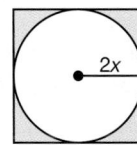

8. The sum of twice a number and 17 is 55. Find the number.
(17)

***9. Error Analysis** Two students solved the proportion $\frac{3}{8} = \frac{x}{4}$. Which student is correct?
(31) Explain the error.

Student A	Student B
$\dfrac{3}{8} = \dfrac{x}{4}$	$\dfrac{3}{8} = \dfrac{x}{4}$
$3 \cdot x = 8 \cdot 4$	$8 \cdot x = 3 \cdot 4$
$x = 10\dfrac{2}{3}$	$x = 1\dfrac{1}{2}$

***10.** (Health) The circle graph shows the prevalence of all listed types of allergies among
(27) people who suffer from allergies. What about the graph may lead someone to an
inaccurate conclusion?

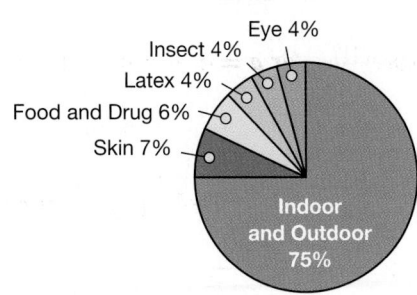

Allergy Prevalence

Eye 4%
Insect 4%
Latex 4%
Food and Drug 6%
Skin 7%
Indoor and Outdoor 75%

11. Write Why is it best to combine like terms in an equation, such as
(26) $3n + 9 - 2n = 6 - 2n + 12$, before attempting to isolate the variable?

12. Verify Is $n = 9$ a solution for $-28 = -4n + 8$? Explain. If false, provide a correct
(23) solution and check.

13. The table lists the ordered pairs from a relation. Determine whether the relation
(25) represents a function. Explain why or why not

Domain (x)	Range (y)
1	5
0	6
2	4
1	8
3	3

14. If there are 60 dozen pencils in 12 cartons, how many are in 1 carton?
(31)

15. Multi-Step How many seconds are in 1 day?
(31)

16. (Roller Coasters) The table shows the number of roller coasters in several countries.
(22) Suppose one student displays the data in a bar graph, and another student makes a
circle graph of the data. Compare the information that each type of display shows.

Roller Coasters Worldwide

Country	Japan	United Kingdom	Germany	France	China	South Korea	Canada	United States
Number	240	160	108	65	60	54	51	624

17. If there are 720 pencils in 6 cartons, how many dozen pencils are in 10 cartons?
(31)

18. Multi-Step How many centimeters are in 1 kilometer?
(31)

*19. (Geography) On a map, Brownsville and Evanstown are 2.5 inches apart. The scale
(31) on the map is 1 inch:25 miles. How far apart are the two towns?

20. Copy and complete the table for $y = |x| + 10$. Then use the table to graph the
(30) equation. Is the graph of the equation a function?

x	-3	-2	-1	0	1	2
y						

*21. Multiple Choice Which expression is simplified?
(32)

A $\dfrac{6xy^2}{z^0}$ **B** $\dfrac{6x^3y^{-2}}{z}$ **C** $\dfrac{6x^3y^2}{z}$ **D** $\dfrac{6x^3y^2z}{z}$

*22. (Chemistry) An electron has a mass of 10^{-28} grams and a proton has a mass of
(32) 10^{-24} grams. How many times greater is the mass of a proton than the mass
of an electron?

23. Multi-Step A border is being built along two sides of a triangular garden. The third side is next to the house.
(17)

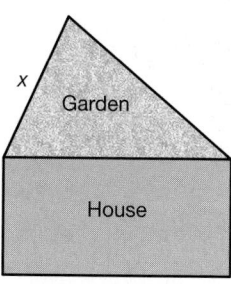

x

Garden

House

  a. The second side of the garden is 4 feet longer than first side. Write an expression for the length of the second side.

  b. If the total amount of border is 28 feet, how long are the sides of the garden that are not next to the house?

24. Multi-Step The temperature of a liquid is 72°F. The first step of a set of instructions requires that a scientist cools the liquid by 15°F. The second step requires that she warms it until it reaches 85°F. By how many degrees will she warm the liquid in the second step?
(19)

25. Analyze Megan and Molly have an age gap of 6 years. Megan is older. If Molly is 8 years old, then how old is Megan?
(29)

26. (Fuel Costs) It cost Rayna $73.25 to fill her truck with gas, not including tax. The gasoline tax is $0.32 per gallon. If the price for gasoline including tax is $3.25 per gallon, how many gallons of gas did she buy?
(24)
  a. Write an equation to represent the problem.

  b. How many gallons of gas did she buy?

27. Expand the expression $(5p - 2c)4xy$ by using the Distributive Property.
(15)

Solve each proportion.

28. $\dfrac{7}{x} = \dfrac{1}{0.5}$
(31)

*29. $\dfrac{1}{x} = \dfrac{-3}{x+2}$
(31)

30. Multi-Step How far Sam bikes in two hours depends on the rate at which he rides. His distance is represented by the equation $y = 25x$, where x is the time in hours and y is the distance in miles.
(20)
  a. Copy and complete the table and graph the solutions.

x	1	2	3	4	5
y					

  b. Connect the points. What do you notice?

  c. Predict If Sam rides at the same rate, how long will it take him to ride 80 miles?

Finding the Probability of Independent and Dependent Events

1. Vocabulary A _____ is the set of all possible outcomes of
₍₁₄₎ an event.

A number cube is labeled 1–6. Suppose the number cube is rolled once.
₍₁₄₎

2. List all the possible outcomes.

3. What is the probability of rolling a prime number?

Simplify.

4. $\dfrac{4}{5} \cdot \dfrac{15}{22}$
₍₁₁₎

5. $\dfrac{18}{55}\left(-\dfrac{33}{54}\right)$
₍₁₁₎

New Concepts

Events where the outcome of one does not affect the probability of the other are called **independent events.** To find the probability of two independent events, multiply the probabilities of the two events.

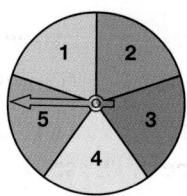 

Spinning a spinner and flipping a coin are independent events. The result of one does not affect the result of the other. What is the probability of spinning a 3 and landing on heads?

$$P(3 \text{ and heads}) = P(3) \cdot P(\text{heads})$$

$$= \dfrac{1}{5} \cdot \dfrac{1}{2}$$

$$= \dfrac{1}{10}$$

Math Reasoning

Write Explain why the first spin does not affect the second spin.

Spinning the spinner twice also creates two independent events. The first spin does not affect the second spin. What is the probability of spinning a 5 and then a 1?

$$P(5 \text{ and } 1) = P(5) \cdot P(1)$$

$$= \dfrac{1}{5} \cdot \dfrac{1}{5}$$

$$= \dfrac{1}{25}$$

With **dependent events,** the outcome of one event does affect the probability of the other event. To find the probability of two dependent events, you multiply the probability of the first event by the probability of the second event, given the results of the first event.

Online Connection
www.SaxonMathResources.com

Type of Events	Definition	Calculating the Probability
Independent Events	The outcome of the first event does not affect the second event.	$P(A \text{ and } B) = P(A) \cdot P(B)$
Dependent Events	The outcome of the first event does affect the second event.	$P(A \text{ and } B) = P(A) \cdot P(B)$, where $P(B)$ is calculated under the new conditions.

Example 1 Identifying Situations Involving Independent and Dependent Events

Identify each set of events as independent or dependent.

a. rolling a 6 on one number cube and a 4 on another number cube

SOLUTION These events are independent. Rolling one number cube does not affect the outcome of rolling the other number cube.

b. rolling a 6 on a number cube and then a 4 on the same number cube

SOLUTION These events are independent. Both rolls of this number cube have the same possible outcomes, and the result of the first roll does not affect the second roll.

c. drawing a red marble from a bag, keeping it out of the bag, and then drawing a blue marble

SOLUTION These events are dependent. By not replacing the first marble, the outcome of the second draw is affected. There are fewer marbles to choose from.

d. drawing a red marble from a bag, putting it back in the bag, and then drawing a blue marble

SOLUTION These events are independent. Because the first marble is replaced, the second draw is not affected. It has the same choices as the first.

Hint

Sometimes independent events are described as events with replacement. Dependent events are without replacement.

A tree diagram can help demonstrate the sample space for events.

Example 2 Using a Tree Diagram

A coin is flipped twice. Make a tree diagram showing all possible outcomes. What is the probability of the coin landing on heads both times?

SOLUTION

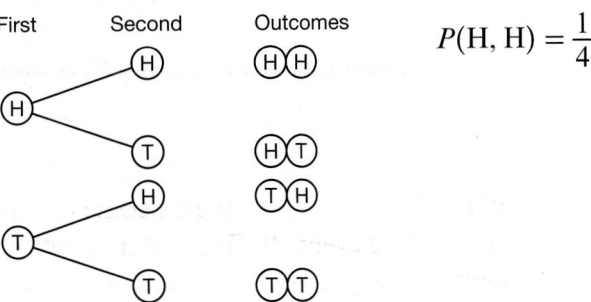

$$P(\text{H, H}) = \frac{1}{4}$$

Example 3   **Calculating the Probability of Dependent Events**

Natalia has two squares and three circles in a bag.

a. Find the probability of drawing a circle, keeping it, and then drawing another circle without the use of a tree diagram.

SOLUTION

For the first draw, the bag has 5 shapes and 3 are circles.

$$P(\text{1st circle}) = \frac{3}{5}$$

For the second draw, a circle has been removed. There is one less circle and one less shape.

$$P(\text{2nd circle}) = \frac{2}{4}$$

To find the probability of these two events, multiply their probabilities.

$$P(\text{1st circle}) \cdot P(\text{2nd circle}) = \frac{3}{5} \cdot \frac{2}{4} = \frac{6}{20} = \frac{3}{10}$$

b. Find the probability of drawing a square, keeping it, and then drawing a circle.

SOLUTION

For the first draw, the bag has 5 shapes and 2 are squares.

$$P(\text{square}) = \frac{2}{5}$$

For the second draw, a square has been removed. There is one less shape, but the number of circles is the same.

$$P(\text{circle}) = \frac{3}{4}$$

To find the probability of these two events, multiply their probabilities.

$$P(\text{square}) \cdot P(\text{circle}) = \frac{2}{5} \cdot \frac{3}{4} = \frac{6}{20} = \frac{3}{10}$$

Math Reasoning

Justify Why do both the numerator and the denominator change for the second event?

Odds are another way of describing the likelihood of an event. Odds are expressed as a ratio, usually written with a colon. Odds can be calculated for something or against something happening.

Definition of Odds
Odds of an event: A ratio expressing the likelihood of an event.
Assume that all outcomes are equally likely, and that there are m favorable and n unfavorable outcomes.
The odds for the event are $m{:}n$.   The odds against the event are $n{:}m$.

Example 4 · Calculating Odds

A bag contains 6 red marbles, 2 yellow marbles, and 1 blue marble.

a. What are the odds of drawing a red marble?

SOLUTION

Look at the favorable outcomes and the unfavorable outcomes.

There are 6 red marbles (favorable outcomes).

There are 3 marbles that are not red (unfavorable outcomes).

The odds of drawing a red marble are 6:3 or 2:1.

b. What are the odds against drawing a blue marble?

SOLUTION

Look at the favorable and the unfavorable outcomes.

There are 8 marbles that are not blue (unfavorable outcome).

There is 1 blue marble (favorable outcome).

The odds against drawing a blue marble are 8:1.

Hint

The sum of the favorable and unfavorable outcomes should be the same as the total possible outcomes.

Example 5 · Solving Multi-Step Problems Involving Probability

Isaac has 6 blue and 4 white shirts in his closet. There are also 2 pairs of navy pants and 3 pairs of khaki pants in his closet.

a. What is the probability Isaac will choose khaki pants and a white shirt from his closet?

SOLUTION

$$P(\text{khaki pants}) = \frac{3}{5}$$

$$P(\text{white shirt}) = \frac{4}{10} = \frac{2}{5}$$

$$P(\text{khaki pants and white shirt}) = \frac{3}{5} \cdot \frac{2}{5} = \frac{6}{25}$$

b. Assume that after the pants and shirt are worn, they are put in the laundry hamper. What is the probability that he will choose khaki pants and a white shirt from the closet to wear the next day?

SOLUTION

$$P(\text{khaki pants}) = \frac{2}{4} = \frac{1}{2}$$

$$P(\text{white shirt}) = \frac{3}{9} = \frac{1}{3}$$

$$P(\text{khaki pants and white shirt}) = \frac{1}{2} \cdot \frac{1}{3} = \frac{1}{6}$$

Identify each set of events as independent or dependent.

a. A card is chosen from a deck of cards, replaced, and then a second card is chosen.
(Ex 1)

b. A marble is drawn from a bag, kept, and then a second marble is drawn.
(Ex 1)

c. A coin is flipped, and a number cube is rolled.
(Ex 1)

d. A spinner is spun and the result is recorded. Then the spinner is spun a second time.
(Ex 1)

e. A coin is flipped and a six-sided number cube is tossed. Make a tree diagram showing all possible outcomes. What is the probability of landing on tails and on an even number?
(Ex 2)

A bag contains 4 red blocks and 3 blue blocks.
(Ex 3)

f. Find the probability of drawing a red block, keeping it, and then drawing another red block.

g. Find the probability of drawing a blue block, keeping it, and then drawing a red block.

Use the spinner to answer the problems.
(Ex 4)

h. What are the odds of spinning black?

i. What are the odds against spinning gray?

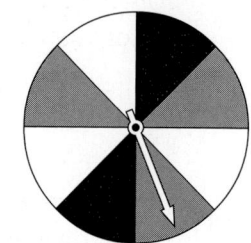

Campers select one inside activity and one outside activity daily. There are 5 inside activities and 8 outside activities.
(Ex 5)

j. What is the probability of choosing pottery and horseback riding on the first day?

k. Inside activities can be repeated, but outside activities cannot be repeated. What is the probability of choosing pottery and swimming the second day?

> **Caution**
>
> The outside events are dependent, so the total number of outcomes changes.

Practice Distributed and Integrated

Solve.

1. $-5v = 6v + 5 - v$
(28)

2. $-3(b + 9) = -6$
(26)

3. $-22 = -p - 12$
(26)

4. $-\dfrac{2}{5} = -\dfrac{1}{3}m + \dfrac{3}{5}$
(26)

5. $\dfrac{2}{x} = \dfrac{30}{-6}$
(31)

6. $\dfrac{x - 4}{6} = \dfrac{x + 2}{12}$
(31)

Simplify.

7. $\dfrac{y^6 x^5}{y^5 x^7}$
(32)

*8. $\dfrac{w^{-5} z^{-3}}{w^{-3} z^2}$
(32)

9. $\dfrac{4x^2 z^0}{2x^3 z}$
(32)

*10. Model There are 10 little marbles and 4 big marbles in a bag. A big marble is drawn
(33) and not replaced. Draw a picture that represents how the contents of the bag
change between the first draw and the second draw.

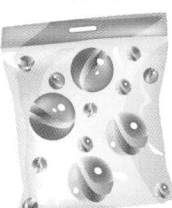

*11. Write Explain the difference between probability and odds.
(33)

*12. True or False: Two rolls of a number cube are independent events.
(33)

*13. Is the set of whole numbers closed under subtraction? Explain.
(1)

*14. Multiple Choice A bag contains 3 blue stones, 5 red stones, and 2 white stones.
(33) What is the probability of picking a blue stone, keeping it, and then picking a
white stone?

A $\dfrac{3}{50}$ **B** $\dfrac{1}{15}$ **C** $\dfrac{3}{28}$ **D** $\dfrac{1}{2}$

15. (**Stock Market**) The value of an investor's stock changed by $-1\frac{3}{4}$ points last week.
(11) This week the value changed by 3 times as much. How much did the value of the
investor's stock change this week?

*16. Predict What is the probability of rolling a 3 twice in a row on a six-sided number
(33) cube?

17. Write Give an example of a situation in which someone may want to use large
(27) intervals on a graph to persuade people to come to a certain conclusion.

*18. Analyze Simplify $x^3 \cdot x^{-3}$. What is the mathematical relationship between x^n and x^{-n}?
(32)

19. (**Time**) A nanosecond is 10^{-9} times as fast as 1 second and a microsecond is
(32) 10^{-6} times as fast as 1 second. How much faster is the nanosecond than the
microsecond?

20. Convert 30 quarts per mile to gallons per mile.
(31)

*21. Error Analysis Two students solved the proportion $\frac{5}{9} = \frac{c}{45}$. Which student is correct?
(31) Explain the error.

Student A	Student B
$\dfrac{5}{9} = \dfrac{c}{45}$	$\dfrac{5}{9} = \dfrac{c}{45}$
$9c = 225$	$9c = 225$
$c = 25$	$c = 2025$

*22. (**Vehicle Rental**) One moving company charges $19.85 plus $0.20 per mile to rent a
(28) van. The company also rents trucks for $24.95 plus $0.17 per mile. At how many
miles is the price the same for renting the vehicles?

23. If a set of ordered pairs is not a relation, can the set still be a function? Explain.
(25)

24. Write Explain how to find the solution of $0.09n + 0.2 = 2.9$.
(24)

25. (**Keeping Cool**) The British thermal unit (BTU) is a unit of energy used globally in
(21) air conditioning industries. The number of BTUs needed to cool a room depends
on the area of the room. To find the number of BTUs recommended for any size
room, use the formula $B = 377lw$, where B is the number of BTUs, l is the length
of the room, and w is the width of the room. The room you want to cool uses the
recomended number of 12,252.5 BTUs and is 5 meters wide. Find the area of the
room.

26. Multi-Step A quarterback throws the ball approximately 30 times per game. He
(20) has already thrown the ball 125 times this season. The equation $y = 30x + 125$
predicts how many times he will have thrown the ball after x more games.

x	y
2	
3	
4	
5	

a. Copy and complete the table using a graphing calculator and then graph the
solutions.

b. When will he have thrown the ball more than 300 times?

27. (**Marathons**) A marathon is 26.2 miles long. In order to qualify for the Boston
(21) Marathon, Jill must first complete a different marathon within $3\frac{2}{3}$ hours. Her
average speed in the last marathon she completed was 7.8 miles per hour. Did she
qualify for the Boston Marathon? Explain.

28. Geometry The rectangles shown are similar.
(31)

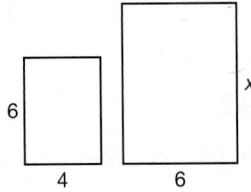

a. Find the ratio of the side lengths of the smaller rectangle to the larger
rectangle.

b. Find the longer side length of the larger rectangle using proportions.

29. Jack is building a square pen for his dog. If he wants the area of the pen to be
(13) 144 square feet, how long should he make each side of the pen?

30. True or False: Whole numbers include negative numbers.
(1)

Recognizing and Extending Arithmetic Sequences

Warm Up

1. Vocabulary Any quantity whose value does not change is called a _____.
(2)

Simplify.

2. $7.2 - 5.8 - (-15)$
(6)

3. $-0.12 - (-43.7) - 73.5$
(6)

4. $6(-2.5)$
(11)

5. $(-15)(-4.2)$
(11)

New Concepts

Sequences of numbers can be formed using a variety of patterns and operations. A **sequence** is a list of numbers that follow a rule, and each number in the sequence is called a **term of the sequence.** Here are a few examples of sequences:

$1, 3, 5, 7, \ldots$

$7, 4, 1, -2, \ldots$

$2, 6, 18, 54, \ldots$

$1, 4, 9, 16, \ldots$

> **Math Language**
>
> The symbol "…" is an **ellipsis** and is read "and so on." In mathematics, the symbol means the pattern continues without end.

In the above examples, the first two sequences are a special type of sequence called an arithmetic sequence. An **arithmetic sequence** is a sequence that has a constant difference between two consecutive terms called the **common difference.**

To find the common difference, choose any term and subtract the previous term. In the first sequence above, the common difference is 2, while in the second sequence, the common difference is -3.

$$1, \quad 3, \quad 5, \quad 7, \ldots \qquad\qquad 7, \quad 4, \quad 1, \quad -2, \ldots$$
$$\;+2 \quad +2 \quad +2 \qquad\qquad\qquad -3 \quad -3 \quad -3$$

If the sequence does not have a common difference, then it is not arithmetic.

Example 1 Recognizing Arithmetic Sequences

Determine if each sequence is an arithmetic sequence. If yes, find the common difference and the next two terms.

a. 7, 12, 17, 22, …

SOLUTION Since $12 - 7 = 5$, $17 - 12 = 5$, and $22 - 17 = 5$, the sequence is arithmetic with a common difference of 5. The next two terms are $22 + 5 = 27$ and $27 + 5 = 32$.

b. 3, 6, 12, 24, …

SOLUTION Since $6 - 3 = 3$ and $12 - 6 = 6$, there is no common difference and the sequence is not arithmetic.

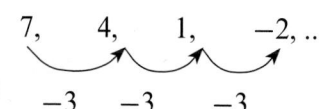
Online Connection
www.SaxonMathResources.com

The first term of a sequence is denoted as a_1, the second term as a_2, the third term a_3, and so on. The nth term of an arithmetic sequence is denoted a_n. The term preceding a_n is denoted a_{n-1}. For example, if $n = 6$, then the term preceding a_6 is a_{6-1} or a_5.

Term Number (n)	Term	Sequence Pattern	Description
1	1st or a_1	7	a_1
2	2nd or a_2	$(7) + 4$	$a_1 + d$
3	3rd or a_3	$(7 + 4) + 4$	$a_2 + d$
4	4th or a_4	$(7 + 4 + 4) + 4$	$a_3 + d$
5	5th or a_5	$(7 + 4 + 4 + 4) + 4$	$a_4 + d$
n	n^{th} or a_n	$a_{n-1} + 4$	$a_{n-1} + d$

Math Reasoning

Generalize Give an example of an arithmetic sequence. State the first 4 terms and the common difference.

Arithmetic sequences can be represented using a formula.

Arithmetic Sequence Formula

Use the formula below to find the next term in a sequence.

$$a_n = a_{n-1} + d$$

$a_1 =$ first term

$d =$ common difference

$n =$ term number

In the arithmetic sequence 7, 11, 15, 19, ..., $a_1 = 7$, $a_2 = 11$, $a_3 = 15$, and $a_4 = 19$. The common difference is 4.

Example 2 **Using a Recursive Formula**

Use a recursive formula to find the first four terms of an arithmetic sequence where $a_1 = -2$ and the common difference $d = 7$.

SOLUTION

$a_n = a_{n-1} + d$	Write the formula.
$a_n = a_{n-1} + 7$	Substitute 7 for d.
$a_1 = -2$	Write the first term.
$a_2 = -2 + 7 = 5$	Find the second term.
$a_3 = 5 + 7 = 12$	Find the third term.
$a_4 = 12 + 7 = 19$	Find the fourth term.

The first four terms of the sequence are -2, 5, 12, and 19.

A rule for finding any term in an arithmetic sequence can be developed by looking at a different pattern in the sequence 7, 11, 15, 19, ...

Term	Term Number (n)	Sequence Pattern	Description
1st or a_1	1	7	a_1
2nd or a_2	2	$7 + 4 = 7 + (1)4$	$a_1 + (1)d$
3rd or a_3	3	$7 + 4 + 4 = 7 + (2)4$	$a_1 + (2)d$
4th or a_4	4	$7 + 4 + 4 + 4 = 7 + (3)4$	$a_1 + (3)d$
5th or a_5	5	$7 + 4 + 4 + 4 + 4 = 7 + 4(4)$	$a_1 + (4)d$
n^{th} or a_n	n	$7 + (n - 1)4$	$a_1 + (n - 1)d$

Finding the nth Term of an Arithmetic Sequence
$$a_n = a_1 + (n - 1)d$$
$a_1 = $ first term $d = $ common difference

Example 3 Finding the nth Term in Arithmetic Sequences

a. Use the rule $a_n = 6 + (n - 1)2$ to find the 4th and 11th terms of the sequence.

SOLUTION

4th term:

$$a_4 = 6 + (4 - 1)2$$
$$= 6 + (3)2$$
$$= 6 + 6$$
$$= 12$$

11th term:

$$a_{11} = 6 + (11 - 1)2$$
$$= 6 + (10)2$$
$$= 6 + 20$$
$$= 26$$

b. Find the 10th term of the sequence 3, 11, 19, 27, ….

SOLUTION

$a_1 = 3$ and the common difference $d = 11 - 3 = 8$

$a_n = 3 + (n - 1)8$ Write the rule, substituting for a, and d.

$a_{10} = 3 + (10 - 1)8$ Substitute the value for n.

$a_{10} = 75$ Simplify using the order of operations.

c. Find the 10th term of the sequence $\frac{1}{4}, \frac{3}{4}, \frac{5}{4}, \frac{7}{4}, \ldots$.

SOLUTION

$a_1 = \frac{1}{4}$ and $d = \frac{3}{4} - \frac{1}{4} = \frac{2}{4} = \frac{1}{2}$

$a_n = \frac{1}{4} + (n - 1)\frac{1}{2}$ Write the rule, substituting for a, and d.

$a_{10} = \frac{1}{4} + (10 - 1)\frac{1}{2}$ Substitute the value for n.

$a_{10} = \frac{19}{4}$ Simplify using the order of operations.

Math Reasoning

Verify Is the sequence
$-1, -5, -9, -13, \ldots$ an
arithmetic sequence?

Example 4 **Application: Seating for a Reception**

The first table at a reception will seat 9 guests while each additional table will seat 6 more guests.

a. Write a rule to model the situation.

SOLUTION $a_1 = 9$ and $d = 6$. The rule is $a_n = 9 + (n - 1)6$.

b. Use the rule to find how many guests can be seated with 10 tables.

SOLUTION

$a_n = 9 + (n - 1)6$

$a_{10} = 9 + (10 - 1)6$

$a_{10} = 63$

63 guests can be seated with 10 tables.

Lesson Practice

Determine if each sequence is an arithmetic sequence. If yes, find the common difference and the next two terms.
(Ex 1)

   a. 7, 6, 5, 4, …

   b. 10, 12, 15, 19, …

   c. Use a recursive formula to find the first four terms of an arithmetic sequence where $a_1 = -3$ and the common difference $d = 4$.
(Ex 2)

   d. Use the rule $a_n = 14 + (n - 1)(-3)$ to find the 4th and 11th terms of an arithmetic sequence.
(Ex 3)

   e. Find the 10th term of the sequence 1, 10, 19, 28, ….
(Ex 3)

   f. Find the 11th term of the sequence $\frac{2}{3}$, 1, $1\frac{1}{3}$, $1\frac{2}{3}$, ….
(Ex 3)

Flowers are purchased to put on tables at a reception. The head table needs to have 12 flowers and the other tables need to have 6 flowers each.
(Ex 4)

   g. Write a rule to model the situation.

   h. Use the rule to find the number of flowers needed for 15 tables.

Practice   Distributed and Integrated

Solve each proportion

1. $\dfrac{2}{10} = \dfrac{x}{-20}$
(31)

2. $\dfrac{32}{4} = \dfrac{x + 4}{3}$
(31)

*3. **(Construction)** An amphitheater with tiered rows is being constructed. The first row
(34) will have 24 seats and each row after that will have an additional 2 seats. If there will be a total of 15 rows, how many seats will be in the last row?

*4. Use a graphing calculator to complete the table of values
(30) for the function $f(x) = 2x^2 - 5$. Graph the function.

x	y
-2	
-1	
0	
1	
2	

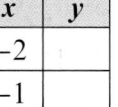

*5. Solve $y = x + \frac{z}{3}$ for z.
(29)

Solve each equation. Check your answer.

6. $4x + 2 = 5(x + 10)$
(28)

7. $2\left(n + \frac{1}{3}\right) = \frac{3}{2}n + 1 + \frac{1}{2}n - \frac{1}{3}$
(28)

8. A bead is drawn from a bag, kept, and then a second bead is drawn. Identify
(33) these events as independent or dependent.

*9. Justify Is the sequence 0.3, -0.5, -1.3, -2.1, ... an arithmetic sequence? Justify
(34) your answer.

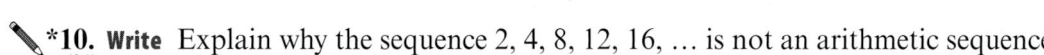

*10. Write Explain why the sequence 2, 4, 8, 12, 16, ... is not an arithmetic sequence.
(34)

*11. Multiple Choice In the rule for the nth term of an arithmetic sequence
(34) $a_n = a_1 + (n - 1)d$, what does d represent?

   A the number of terms   **B** the first term

   C the nth term   **D** the common difference

*12. Is the sequence 7, 14, 21, 28, ... an arithmetic sequence? If it is, then find the
(34) common difference and the next two terms. If it is not, then find the next two
terms.

13. Statistics A poll is taken and each person is asked two questions.
(33) The results are shown in the table. What is the probability
that someone answered "yes" to both questions?

	Question 1	Question 2
Yes	55	30
No	45	70

14. Predict A number cube labeled 1–6 is rolled two times. What is the probability of
(33) rolling a 2 and then a 3?

*15. Geometry A rectangle with perimeter 10 units has a length of 3 units and a width
(34) of 2 units. Additional rectangles are added as shown below.

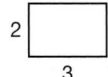 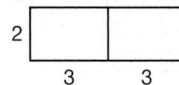 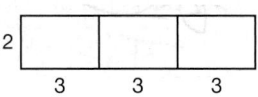 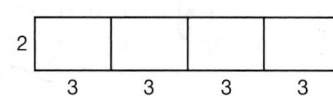

$P = 10$ units $P = 16$ units $P = 22$ units $P = 28$ units

   a. Write a rule for the perimeter of n rectangles.

   b. Use the rule to find the perimeter of 12 rectangles.

*16. Work uniforms include pants or a skirt, a shirt, and a tie or a vest. There are
(33) 3 pairs of pants, 5 skirts, 10 shirts, 2 ties, and 1 vest in a wardrobe.

   a. What is the probability of choosing a pair of pants, a shirt, and a tie?

   b. The pants and shirt from the previous day must be washed, but the tie returns
to the wardrobe. What is the probability of choosing pants, a shirt, and a tie the
next day?

17. Evaluate the expression $d = 6 \cdot \frac{1}{c^{-2}}$ for $c = 2$.
(32)

18. (**Physical Science**) The wavelengths of microwaves can range from 10^{-3} m to 10^{-1} m.
(32) Express the range of wavelengths using positive exponents.

19. **Multiple Choice** Ms. Markelsden baked 36 cookies in 45 minutes. How many cookies
(31) can she bake in 3 hours?

    A 45 cookies   **B** 81 cookies

    C 64 cookies   **D** 144 cookies

20. Does $y = x^2 + 2$ represent a function? Explain how you know.
(30)

21. (**Architecture**) A model of a building is 15 inches tall. In the scale drawing, 1 inch
(31) represents 20 feet. How tall is the building?

*22. **Generalize** Given $\frac{2}{b} = \frac{1}{a}$, where a and b are positive numbers, write an equation
(31) that shows how to find a.

23. The line graph at right shows the costs of tuition at a
(27) university over the past 5 years. How might this graph be
misleading?

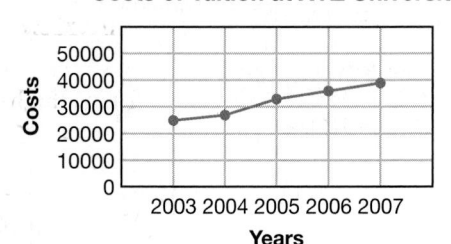

Costs of Tuition at XYZ University

24. **Write** The equation $x + 5 = x - 5$ has no solution. Explain
(28) why it has no solution.

25. **Verify** Solve $16x + 4(2x - 6) = 60$ for x. Check your answer.
(26)

26. True or False: Any irrational number divided by an irrational number will be
(1) an irrational number. Explain your answer.

27. (**Savings**) Hector has $400 in his savings account. Each week he deposits his $612.50
(23) paycheck and takes out $250 to live on for the week. If he wants to buy a car for
$5500, about how many months will it take him to save up for the car?

28. **Multi-Step** Jamal is riding his bike at a rate of about 8 miles per hour. How many
(31) hours will it take Jamal to ride 50 miles?

29. (**Car Rental**) A family rented a car that cost $45 per day plus $0.23 per mile. If the
(24) family rented the car for 7 days and paid $395.50 altogether, how many miles did
they drive?

30. **Error Analysis** Two students determine whether the ordered pairs in the table
(25) represent a function. Which student is correct? Explain the error.

x	y
7	10
−2	−3
7	12
5	4

Student A	Student B
(7, 12) and (7, 10) The x-values are the same, so it is not a function.	All the y-values are different, so it is not a function.

Locating and Using Intercepts

Warm Up

1. *(20)* **Vocabulary** A pair of numbers that can be used to locate a point on a coordinate plane is called a(n) _____.

Evaluate.

2. *(16)* $3x + 14$; $x = -9$

3. *(16)* $7.5w - 84.3$; $w = 15$

Solve.

4. *(23)* $7x - 18 = -74$

5. *(23)* $57 + 19y = -76$

New Concepts

Linear equations can be graphed by making a table of ordered pairs that satisfy the equation and then graphing the corresponding points (x, y). An ordered pair or set of ordered pairs that satisfy an equation is called the **solution of a linear equation in two variables.** When an equation is in standard form, the linear equation can be graphed another way.

> **Math Language**
>
> An **ordered pair** can be used to locate a point on a coordinate plane.

Standard Form of a Linear Equation
The **standard form of a linear equation** is $Ax + By = C$, where A, B, and C are real numbers and A and B are not both zero.

The x-coordinate of the point where the graph of an equation intersects the x-axis is called the **x-intercept.** The y-coordinate of the point where the graph of an equation intersects the y-axis is called the **y-intercept.** The coordinate pairs $(x, 0)$ and $(0, y)$ that satisfy a linear equation are two solutions of the linear equation in two variables.

Example 1 Finding x- and y-Intercepts

Find the x- and y-intercepts for $3x + 4y = 24$.

SOLUTION

To find the intercepts, make a table. Substitute 0 for y and solve for x. Substitute 0 for x and solve for y.

$$3x + 4y = 24$$
$$3x + 4(0) = 24$$
$$3x = 24$$
$$\frac{3x}{3} = \frac{24}{3}$$
$$x = 8$$

$$3x + 4y = 24$$
$$3(0) + 4y = 24$$
$$4y = 24$$
$$\frac{4y}{4} = \frac{24}{4}$$
$$y = 6$$

x	y
8	0
0	6

The x-intercept is 8. The y-intercept is 6.

Online Connection
www.SaxonMathResources.com

An efficient method for graphing a linear equation in two variables is to plot the x- and y-intercepts and then to draw a line through them.

Example 2 Graphing Using the x- and y-Intercepts

Graph $5x - 6y = 30$ using the x- and y-intercepts.

SOLUTION

To find the intercepts, make a table. Substitute 0 for y and solve for x. Substitute 0 for x and solve for y.

$$5x - 6y = 30$$
$$5x - 6(0) = 30$$
$$5x = 30$$
$$\frac{5x}{5} = \frac{30}{5}$$
$$x = 6$$

$$5x - 6y = 30$$
$$5(0) - 6y = 30$$
$$-6y = 30$$
$$\frac{-6y}{-6} = \frac{30}{-6}$$
$$y = -5$$

x	y
6	0
0	−5

The x-intercept is 6. The y-intercept is −5.

To graph the equation, plot the points $(6, 0)$ and $(0, -5)$. Then draw a line through them.

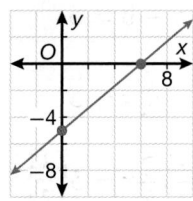

Math Reasoning

Write Explain why the y-value of the x-intercept is 0 and the x-value of the y-intercept is 0.

Example 3 Locating x- and y-Intercepts on a Graph

Find the x- and y-intercepts on the graph.

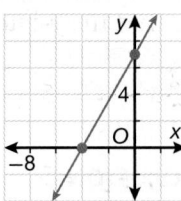

SOLUTION

The x-intercept is the x-coordinate of the point where the line crosses the x-axis. The point where the line crosses the x-axis is $(-4, 0)$. The x-intercept is −4.

The y-intercept is the y-coordinate of the point where the line crosses the y-axis. The point where the line crosses the y-axis is $(0, 7)$. The y-intercept is 7.

Caution

The interval used on the x- and y-axis varies. Check the labels before naming the coordinates of a point.

Any linear equation can be rearranged into standard form. Put both variables and their coefficients on one side of the equal sign and the constants on the other side.

Example 4 Using Standard Form to Graph

Write the equation $y = -\frac{2}{3}x + 5$ in standard form. Then graph the equation using the x- and y-intercepts.

SOLUTION

Write the equation in standard form.

$$y = -\frac{2}{3}x + 5$$

$$+\frac{2}{3}x = +\frac{2}{3}x$$

$$\frac{2}{3}x + y = 5$$

To find the x-intercept, substitute 0 for y and solve for x.

$$\frac{2}{3}x + y = 5$$

$$\frac{2}{3}x + 0 = 5$$

$$\frac{2}{3}x = 5$$

$$\left(\frac{3}{2}\right)\frac{2}{3}x = 5\left(\frac{3}{2}\right)$$

$$x = 7\frac{1}{2}$$

The x-intercept is $7\frac{1}{2}$.

To find the y-intercept, substitute 0 for x and solve for y.

$$\frac{2}{3}x + y = 5$$

$$\frac{2}{3}(0) + y = 5$$

$$y = 5$$

The y-intercept is 5.

Graph the x- and y-intercepts and draw a line through them.

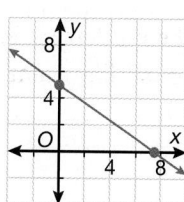

Hint

Use inverse operations to write the equation so that both variables are on the same side.

Example 5   Application: Play Tickets

At a school play, student tickets are $5 and adult tickets are $8. Let x be the number of student tickets sold. Let y be the number of adult tickets sold. The equation $5x + 8y = 400$ shows that one drama club member raised $400 from ticket sales. Find the intercepts and explain what each means.

SOLUTION

Substitute 0 for y and solve for x. Then substitute 0 for x and solve for y.

$$5x + 8y = 400 \qquad\qquad 5x + 8y = 400$$
$$5x + 8(0) = 400 \qquad\qquad 5(0) + 8y = 400$$
$$5x = 400 \qquad\qquad 8y = 400$$
$$\frac{5x}{5} = \frac{400}{5} \qquad\qquad \frac{8y}{8} = \frac{400}{8}$$
$$x = 80 \qquad\qquad y = 50$$

The x-intercept is 80. The y-intercept is 50.

The x-intercept shows that if the drama club member sold no adult tickets, 80 student tickets were sold. The y-intercept shows that if no student tickets were sold, 50 adult tickets were sold.

Lesson Practice

a. Find the x- and y-intercepts for $-6x + 9y = 36$.
(Ex 1)

b. Graph $4x + 7y = 28$ using the x- and y-intercepts.
(Ex 2)

c. Find the x- and y-intercepts on the graph.
(Ex 3)

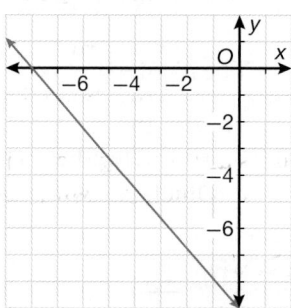

d. Write $4y = 12x - 12$ in standard form. Then graph the equation using the x- and y-intercepts.
(Ex 4)

e. (Athletics) Hirva jogs 6 miles per hour and bikes 12 miles per hour. The equation $6x + 12y = 24$ shows that she has gone a total of 24 miles. Find the intercepts and explain what each means.
(Ex 5)

Solve.

1. $\dfrac{-2.25}{x} = \dfrac{9}{6}$
(31)

*2. $\dfrac{y+2}{y+7} = \dfrac{11}{31}$
(31)

3. $2(f+3) + 4f = 6 + 6f$
(28)

4. $3x + 7 - 2x = 4x + 10$
(28)

Evaluate each expression for the given value of the variable.

5. $(m+6) \div (2-5)$ for $m = 9$
(9)

6. $-3(x + 12 \cdot 2)$ for $x = -8$
(9)

Simplify by combining like terms.

7. $10y^3 + 5y - 4y^3$
(18)

8. $10xy^2 - 5x^2y + 3y^2x$
(18)

9. Identify the subsets of real numbers to which the number $\sqrt{7}$ belongs.
(1)

*10. Find the x- and y-intercepts for $5x + 10y = -20$.
(35)

*11. Find the x- and y-intercepts for $-8x + 20y = 40$.
(35)

*12. Write Explain how knowing the x- and y-intercepts is helpful in graphing a linear
(35) equation.

*13. Multiple Choice What is the x-intercept for the equation $15x + 9y = 45$?
(35)
　　A $(0, 3)$ 　　　　**B** $(3, 0)$ 　　　　**C** $(5, 0)$ 　　　　**D** $(0, 5)$

*14. (**Fishery**) A Pacific salmon can swim at a maximum speed of 8 miles per hour. The
(35) function $y = 8x$ describes how many miles y the fish swims in x hours. Graph the
function. Use the graph to estimate the number of miles the fish swims in 2.5 hours.

15. Determine if the sequence 34, 29, 24, 19, … is an arithmetic sequence or not. If yes,
(34) find the common difference and the next two terms. If no, find the next two terms.

16. Error Analysis Two students are finding the common difference for the arithmetic
(34) sequence 18, 15, 12, 9, …. Which student is correct? Explain the error.

Student A	Student B
$18 - 15 = 3$	$15 - 18 = -3$
$15 - 12 = 3$	$12 - 15 = -3$
$12 - 9 = 3$	$9 - 12 = -3$

*17. Geometry A right triangle is formed by the origin and the x- and y-intercepts of
(35) $14x + 7y = 56$. Find the area of the triangle.

18. Data Analysis The table shows the weights of a newborn baby
(34) who was 7.5 lb at birth.

    a. Write a recursive formula for the baby's weight gain.

    b. If the pattern continues, how much will the baby weigh
    after 7 weeks?

Week Number	Weight (lb)
1	9
2	10.5
3	12
4	13.5

*19. Multi-Step Use the arithmetic sequence $-65, -72, -79, -86, \ldots$.
(34)   **a.** What is the value of a_1?

    b. What is the common difference d?

    c. Write a rule for the nth term of the sequence.

20. Write A coin is flipped and lands on heads. It is flipped again and lands on tails.
(33) Identify these events as independent or dependent.

21. (Economics) You have agreed to a babysitting job that will last 14 days. On the first
(34) day, you earn \$25, but on each day after that you will earn \$15. How much will
you earn if you babysit for 7 days?

22. Probability A bag holds 5 red marbles, 3 white marbles, and 2 green marbles.
(33) A marble is drawn, kept out, and then another marble is drawn. What is the
probability of drawing two white marbles?

*23. Multiple Choice Which of the following expressions is the simplified solution
(32) of $\dfrac{m^3 n^{-10} p^5}{m n^0 p^{-2}}$?

  A $\dfrac{m^3 p^3}{n^{10}}$ **B** $\dfrac{m^3 p^7}{n^{10}}$ **C** $\dfrac{m^2 p^3}{n^9}$ **D** $\dfrac{m^2 p^7}{n^{10}}$

*24. Verify Is the statement $4^{-2} = -16$ correct? Explain your reasoning.
(32)

25. Convert 45 miles per hour to miles per minute.
(31)

26. Rewrite the following question so it is not biased: Would you rather buy a brand
(Inv 3) new luxury SUV or a cheap used car?

27. Identify the independent variable and the dependent variable: money earned,
(20) hours worked.

28. (Temperature) Use the formula $F = \frac{9}{5}C + 32$ to find an equivalent Fahrenheit
(23) temperature when the temperature is $-12°C$.

29. (Homework) A student has to write a book report on a book that contains 1440
(25) pages. Suppose she plans to read 32 pages per day. Using function notation,
express how many pages remain after reading for d days.

30. (Soccer) For every hour a player practices soccer, he must drink 8 fluid ounces of
(25) liquid to stay hydrated. Write an equation describing this relation and determine
whether it is a function.

Writing and Solving Proportions

Warm Up

1. Vocabulary A _____ is a comparison of two quantities using division.
(31)

Solve.

2. $\dfrac{13}{52} = \dfrac{x}{36}$
(31)

3. $\dfrac{42}{56} = \dfrac{63}{w}$
(31)

4. $15x - 37 = 143$
(23)

5. $78 + 22y = -230$
(23)

New Concepts

Proportions are frequently used to solve problems in mathematics. Proportional reasoning can be applied in many situations, including reading and drawing maps, architecture, and construction. Solving problems in these situations requires knowledge of similar figures.

> **Reading Math**
>
> The ~ symbol indicates similar figures and reads "is similar to." The ≅ symbol indicates congruent figures and reads "is congruent to."

If two geometric objects or figures are **similar,** they have the same shape but are not necessarily the same size. The triangles below are similar.

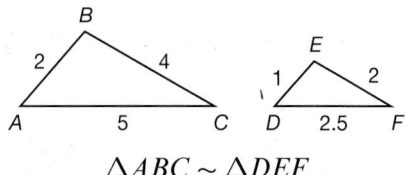

$$\triangle ABC \sim \triangle DEF$$

When two figures are similar, they have sides and angles that correspond. Corresponding sides and angles are found using the order of the letters in the similarity statement. In the triangles above, $\angle A$ and $\angle D$ correspond, $\angle B$ and $\angle E$ correspond, and $\angle C$ and $\angle F$ correspond. Corresponding angles of similar figures are **congruent,** or have the same measure.

$$\angle A \cong \angle D \qquad \angle B \cong \angle E \qquad \angle C \cong \angle F$$

> **Reading Math**
>
> $\overline{AB}$ is read "segment AB."

Sides of similar figures also correspond. In the example above, $\overline{AB}$ and $\overline{DE}$ correspond, $\overline{BC}$ and $\overline{EF}$ correspond, and $\overline{AC}$ and $\overline{DF}$ correspond. Corresponding sides of similar figures do not have to be congruent. However, they do have to be in proportion. The ratio of the all pairs of corresponding sides must be the same.

$$\frac{AB}{DE} = \frac{BC}{EF} = \frac{AC}{DF}$$

In the example above, the ratio of the sides of $\triangle ABC$ to $\triangle DEF$ is 2 to 1. This ratio, which can also be written as $\frac{2}{1}$ or 2:1, is called the scale factor of $\triangle ABC$ to $\triangle DEF$.

$$\frac{AB}{DE} = \frac{BC}{EF} = \frac{AC}{DF} = \frac{2}{1}$$

A **scale factor** is the ratio of a side length of a figure to the side length of a similiar figure. The scale factor of $\triangle DEF$ to $\triangle ABC$ is 1 to 2.

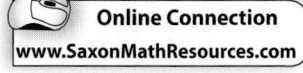

Online Connection
www.SaxonMathResources.com

Example 1 Finding Measures in Similar Figures

$PQRS \sim WXYZ$

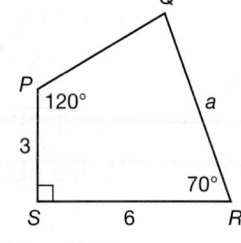
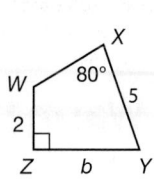

a. Find m$\angle Q$ and m$\angle W$.

SOLUTION

$\angle Q$ and $\angle X$ correspond, so they are equal, and m$\angle Q = 80°$. $\angle W$ and $\angle P$ correspond, so they are equal and m$\angle W = 120°$.

b. Find the scale factor of $PQRS$ to $WXYZ$.

SOLUTION

$\overline{PS}$ and $\overline{WZ}$ correspond, so the scale factor of $PQRS$ to $WXYZ$ is $\frac{PS}{WZ} = \frac{3}{2}$.

c. Use the scale factor to find QR and ZY.

SOLUTION

All corresponding side lengths must be in a ratio of 3 to 2. $\overline{QR}$ corresponds with $\overline{XY}$ and $\overline{ZY}$ corresponds with $\overline{SR}$.

$$\frac{PS}{WZ} = \frac{QR}{XY} \qquad\qquad \frac{PS}{WZ} = \frac{SR}{ZY}$$

$$\frac{3}{2} = \frac{a}{5} \qquad\qquad\qquad \frac{3}{2} = \frac{6}{b}$$

$$2a = 15 \qquad\qquad\qquad 3b = 12$$

$$a = 7.5 \qquad\qquad\qquad b = 4$$

So, $QR = 7.5$ and $ZY = 4$.

Another application of proportional reasoning is indirect measurement. Indirect measurement involves using similar figures to find unknown lengths.

Example 2 Using Indirect Measurement

A radio tower casts a shadow 10 feet long. A woman who is 5.5 feet tall casts a shadow 4 feet long. The triangle drawn with the tower and its shadow is similar to the triangle drawn with the woman and her shadow. How tall is the radio tower?

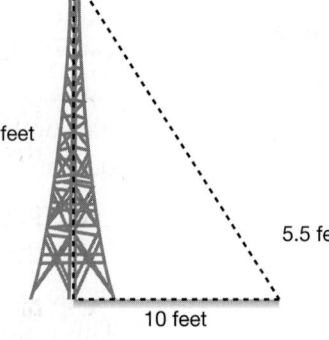

SOLUTION Set up a proportion to solve the problem.

$$\frac{10}{4} = \frac{x}{5.5}$$

$$10(5.5) = 4 \cdot x$$

$$55 = 4x$$

$$13.75 = x$$

The radio tower is 13.75 feet tall.

Math Reasoning

Generalize Will the proportions $\frac{x}{4} = \frac{5}{6}$ and $\frac{4}{x} = \frac{6}{5}$ give the same values for x? Explain your reasoning.

A **scale drawing** is a drawing that reduces or enlarges the dimensions of an object by a constant factor. Maps and blueprints are examples of scale drawings. The **scale** is a ratio showing the relationship between a scale drawing or model and the actual object.

Example 3   Application: Scale Drawings

A desk is designed to have three drawers on the right side. In the scaled design drawing, the width of the drawers is 4 centimeters. If the scale of the drawing is 1 cm:7 cm, how wide will the actual desk drawers be?

SOLUTION Set up a proportion to solve the problem.

$$\frac{\text{drawing length}}{\text{actual length}} = \frac{1}{7} = \frac{4}{x}$$

$$1 \cdot x = 4 \cdot 7$$

$$x = 28$$

The width of the actual desk drawers will be 28 centimeters.

Scale factors of side lengths can also be used to determine the ratios of perimeters, areas, and volumes of figures and solids.

Exploration   Changing Dimensions

Materials

• 64 cubes per pair or group

Alternate Materials (blocks, cheese or sugar cubes are possible examples)

Students may work in groups of two or three.

a. Begin with 1 cube and let the length of an edge equal 1 unit. Then the perimeter of the base of the cube is $4 \cdot 1 = 4$ units, the area of the base of the cube is $1 \cdot 1 = 1$ square unit, and the volume of the cube is $1 \cdot 1 \cdot 1 = 1$ cubic unit. Copy and complete the table below.

Length of Edge (units)	Perimeter of the Base (units)	Area of the Base (square units)	Volume of the Base (cubic units)
1			
2			
3			

b. Use the cubes to build another cube with edge lengths of 2 units. Record your answers in the table.

c. Repeat for a cube with a side length of 3 units. Record your answers in the table.

Use the rows with edge lengths of 2 and 3 from the table.

d. What is the scale factor of the edge lengths?

e. Find the ratio of the perimeters. How does this ratio compare to the scale factor?

f. Find the ratio of the areas. How does this ratio compare to the scale factor?

g. Find the ratio of the volumes. How does this ratio compare to the scale factor?

Ratios of the Perimeter, Area, and Volume of Similar Figures
If two similar figures have a scale factor of $\frac{a}{b}$, then the ratio of their perimeters is $\frac{a}{b}$, the ratio of their areas is $\frac{a^2}{b^2}$, and the ratio of their volumes is $\frac{a^3}{b^3}$.

Example 4 Application: Changing Dimensions

A dartboard is composed of concentric circles. The radius of the smallest inner circle is 1 inch, and with each consecutive circle, the radius increases by 1 inch.

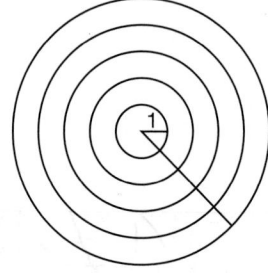

a. What is the ratio of the circumference of the two inner circles to the circumference of the outermost circle?

SOLUTION

$$\frac{\text{circumference of two inner circles}}{\text{circumference of outermost circle}} = \frac{2\pi(2)}{2\pi(5)} = \frac{2}{5}$$

b. What is the ratio of the area of the two inner circles to the area of the outermost circle?

SOLUTION

$$\frac{\text{area of two inner circles}}{\text{area of outermost circle}} = \frac{\pi(2)^2}{\pi(5)^2}$$

$$= \frac{4\pi}{25\pi}$$

$$= \frac{4}{25}$$

Lesson Practice

a. $\triangle ABC \sim \triangle LKM$. Find $m\angle K$ and $m\angle C$.
(Ex 1)

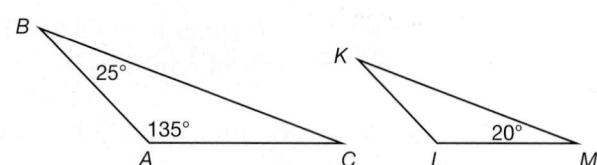

b. The figures are similar. Find the scale factor. Then use the scale factor to find x.
(Ex 1)

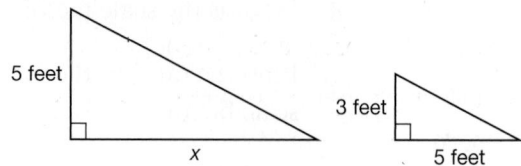

c. The side of a building casts a shadow 21 meters long. A statue that is 5 meters tall casts a shadow 4 meters long. The triangles are similar. How tall is the building?
(Ex 2)

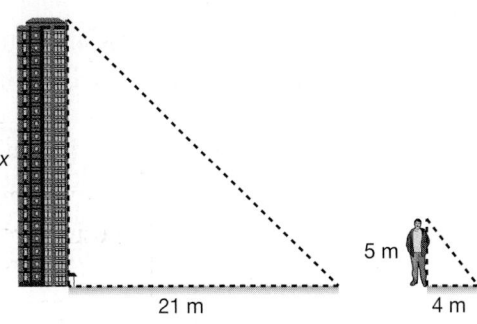

d. The scale drawing of the kitchen tabletop has dimensions 5 inches by 2.5 inches. If the scale factor of the drawing to the actual table is 1 in.:18 in., what are the dimensions of the actual table?
(Ex 3)

e. Small toy cars are constructed using a scale factor of 1 in.:64 in. What is the ratio of the areas of the toy car and the actual car?
(Ex 4)

Practice Distributed and Integrated

Solve each proportion.

*1. $\dfrac{3}{4} = \dfrac{x}{100}$
(36)

*2. $\dfrac{5.5}{x} = \dfrac{1.375}{11}$
(36)

Simplify each expression.

3. $2^2 + 6(8 - 5) \div 2$
(4)

4. $\dfrac{(3 + 2)(4 + 3) + 5^2}{6 - 2^2}$
(4)

5. $\dfrac{14 - 8}{-2^2 + 1}$
(4)

6. The point $(3, 5)$ is graphed in which quadrant of a coordinate plane?
(20)

7. True or False: The set of ordered pairs below defines a function.
(25)

$$\{(1, 3), (2, 3), (3, 3), (4, 3)\}$$

*8. The triangles at right are similar. Find the missing length.
(36)

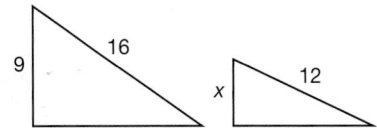

*9. Multiple Choice One triangle has side lengths 3, 5, and 6. A similar triangle has side lengths 18, 15, and 9. Which of the following ratios is the scale factor of the triangles?
(36)

A $\dfrac{1}{6}$ **B** $\dfrac{1}{3}$ **C** $\dfrac{1}{5}$ **D** $\dfrac{2}{3}$

*10. (Landscaping) A landscaping company needs to measure the height of a tree. The tree casts a shadow that is 6 feet long. A person who is 5 feet tall casts a shadow that is 2 feet long.
(36)

a. Draw a picture to represent the problem.

b. Use your picture to find the height of the tree.

*11. A real estate company sells small models of houses. The scale factor of the models
(36) to the actual houses is 0.5 ft:10 ft. Find the ratio of the areas of the model to the
actual house.

12. (Entrepreneurship) A small child decided to sell his artwork. He sold black-and-
(35) white drawings for $2 and colored drawings for $3. The equation $2x + 3y = 24$
shows that he earned $24. Find the x- and y-intercepts.

*13. Verify A tree casts a shadow 14 feet long. A flagpole that is 20 feet tall casts
(36) a shadow 8 feet long. The triangle formed by the tree and its shadow is similar
to the triangle formed by the flagpole and its shadow. Verify that the tree is
35 feet tall.

14. Find the x-intercept for $11x - 33y = 99$.
(35)

15. Find the y-intercept for $-7x - 8y = 56$.
(35)

*16. Geometry A right triangle is formed by the origin and the x- and y-intercepts
(35) of the line $11x - 4y = 22$. Find the area of the triangle.

17. Multi-Step A car wash is held as a school fundraiser to earn $ 280 for a field trip.
(35) The charge is $7 for a car and $10 for an SUV. Let x be the number of cars and
y be the number of SUVs washed. The profits are calculated using the equation
$7x = -10y + 280$.

a. Rewrite the profit equation in standard form.

b. Calculate the y-intercept and explain its real-world meaning.

c. Calculate the x-intercept and explain its real-world meaning.

18. Determine if the sequence $0.4, 0.1, -0.2, -0.5, \ldots$ is an arithmetic sequence or
(34) not. If yes, find the common difference and the next two terms. If no, find the next
two terms.

*19. Error Analysis Two students are writing an example of an arithmetic sequence.
(34) Which student is correct? Explain the error.

Student A	Student B
5, 1, −3, −7, ...	1, 4, 16, 44, ...

*20. Verify At a raffle, 5 students' names are in a hat. There are 3 prizes in a bag:
(33) 2 books and a free lunch. Once the name and a prize are drawn, they are not
replaced. After giving out a book in the first drawing, a remaining student quickly
calculates her probability of winning a book in the second drawing as $\frac{1}{8}$. Show
that she is correct.

21. (Astronomy) The force of gravity on the moon is about one-sixth of that on Earth.
(31) If an object on Earth weighs 200 pounds, about how much does it weigh on the
moon?

22. Multiple Choice What are the odds against spinning a B on the spinner?
(33)

A 1:2   **B** 1:3

C 2:1   **D** 3:1

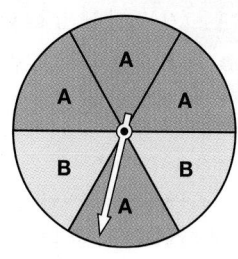

23. Multi-Step Steve has $300 in the bank. Each week he spends $10. Mario has $100 in
(18) the bank and deposits $5 each week.

   a. Write expressions to represent how many dollars each person has in the bank
   after w weeks.

   b. Write an expression that represents how many dollars they have altogether.

   c. After 6 weeks, how much money do they have?

24. Identify the independent variable and the dependent variable in the following
(20) statement: The fire was very large, so many firefighters were there.

25. Multi-Step The measure of angle B is three times the measure of
(23) angle A. The sum of the angle measures is 128°. Find the value of x.

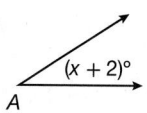

26. (Piano Lessons) A piano student has a $250 scholarship and an additional $422 saved
(23) for piano lessons. If each lesson costs $42, how many lessons will he have?

27. Simplify $\dfrac{4x^2z^0}{2x^3z}$.
(32)

28. (Meteorology) Meteorologists sometimes use a measure known as virtual
(26) temperature (T_v) in kelvins (K) to compare dry and moist air. It can be calculated
as $T_v = T(1 + 0.61r)$, where T is the temperature of the air and r is the mixing ratio
of water vapor and dry air. For temperatures of $T = 282.5$ K and $T_v = 285$ K, find
the mixing ratio to the nearest thousandth.

29. Measurement For a science project, Joe must measure out 5 samples of a liquid. The
(27) graph shows the size of his samples. Why might the data require smaller intervals
on the graph?

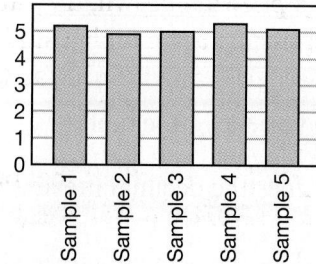

30. Justify Solve the equation $34 - 2(x + 17) = 23x - 15 - 3x$. Write out and justify
(28) each step.

Using Scientific Notation

1. **Vocabulary** The _____ tells how many times the base of a power is
   (3)
   used as a factor.

Simplify.

2. 7^4
   (3)

3. $(8.34)(-4)(100)$
   (11)

4. 5^{-5}
   (32)

5. $\dfrac{3x^{-3}}{5xy^{-5}}$
   (32)

New Concepts   Very large or very small numbers are often written in **scientific notation,** a
method of writing a number as the product of a number greater than or
equal to 1 but less than 10 and a power of ten.

Exploration   **Applying Scientific Notation**

a. Copy the table. Multiply to find each number in standard form.

Scientific Notation	Standard Form
1.08×10^2	
1.08×10^3	
1.08×10^4	
1.08×10^5	

b. What pattern do you see in the table?

c. Copy the table. Multiply to find each number in standard form.

Scientific Notation	Standard Form
1.08×10^{-1}	
1.08×10^{-2}	
1.08×10^{-3}	
1.08×10^{-4}	

d. What pattern do you see in the table?

e. Which direction does the decimal move when the exponent is positive?

f. Which direction does the decimal move when the exponent is negative?

Scientific Notation
A number written as the product of two factors in the form $a \times 10^n$, where $1 \leq a < 10$ and n is an integer.

 **Example 1** **Writing Numbers in Scientific Notation**

Write each number in scientific notation.

a. 856,000

SOLUTION

Because this is a number greater than 1, the exponent will be positive.

The decimal point moves to be after the 8 so that there is one digit to the left of the decimal.

$$856{,}000.$$
$$5\ 4\ 3\ 2\ 1$$

Move the decimal five places, and write the number as 8.56000×10^5.

So, $856{,}000 = 8.56 \times 10^5$.

b. 0.0005

SOLUTION

Because this is a number between 0 and 1, the exponent will be negative.

The decimal point moves to be after the 5, so that there is one digit to its left.

$$0.0005.$$
$$1\ 2\ 3\ 4$$

Move the decimal four places, and write the number as 5×10^{-4}.

Caution

8.56×10^5 is in scientific notation.
85.6×10^4 is not in scientific notation.

Math Reasoning

Analyze Why is there no decimal point in the answer?

To multiply numbers in scientific notation, multiply the coefficients and then multiply the powers. If the result is not in scientific notation, adjust it so that it is.

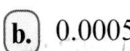 **Example 2** **Multiplying Numbers in Scientific Notation**

Find the product. Write the answer in scientific notation.

$$(5.7 \times 10^5)(1.8 \times 10^3)$$

SOLUTION

$$(5.7 \times 10^5)(1.8 \times 10^3)$$

$= (5.7 \cdot 1.8)(10^5 \cdot 10^3)$ Use the Commutative and Associative Properties of Multiplication to group the numbers and the powers.

$= 10.26 \times 10^8$ Simplify.

Notice that the result is not in scientific notation. There is more than one digit before the decimal point. Move the decimal to the left one place and add one to the exponent.

$$10.26 \times 10^8 = 1.026 \times 10^9$$

Hint

When you multiply powers with like bases, keep the base the same and add the exponents.
$10^5 \cdot 10^3 = 10^{5+3}$

To divide numbers in scientific notation, divide the coefficients, and then divide the powers. If the result is not in scientific notation, adjust it so that it is.

Example 3 Dividing Numbers in Scientific Notation

Find the quotient. Write the answer in scientific notation.

$$\frac{1.2 \times 10^3}{9.6 \times 10^6}$$

SOLUTION

$$\frac{1.2 \times 10^3}{9.6 \times 10^6}$$

$$= \frac{1.2}{9.6} \times \frac{10^3}{10^6} \qquad \text{Divide the coefficients and divide the powers.}$$

$$= 0.125 \times 10^{-3} \qquad \text{Simplify.}$$

Notice that this number is not in scientific notation. There is not one nonzero digit before the decimal point. Move the decimal to the right one place and subtract one from the exponent.

$$0.125 \times 10^{-3} = 1.25 \times 10^{-4}$$

Hint

When you divide powers with like bases, keep the base the same and subtract the exponents.

$$\frac{10^3}{10^6} = 10^{3-6}$$

Example 4 Comparing Expressions with Scientific Notation

Compare. Use $<$, $>$, or $=$.

$$\frac{7.2 \times 10^6}{3.6 \times 10^4} \bigcirc \frac{1.05 \times 10^7}{3.5 \times 10^5}$$

SOLUTION

$$\frac{7.2 \times 10^6}{3.6 \times 10^4} \qquad\qquad \frac{1.05 \times 10^7}{3.5 \times 10^5}$$

$$= \frac{7.2}{3.6} \times \frac{10^6}{10^4} \qquad\qquad = \frac{1.05}{3.5} \times \frac{10^7}{10^5}$$

$$= 2 \times 10^2 = 200 \qquad = 0.3 \times 10^2 = 30$$

Since $200 > 30$, then $\dfrac{7.2 \times 10^6}{3.6 \times 10^4} > \dfrac{1.05 \times 10^7}{3.5 \times 10^5}$.

Example 5 Application: Speed of Light

The speed of light is 3×10^8 meters per second. If Earth is 1.47×10^{11} meters from the sun, how many seconds does it take light to reach Earth from the sun? Write the answer in scientific notation.

SOLUTION Divide the earth's distance from the sun by the speed of light.

$$\frac{1.47 \times 10^{11}}{3 \times 10^8} = 0.49 \times 10^3$$

$$= 4.9 \times 10^2 \qquad \text{Write the answer in scientific notation.}$$

It takes light about 4.9×10^2 seconds to reach the earth from the sun.

Write each number in scientific notation.
(Ex 1)

    a. 1,234,000.   **b.** 0.0306.

    c. Find the product. Write the answer in scientific notation.
(Ex 2)

$$(5.82 \times 10^3)(6.13 \times 10^{11})$$

    d. Find the quotient. Write the answer in scientific notation.
(Ex 3)

$$\frac{(7.29 \times 10^{-2})}{(8.1 \times 10^{-6})}$$

    e. Compare. Use $<$, $>$, or $=$.
(Ex 4)

$$\frac{4.56 \times 10^9}{3 \times 10^5} \bigcirc \frac{5.2 \times 10^8}{1.3 \times 10^5}.$$

    f. (**Astronomy**) The speed of light is 3×10^8 meters per second. If Mars is
(Ex 5) 2.25×10^{11} meters from the Sun, how many seconds does it take light to
reach Mars from the Sun? Write the answer in scientific notation.

Practice   Distributed and Integrated

Simplify each expression.

  1. $18 \div 3^2 - 5 + 2$ **2.** $7^2 + 4^2 + 3$ **3.** $3[-2(8 - 13)]$
  (4)   *(4)*   *(4)*

Simplify each expression by combining like terms.

  4. $13b^2 + 5b - b^2$ **5.** $-3(8x + 4) + \frac{1}{2}(6x - 24)$
  (18)   *(18)*

  *6. Write 7.4×10^{-9} in standard notation.
  (37)

  *7. Write Explain how to recognize if a number is in scientific notation.
  (37)

  *8. Write Explain why anyone would want to use scientific notation.
  (37)

  *9. Multiple Choice What is $(3.4 \times 10^{10})(4.8 \times 10^5)$ in scientific notation?
  (37)   **A** 1.632×10^{15} **B** 1.632×10^{16} **C** 16.32×10^{15} **D** 16.32×10^{16}

  *10. (**Physiology**) The diameter of a red blood cell is about 4×10^{-5} inches. Write this
  (37)   number in standard notation.

  11. The triangles shown are similar. Find the missing length.
  (36)

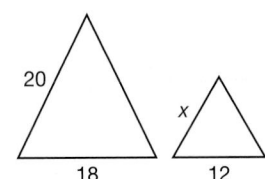

  12. A student's final grade is determined by adding four test grades and dividing by
  (26)   4. The student's first three test grades are 79, 88, and 94. What must the student
make on the last test to get a final grade of 90?

*13. Graph $50x - 100y = 300$ using the x- and y-intercepts.
(35)

14. Geometry A square has side lengths of 3 centimeters. Another square has side
(36) lengths of 6 centimeters.

   a. What is the scale factor of the sides of the smaller square to the larger
   square?

   b. What is the perimeter of each square?

   c. What is the ratio of the perimeter of the smaller square to the perimeter of the
   larger square?

   d. What is the area of each square?

   e. What is the ratio of the area of the smaller square to the area of the larger
   square?

*15. Error Analysis In the figures at right, $\angle A$ and $\angle F$ correspond. Two students
(36) are finding the measure of $\angle F$. Which student is correct? Explain
the error.

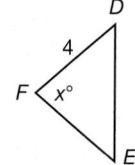

Student A	Student B
$\dfrac{5}{4} = \dfrac{80}{x}$	$m\angle A = m\angle F$
$5x = 320$	$80° = m\angle F$
$x = 64$	
$m\angle F = 64°$	

16. (**Architecture**) A room is 10 feet by 12 feet. If the scale of the blueprints to the room
(36) is 1 inch to 2 feet, find the dimensions of the room on the blueprints.

*17. Measurement What is the ratio of the area of the smaller circle to the area of the
(36) larger circle?

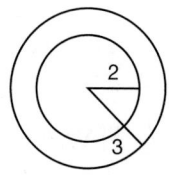

18. Verify Verify that the sequence $4, 2\frac{2}{3}, 1\frac{1}{3}, 0, \ldots$ is an arithmetic sequence.
(34)

19. A piece of fruit is chosen from a box, eaten, and then a second piece of fruit is
(33) chosen. Identify these events as independent or dependent.

20. Predict An estimate of the number of tagged foxes to the total number of foxes
(31) in a forest is 3 to 13. A forest warden noted 21 tagged foxes during a trip in the
forest. Write a proportion to indicate the total number of foxes that might be in
the forest.

21. Multiple Choice In the rule for the nth term of arithmetic sequence
(34) $a_n = a_1 + (n - 1)d$, what does a_1 represent?

   A the number of terms   **B** the first term

   C the nth term   **D** the common difference

*22. (**Physical Science**) The wavelengths of ultraviolet light can range from 10^{-9} meter to
(32) 10^{-7} meter. Express the range of wavelengths using positive exponents.

23. Estimate Between which two whole numbers is the solution to $\frac{13}{14} = \frac{x}{10}$?
(31)

24. (Dog Breeds) The table shows the number of dogs of the top five breeds registered
(27) with the American Kennel Club in 2006. Describe how the data could be displayed
in a potentially misleading way.

Breed	Labrador Retriever	Yorkshire Terrier	German Shepherd	Golden Retriever	Beagle
Number	123,760	48,346	43,575	42,962	39,484

25. Choose an appropriate graph to display a survey showing what type of sport
(22) most people like. Explain your answer.

26. (Exercising) A weightlifter averages 2 minutes on each exercise. Each workout
(25) includes a 20-minute swim. Write a rule in function notation to describe the time it
takes to complete w exercises and the swim.

27. Estimate Using the order of magnitude, estimate the value of 89,678 multiplied
(3) by 11,004,734.

28. Justify Solve for x: $7x + 9 = 2(4x + 2)$. Justify each step.
(29)

***29.** An oceanographer wants to convert measurements that are above and below sea
(30) level from yards to feet. He takes measurements of depths and heights in yards
and feet.

yards	−679	−125	32	79
feet	−2037	−375	96	237

 a. Formulate Use the table to write a formula to convert from yards to feet.

 b. Predict Use the formula to convert 27.5 yards to feet.

 c. Write a formula to convert yards to inches.

30. Multi-Step A rectangle has a perimeter of $38 + x$ centimeters. The rectangle has a
(28) length of $3x - 2$ centimeters and a width of x centimeters. What is the length of
the rectangle?
 a. Substitute the dimensions of the rectangle into the perimeter formula
 $P = 2w + 2l$.

 b. Solve for x.

 c. Find the length of the rectangle.

Simplifying Expressions Using the GCF

Warm Up

1. Vocabulary When two or more quantities are multiplied, each is a
(2)
_____ (**term, factor**) of the product.

Simplify.

2. $2x(3x - 5)$
(16)

3. $-3x^2y(4x^2 - 7xy)$
(16)

4. $\dfrac{x^5}{x^{-3}}$
(32)

5. $\dfrac{1}{-(-4)^3}$
(32)

New Concepts

Simplifying expressions that contain numbers often requires knowledge of prime numbers and factors. Recall that a prime number is a whole number that is only divisible by itself and 1.

$$2 = 1 \cdot 2 \qquad 5 = 1 \cdot 5 \qquad 13 = 1 \cdot 13 \qquad 19 = 1 \cdot 19$$

All whole numbers other than 1 that are not prime are composite numbers.

Composite numbers have whole-number factors other than 1 and the number itself. They can be written as a product of prime numbers, which is called the prime factorization of a number.

$$4 = 2 \cdot 2 \qquad 6 = 2 \cdot 3 \qquad 8 = 2 \cdot 2 \cdot 2$$

Several methods can be used to find the prime factorization of a number. The process requires breaking down the composite numbers until all the factors are prime numbers.

The prime factorization for the number 24 can be found in at least three ways.

Math Reasoning

Formulate Find all of the prime numbers that are less than 100.

$$24 = 2 \cdot 12$$
$$= 2 \cdot 2 \cdot 6$$
$$= 2 \cdot 2 \cdot 2 \cdot 3$$

2	24
2	12
2	6
3	3
	1

It does not matter which method is used to find a prime factorization. The final product, however, must consist of only prime numbers. The factors are usually written in ascending order.

Online Connection
www.SaxonMathResources.com

Example 1 Finding the Prime Factorization of a Number

Find the prime factorization of each number.

a. 120

SOLUTION

Method 1: List the factors and then the prime factors.

$$120 = 2 \cdot 60$$
$$= 2 \cdot 2 \cdot 30$$
$$= 2 \cdot 2 \cdot 2 \cdot 15$$
$$= 2 \cdot 2 \cdot 2 \cdot 3 \cdot 5$$

Method 2: Use a factor tree.

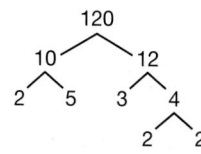

The prime factors are 2, 2, 2, 3, and 5.

Method 3: Use division by primes.

$$
\begin{array}{c|c}
2 & 120 \\
2 & 60 \\
2 & 30 \\
3 & 15 \\
5 & 5 \\
\hline
 & 1
\end{array}
$$

The prime factors are 2, 2, 2, 3, and 5.

The prime factorization of $120 = 2 \cdot 2 \cdot 2 \cdot 3 \cdot 5$.

b. 924

SOLUTION

$$924 = 2 \cdot 462$$
$$= 2 \cdot 2 \cdot 231$$
$$= 2 \cdot 2 \cdot 3 \cdot 77$$
$$= 2 \cdot 2 \cdot 3 \cdot 7 \cdot 11$$

The prime factorization of $924 = 2 \cdot 2 \cdot 3 \cdot 7 \cdot 11$.

<aside>

Hint

One method for finding the prime factorization of a number is to divide out all 2's first, then all 3's, then all 5's, and so on, if they are factors.

</aside>

Prime factorization can be used when determining the **greatest common factor (GCF) of monomials,** which is the product of the greatest integer that divides without a remainder into the coefficients and the greatest power of each variable that divides without a remainder into each term.

Finding the GCF means finding the largest monomial that divides without a remainder into each term of a polynomial.

Example 2 Determining the GCF of Algebraic Expressions

Find the GCF of each expression.

a. $6a^2b^3 + 8a^2b^2c$

SOLUTION

Write the prime factorization for both terms.

$$6a^2b^3 = 2 \cdot 3 \cdot a \cdot a \cdot b \cdot b \cdot b \qquad 8a^2b^2c = 2 \cdot 2 \cdot 2 \cdot a \cdot a \cdot b \cdot b \cdot c$$

Find all factors that are common to both terms.

$$6a^2b^3 = 2 \cdot 3 \cdot a \cdot a \cdot b \cdot b \cdot b$$
$$8a^2b^2c = 2 \cdot 2 \cdot 2 \cdot a \cdot a \cdot b \cdot b \cdot c$$

Each term has one factor of 2, two factors of a and two factors of b, so the GCF of $6a^2b^3$ and $8a^2b^2c$ is $2 \cdot a \cdot a \cdot b \cdot b = 2a^2b^2$.

b. $8c^4d^2e - 12c^3d^4e^2$

SOLUTION

$$8c^4d^2e = 2 \cdot 2 \cdot 2 \cdot c \cdot c \cdot c \cdot c \cdot d \cdot d \cdot e$$
$$12c^3d^4e^2 = 2 \cdot 2 \cdot 3 \cdot c \cdot c \cdot c \cdot d \cdot d \cdot d \cdot d \cdot e \cdot e$$

The GCF is $4c^3d^2e$.

Finding the GCF of a polynomial allows you to factor it and to write the polynomial as a product of factors instead of the sum or difference of monomials.

Factoring a polynomial is the inverse of the Distributive Property. Using the Distributive Property will "undo" the factoring of the GCF.

Example 3 **Factoring a Polynomial**

Factor each polynomial completely.

a. $6x^3 + 8x^2 - 2x$

SOLUTION

Find the GCF of the terms. The GCF is $2x$.

Write each term of the polynomial with the GCF as a factor.

$$6x^3 + 8x^2 - 2x = 2x \cdot 3x^2 + 2x \cdot 4x - 2x \cdot 1$$
$$2x(3x^2 + 4x - 1)$$

Check

$$2x(3x^2 + 4x - 1)$$
$$2x(3x^2) + 2x(4x) - 2x(1) \qquad \text{Use the Distributive Property.}$$
$$6x^3 + 8x^2 - 2x \qquad \text{Multiply each term by the GCF.}$$

The factored polynomial is the same as the original polynomial.

Hint

You can also divide each term by the GCF.
$$\frac{6x^3}{2x} = 3x^2$$

b. $9x^4y^2 - 9x^6y$

SOLUTION

The GCF of the polynomial is $9x^4y$.

$$9x^4y^2 - 9x^6y = 9x^4y \cdot y - 9x^4y \cdot x^2$$

The factored polynomial is $9x^4y(y - x^2)$.

Fractions can be simplified if the numerator and denominator contain common factors. This is because the operations of multiplication and division undo each other.

numeric fractions: $\dfrac{4}{10} = \dfrac{2}{5}$ and $\dfrac{8}{4} = \dfrac{2}{1}$ or 2

algebraic fractions: $\dfrac{4x}{10} = \dfrac{2x}{5}$ and $\dfrac{8x}{4} = 2x$

Notice that there is no addition or subtraction involved in the fractions above. Simplifying fractions with addition or subtraction in the numerator follows similar rules to adding or subtracting numeric fractions. A fraction can only be simplified if the numerator and the denominator have common factors.

Example 4 **Simplifying Algebraic Fractions**

Simplify each expression.

a. $\dfrac{3p + 3}{3}$

SOLUTION

$$\dfrac{3p + 3}{3}$$

$$= \dfrac{\cancel{3}(p + 1)}{\cancel{3}} \qquad \text{Factor out the GCF.}$$

$$= p + 1 \qquad \text{Simplify.}$$

b. $\dfrac{5x - 25x^2}{5xy}$.

SOLUTION

$$\dfrac{5x - 25x^2}{5xy}$$

$$= \dfrac{\cancel{5x}(1 - 5x)}{\cancel{5x}y} \qquad \text{Factor out the GCF.}$$

$$= \dfrac{1 - 5x}{y} \qquad \text{Simplify.}$$

Verify Show that the polynomial $-2x^3y - 6xy^3$ equivalent to $-2xy(x^2 + 3y^2)$?

Example 5 Application: Finding the Height of an Object

The formula $h = -16t^2 + 72t + 12$ can be used to represent the height of an object that is launched into the air from 12 feet off the ground with an initial velocity of 72 feet/second. Rewrite the formula by factoring the right side using the GCF and making the t^2-term positive.

SOLUTION

The GCF of the monomials is 4. To keep the t^2-term positive, factor out -4. So $h = -4(4t^2 - 18t - 3)$.

Lesson Practice

Find the prime factorization of each number.
(Ex 1)

   a. 100   **b.** 51

Find the GCF of each expression.
(Ex 2)

   c. $24m^3n^4 + 32mn^5p$ **d.** $5p^2q^5r^2 - 10pq^2r^2$

Factor each polynomial completely.
(Ex 3)

   e. $8d^2e^3 + 12d^3e^2$ **f.** $12x^4y^2z - 42x^3y^3z^2$

Factor each expression completely.
(Ex 4)

   g. $\dfrac{6x + 18}{6}$ **h.** $\dfrac{18x + 45x^3}{9x}$

   i. The formula $h = -16t^2 + 60t + 4$ can be used to find the height of an
(Ex 5) object that is launched into the air from 4 feet off the ground with an initial velocity of 60 feet/second. Rewrite the formula by factoring the right side of the equation using the GCF and making the t^2-term positive.

Practice   Distributed and Integrated

Solve each equation for the variable indicated.

   1. $6 = hj + k$ for j **2.** $\dfrac{a + 3}{b} = c$ for a
(29)   *(29)*

Draw a graph that represents each situation.

   3. A tomato plant grows taller at a steady pace.
(Inv 2)

   4. A tomato plant grows at a slow pace, and then grows rapidly with more sun and
(Inv 2) water.

   5. A tomato plant grows slowly at first, remains a constant height during a dry spell,
(Inv 2) and then grows rapidly with more sun and water.

Find each unit rate.

   6. Thirty textbooks weigh 144 pounds.   **7.** Doug makes $43.45 in 5.5 hours.
(31)   *(31)*

8. Write 2×10^6 in standard notation.
(37)

9. Solve $\dfrac{p}{3} = \dfrac{18}{21}$.
(31)

*10. Find the prime factorization of 140.
(38)

*11. Multiple Choice Which of the following expressions is the correct simplification
(38) of $\dfrac{10x + 5}{5}$?

   A $2x + 5$ **B** $2x + 1$ **C** $10x + 1$ **D** $5x$

*12. **Free Fall** The function $h = 40 - 16t^2$ can be used to find the height of an object
(38) as it falls to the ground after being dropped from 40 feet in the air. Rewrite the
equation by factoring the right side.

*13. Write Explain how the Distributive Property and factoring a polynomial are related.
(38)

*14. Generalize Explain why the algebraic fraction $\dfrac{6(x - 1)}{6}$ can be reduced, and why
(38) the fraction $\dfrac{6x - 1}{6}$ cannot be reduced.

15. **Biology** The approximate diameter of a DNA helix is 0.000000002 meters.
(37) Write this number in scientific notation.

16. Measurement A nanosecond is one-billionth of a second. Write this number in
(37) scientific notation.

17. Write 78,000,000 in scientific notation.
(37)

*18. Geometry A square has side length 6.04×10^{-5} meters. What is its area?
(37)

*19. The triangles are similar. Find the missing length.
(36)

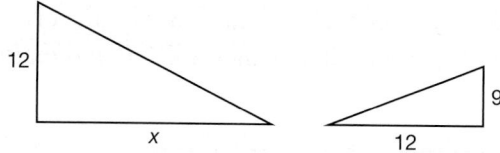

20. Multi-Step An adult brain weighs about 3 pounds.
(37)
   a. There are about 100 billion brain cells in the brain. Write this number in
scientific notation.

   b. Divide the weight of an adult brain by the number of cells and find how many
pounds one brain cell weighs. Write the answer in scientific notation.

*21. Analyze Find the x- and y-intercepts for $y = 12x$ and explain how they relate to the
(35) graph of the equation.

22. **Fundraising** The math club has a carwash to raise money. Out of the first 40 vehicles,
(33) 22 are SUVs and 18 are cars. What are the odds against the next one being a car ?

*23. Justify Explain why the statement $3^{-2} = -6$ is false.
(32)

24. **Analysis** A bookstore wants to show the number of different types of books that
$(Inv\ 3)$ were sold on a given day. Why is this graph misleading?

Number of Books Sold

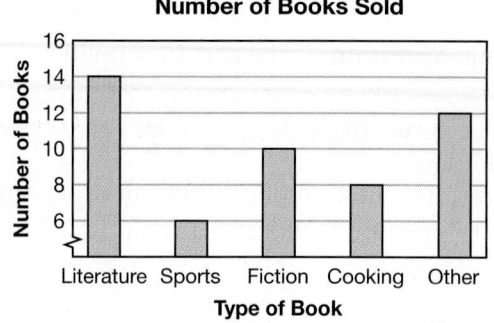

Type of Book

*__**25.**__ Determine if the sequence $\frac{5}{4}, 2, \frac{11}{4}, \frac{7}{2}, \ldots$ is an arithmetic sequence. If yes, find the
(34) common difference and the next two terms.

26. **Multiple Choice** Which equation is in standard form?
(35)
  A $y - 6 = 3(x + 4)$ **B** $y = -6x + 13$

  C $10y = 12y + 25$ **D** $9x + 11y = 65$

27. How is the value 30 represented in a stem-and-leaf plot?
(22)

28. (**Pool Charges**) Barton Springs Pool charges $2 a visit plus a membership fee of $20.90
(28) a month. Blue Danube Pool charges $2.95 a visit, with no membership fee. At what
number of visits per month will the total fees for each pool be the same?

29. (**Stock Market**) On a day of heavy trading, one share of ABC Industries' stock
(26) originally decreased by $5 only to increase later in the day by twice the original
value. The stock ended the day at $43 a share. What was the starting price of
one share?

30. **Multi-Step** The table shows the total number of shrubs a gardener planted after
(30) each half hour.

Time (hr)	0.5	1	1.5	2
Number of Shrubs	1	3	7	8

  a. Plot this data on a coordinate grid.

  b. Determine if the graph is a function. Explain.

  c. **Predict** Can you predict the number of shrubs the gardener will plant
     in 3 hours? Why or why not?

Using the Distributive Property to Simplify Rational Expressions

---

Warm Up

1. **Vocabulary** The set of _____ numbers includes all rational and irrational numbers.
(1)

Simplify.

2. $-3x^2y\left(4x^2y^{-1} - xy\right)$
(15)

3. $mn(2x - 3my + 5ny)$
(15)

4. $\dfrac{5x - 25x^2}{5x}$
(38)

5. Factor. $3a^2b^3 - 6a^4b + 12ab$
(38)

New Concepts

A **rational expression** is an expression with a variable in the denominator. Rational expressions can be treated just like fractions. As with fractions, the denominator cannot equal zero. Therefore, any value of the variable that makes the denominator equal to zero is not permitted.

Variables stand for unknown real numbers. So, all properties that apply to real numbers also apply to rational expressions. The Distributive Property can be used to simplify rational expressions.

> **Math Reasoning**
>
> **Write** Why isn't division by zero allowed?

Example 1 Distributing Over Addition

Simplify $\dfrac{x^2}{y^2}\left(\dfrac{x^2}{y} + \dfrac{3y^3}{m}\right)$.

SOLUTION

$$\dfrac{x^2}{y^2}\left(\dfrac{x^2}{y} + \dfrac{3y^3}{m}\right)$$

$$= \left(\dfrac{x^2}{y^2} \cdot \dfrac{x^2}{y}\right) + \left(\dfrac{x^2}{y^2} \cdot \dfrac{3y^3}{m}\right) \qquad \text{Multiply } \dfrac{x^2}{y^2} \text{ by each term inside the parentheses.}$$

$$= \dfrac{x^4}{y^3} + \dfrac{3x^2y^3}{y^2m} \qquad \text{Simplify.}$$

$$\dfrac{x^4}{y^3} + \dfrac{3x^2y}{m}; \, y \neq 0, \, m \neq 0$$

Note that $y \neq 0$ and $m \neq 0$ because either value would make the denominator equal to zero.

> **Hint**
>
> When multiplying powers, add the exponents. When dividing powers, subtract the exponents.

Online Connection
www.SaxonMathResources.com

Math Reasoning

Justify Why can the final expression not be simplified further?

Example 2 **Distributing Over Subtraction**

Simplify $\dfrac{m}{z}\left(\dfrac{axp}{mk} - 2m^4p^4\right)$.

SOLUTION

$\dfrac{m}{z}\left(\dfrac{apx}{mk} - 2m^4p^4\right)$

$= \dfrac{mapx}{zmk} - \dfrac{m \cdot 2m^4p^4}{z}$ Distribute $\dfrac{m}{z}$.

$= \dfrac{apx}{zk} - \dfrac{2m^5p^4}{z}; z \neq 0, k \neq 0, m \neq 0$ Simplify.

Note that $z \neq 0$, $k \neq 0$, and $m \neq 0$ because any of those values would make a denominator equal to zero. Although there is not an m in the denominator of the final expression, there is one in the denominator of the original expression; that is why $m \neq 0$.

When simplifying an expression with negative exponents, the final expression should not have negative exponents.

Example 3 **Simplifying with Negative Exponents**

Simplify each expression.

a. $\dfrac{b^3}{d^{-3}}\left(\dfrac{2b^2}{d} - \dfrac{f^{-3}d}{b}\right)$

SOLUTION

$\dfrac{b^3}{d^{-3}}\left(\dfrac{2b^2}{d} - \dfrac{f^{-3}d}{b}\right)$

$= \dfrac{b^3 \cdot 2b^2}{d^{-3} \cdot d} - \dfrac{b^3 \cdot f^{-3}d}{d^{-3}b}$ Distribute $\dfrac{b^3}{d^{-3}}$.

$= \dfrac{2b^5}{d^{-2}} - \dfrac{b^3f^{-3}d}{d^{-3}b}$ Product Property of Exponents

$= 2b^5d^2 - \dfrac{b^2d^4}{f^3}; d \neq 0, b \neq 0, f \neq 0$ Simplify.

b. $\dfrac{n^{-1}}{m}\left(\dfrac{mx}{cn^{-3}p^{-5}} + 5n^{-4}p^{-5}\right)$

SOLUTION

$\dfrac{n^{-1}}{m}\left(\dfrac{mx}{cn^{-3}p^{-5}} + 5n^{-4}p^{-5}\right)$

$= \dfrac{n^{-1}mx}{mcn^{-3}p^{-5}} + \dfrac{n^{-1} \cdot 5n^{-4}p^{-5}}{m}$ Distribute $\dfrac{n^{-1}}{m}$.

$= \dfrac{n^{-1}x}{cn^{-3}p^{-5}} + \dfrac{5n^{-5}p^{-5}}{m}$ Simplify.

$= \dfrac{n^2xp^5}{c} + \dfrac{5}{mn^5p^5}; c \neq 0, m \neq 0, n \neq 0, p \neq 0$ Simplify.

Simplify each expression.

a. $\dfrac{ab}{c^2}\left(\dfrac{axb}{c} + 2bx - \dfrac{4}{c^2}\right)$

SOLUTION

$$\dfrac{ab}{c^2}\left(\dfrac{axb}{c} + 2bx - \dfrac{4}{c^2}\right)$$

$$= \dfrac{ab \cdot axb}{c^2 \cdot c} + \dfrac{ab \cdot 2bx}{c^2} - \dfrac{ab \cdot 4}{c^2 \cdot c^2} \qquad \text{Distribute } \dfrac{ab}{c^2}.$$

$$= \dfrac{a^2b^2x}{c^3} + \dfrac{2ab^2x}{c^2} - \dfrac{4ab}{c^4}; c \neq 0 \qquad \text{Simplify.}$$

b. $\dfrac{g^2h}{d^2}\left(\dfrac{g^{-2}xh}{d^{-1}} - 2h^4x^{-1} + \dfrac{9}{d^{-3}}\right)$

SOLUTION

$$\dfrac{g^2h}{d^2}\left(\dfrac{g^{-2}xh}{d^{-1}} - 2h^4x^{-1} + \dfrac{9}{d^{-3}}\right)$$

$$= \dfrac{g^0xh^2}{d} - \dfrac{2h^5x^{-1}g^2}{d^2} + \dfrac{9g^2h}{d^{-1}} \qquad \text{Distribute } \dfrac{g^2h}{d^2}.$$

$$= \dfrac{xh^2}{d} - \dfrac{2h^5g^2}{xd^2} + 9dg^2h; d \neq 0 \text{ and } x \neq 0 \qquad \text{Simplify.}$$

> **Hint**
>
> When a variable has no exponent, it is implied that the exponent is 1.
>
> Any variable or number raised to the 0 power equals 1.

A tabletop that is in the shape of a trapezoid has height $\dfrac{a^2c}{b}$, and bases $\dfrac{b^3}{c}$ and $\dfrac{da}{c^2}$. The area of the tabletop is represented by the expression $\dfrac{a^2c}{2b}\left(\dfrac{b^3}{c} + \dfrac{da}{c^2}\right)$. Simplify the expression.

> **Hint**
>
> The formula for the area of a trapezoid is
>
> $A = \dfrac{1}{2}h(b_1 + b_2)$.

SOLUTION

$$\dfrac{a^2c}{2b}\left(\dfrac{b^3}{c} + \dfrac{da}{c^2}\right)$$

$$= \dfrac{a^2cb^3}{2bc} + \dfrac{a^2c \cdot da}{2bc^2} \qquad \text{Distribute.}$$

$$= \dfrac{a^2b^3c}{2bc} + \dfrac{a^3cd}{2bc^2} \qquad \text{Multiply.}$$

$$= \dfrac{a^2b^2}{2} + \dfrac{a^3d}{2bc} \qquad \text{Simplify.}$$

The area of the tabletop can be represented by the simplified expression $\dfrac{a^2b^2}{2} + \dfrac{a^3d}{2bc}$ where b and $c \neq 0$.

Simplify each expression.

a. $\dfrac{r^2}{q}\left(\dfrac{r^2}{q^3}+\dfrac{7q^3}{w}\right)$
(Ex 1)

b. $\dfrac{t}{z}\left(\dfrac{uay}{tq}-2t^3y^2\right)$
(Ex 2)

c. $\dfrac{j^{-2}}{m}\left(\dfrac{j^{-3}}{m^{-2}}+\dfrac{9m^3}{k}\right)$
(Ex 3)

d. $\dfrac{n^{-2}}{z}\left(\dfrac{v^{-2}cb}{nv^{-1}}-4n^5b^{-3}\right)$
(Ex 3)

e. $\dfrac{fs}{d^4}\left(\dfrac{fhs}{d}+2sk-\dfrac{7}{d^6}\right)$
(Ex 4)

f. $\dfrac{zx}{w^{-2}}\left(\dfrac{zd^{-2}x}{w}+5tz-\dfrac{2}{w^{-4}}\right)$
(Ex 4)

g. (**Painting**) A rectangular canvas is to be painted. The area of the canvas
(Ex 5) with length $\left(\dfrac{t^{-3}}{y^{-2}}+\dfrac{z^{-4}}{y^5t}\right)$ and width $\dfrac{t^2y}{z}$ is represented by the expression
$\dfrac{t^2y}{z}\left(\dfrac{t^{-3}}{y^{-2}}+\dfrac{z^{-4}}{y^5t}\right)$ where t, y and $z\neq 0$. Simplify the expression.

Math Reasoning

Generalize For problem **f,** which variable in the numerator cannot equal zero? Explain.

Practice   Distributed and Integrated

Solve each equation. Check your answer.

1. $4\left(y+\dfrac{3}{2}\right)=-18$
(26)

2. $x-4+2x=14$
(26)

3. True or False: The set of integers is closed under division. If false, give a
(1) counterexample.

Translate words into algebraic expressions.

4. the sum of a and 3
(17)

5. 2.5 more than k
(17)

6. 3 less than x
(17)

7. 2 more than the product of 3 and y
(17)

*8. Simplify $\dfrac{d^2}{s^2}\left(\dfrac{d^2}{s}+\dfrac{9s^3}{h}\right)$.
(39)

*9. Write Why isn't division by zero allowed?
(39)

*10. Justify Simplify $\dfrac{x^{-2}}{n^{-1}}(2x^{-4}+n^{-3})$ and explain each step.
(39)

*11. Multiple Choice Simplify $\dfrac{g^{-2}s}{b^2}\left(\dfrac{g^{-3}s^{-1}}{b^{-1}}+\dfrac{4}{b^3}\right)$ where b, g and $s\neq 0$.
(39)

A $\dfrac{4g^{-5}s^{-1}}{b^4}$

B $\dfrac{g^{-5}s^{-1}}{b}+\dfrac{4g^{-2}s}{b^5}$

C $\dfrac{g^{-5}}{b}+\dfrac{4g^{-2}s}{b^5}$

D $\dfrac{1}{bg^5}+\dfrac{4s}{b^5g^2}$

*12. Simplify the expression $\dfrac{w^2p}{t}\left(\dfrac{4}{w^4} - \dfrac{t^2}{p^5}\right)$.
(39)

*13. Find the prime factorization of 918.
(38)

*14. **Error Analysis** Two students factor the polynomial $16x^4y^2z + 28x^3y^4z^2 + 4x^3y^2z$ as
(38) shown below. Which student is correct? Explain the error.

Student A	Student B
$4x^3y^2z(4x + 7y^2z)$	$4x^3y^2z(4x + 7y^2z + 1)$

15. **Geometry** The area of a rectangle is represented by the polynomial $6a^2b + 15ab$.
(38) Find two factors that could be used to represent the length and width of the
rectangle.

16. **Multiple Choice** Complete the following statement: The side lengths of similar
(36) figures _____.

 A must be congruent   **B** cannot be congruent

 C are in proportion   **D** must be whole numbers

17. **Multi-Step** Use the expression $24x^2y^3 + 18xy^2 + 6xy$.
(38) **a.** What is the GCF of the polynomial?

 b. Use the GCF to factor the polynomial completely.

*18. **Probability** The probability that a point selected at random is in the shaded
(38) region of the figure is represented by the fraction $\dfrac{\text{area of shaded rectangle}}{\text{area of entire rectangle}}$. Find the
probability. Write your answer in simplest form.

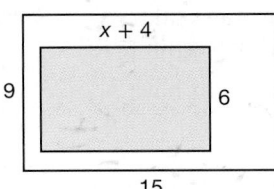

*19. **Analyze** In order to double the volume of water in a fish tank, is it necessary
(36) to double the length, width, and height of the tank? If yes, explain why. If no,
explain how to double the volume of water.

*20. Graph $27x + 9y = 54$ using the x- and y-intercepts.
(35)

*21. (**Fundraising**) For a fundraiser, the science club sold posters for $5 and mugs
(35) for $8. The equation $5x + 8y = 480$ shows that they made $480. Find the
x- and y-intercepts.

22. (**Entertainment**) A contestant is in the bonus round of a game show where
(34) she can win $1500 for answering the first question correctly and then an
additional $500 for each correct response to each of the next five questions.
If she answers all of the questions correctly, how much money will she
receive when she answers the sixth question?

23. Write 0.00608 in scientific notation.
(37)

24. Error Analysis Two students write 1.32×10^{-5} in standard form. Which student is
(37) correct? Explain the error.

Student A	Student B
0.00000132	0.0000132

25. Verify Show that $4\frac{3}{4}$ is the solution to $\frac{1}{n-1} = \frac{4}{15}$.
(31)

26. Evaluate the expression $\dfrac{x^2 y^{-2}}{z^2}$ if $x = 3$, $y = 4$, and $z = -2$.
(32)

27. Analyze The odds of winning a CD in a raffle are 3:7. Explain how to find the
(33) probability of not winning a CD.

28. ⟮**Stamp Collecting**⟯ The table shows some collectible stamps with their estimated
(25) values. Explain whether the ordered pairs, such as (2, \$2) and (2, \$3), will be a
function.

Number	Stamp	Value (low)	Value (high)
1	11¢ President Hayes (1931)	\$2	\$4
2	14¢ American Indian (1931)	\$2	\$3
3	4¢ President Taft (1930)	\$1	\$3
4	1¢ Benjamin Franklin (1911)	\$5	\$50

29. ⟮**Salaries**⟯ In an interview with a potential employee, an
(27) employer shows a line graph displaying the average salary
of employees over several years. Explain why the graph is
potentially misleading and why the employer might have
shown this graph.

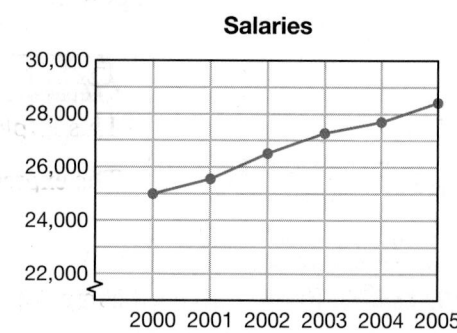

30. Formulate Write a rule for the table in function notation.
(30)

g	2	4	6	8	10
$f(g)$	1.5	2.5	3.5	4.5	5.5

Simplifying and Evaluating Expressions Using the Power Property of Exponents

1. Vocabulary The _____ is the number that tells how many times the
$^{(3)}$ base of a power is used as a factor.

Simplify.

2. $(4x^2y^3)(5x^4y^4)$
$^{(3)}$

3. $\dfrac{24x^3y^6}{36x^5y^3}$
$^{(32)}$

4. $(-3)^2 - 3^2$
$^{(11)}$

5. Compare: $4^2 + \sqrt{36} \bigcirc -(-3)^2 + \sqrt{25}$. Use >, <, or =.
$^{(13)}$

New Concepts

Previous lessons have explored expressions involving exponents. Several rules and definitions have been developed.

$$x^0 = 1 \qquad\qquad x^m \cdot x^n = x^{m+n}$$

$$x^1 = x \qquad\qquad x^{-n} = \dfrac{1}{x^n}$$

$$\dfrac{x^m}{x^n} = x^{m-n}$$

There is another property of exponents that involves raising a power to a power.

Exploration **Raising a Power to a Power**

This Exploration shows how to raise a power to a power.

The expression $(2^4)^3$ means to use 2^4 as a factor three times.

$$(2^4)^3 = 2^4 \cdot 2^4 \cdot 2^4 = 2^{12}$$

Simplify.

a. $(3^2)^3$ **b.** $(4^5)^2$ **c.** $(7^2)^4$

d. Are there any patterns? What conclusions can you draw from the patterns?

The expression $(a^2)^3$ means to use a^2 as a factor three times.

$$(a^2)^3 = a^2 \cdot a^2 \cdot a^2 = a^6$$

Simplify.

e. $(a^3)^5$ **f.** $(b^6)^2$

g. $(d^4)^4$

h. Using the results from **a** through **g** above, write a rule for raising a power to a power.

> **Hint**
>
> Write in a 1 if there is no exponent for variables or numbers. For example, $4 = 4^1$ and $x = x^1$.

> **Math Reasoning**
>
> **Generalize** Use the meaning of powers and exponents to explain why $(a^2)^3 = a^6$.

> **Online Connection**
> www.SaxonMathResources.com

The pattern in the Exploration leads to the Power of a Power Property.

Power of a Power Property
If m and n are real numbers and $x \neq 0$, then $$(x^m)^n = x^{mn}.$$

Example 1 **Simplifying a Power of a Power**

Simplify each expression.

a. $(2^3)^2$

SOLUTION

$(2^3)^2$

$= 2^{3 \cdot 2}$

$= 2^6$

b. $(a^6)^3$

SOLUTION

$(a^6)^3$

$= a^{6 \cdot 3}$

$= a^{18}$

The Power of a Power Property and the Product Property of Exponents can be used together to formulate a rule for the power of a product. Look at the expression $(5x^2)^3$. The outer exponent of 3 means to use everything inside the parentheses as a factor three times, or to multiply $5x^2$ three times.

$$(5x^2)^3 = 5x^2 \cdot 5x^2 \cdot 5x^2$$
$$= (5 \cdot 5 \cdot 5) \cdot (x^2 \cdot x^2 \cdot x^2) = 5^3 \cdot x^6 = 125x^6$$

This pattern is summarized in the Power of a Product Property.

Power of a Product Property
If m is a real number with $x \neq 0$ and $y \neq 0$, then $$(xy)^m = x^m y^m.$$

Example 2 **Simplifying a Power of a Product**

Simplify each expression.

a. $(7a^3b^5)^3$

SOLUTION

$(7a^3b^5)^3$

$= 7^3 \cdot a^{3 \cdot 3} \cdot b^{5 \cdot 3}$

$= 343a^9b^{15}$

b. $(-2y^4)^3$

SOLUTION

$(-2y^4)^3$

$= (-2)^3 \cdot y^{4 \cdot 3}$

$= -8y^{12}$

Math Reasoning

Write Explain the difference between the expression $x^m \cdot x^n$ and $(x^m)^n$.

Example 3 **Application: Interior Design**

A square family room is being measured for carpeting. If the length of one side of the room is $2x$ feet, what is the area of the room?

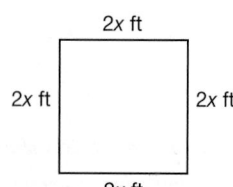

2x ft

2x ft   2x ft

2x ft

SOLUTION

The area is $(2x)^2 = 4x^2$ square feet.

Power of a Quotient Property
If x and y are any nonzero real numbers and m is an integer, then $$\left(\frac{x}{y}\right)^m = \frac{x^m}{y^m}.$$

Example 4 Simplifying a Power of a Quotient

Simplify each expression.

a. $\left(\dfrac{2x}{5}\right)^2$

SOLUTION

$$\left(\frac{2x}{5}\right)^2$$

$$= \frac{2^2 x^2}{5^2}$$

$$= \frac{4x^2}{25}$$

b. $\left(\dfrac{-x^2}{3y^3}\right)^4$

SOLUTION

$$\left(\frac{-x^2}{3y^3}\right)^4$$

$$= \frac{(-1)^4 (x^2)^4}{(3)^4 (y^3)^4}$$

$$= \frac{x^8}{81y^{12}}$$

The rules for exponents apply to many expressions with powers. When simplifying expressions, be sure to follow the order of operations.

Example 5 Simplifying Expressions with Powers

Simplify each expression.

Math Reasoning

Justify Is $5(x^2)^3$ equivalent to $(5x^2)^3$? Justify your answer.

a. $(4xy^2)^2(2x^3y)^2$

SOLUTION

$$(4xy^2)^2(2x^3y)^2$$

$$= (4^2 x^2 y^4)(2^2 x^6 y^2)$$

$$= (16x^2 y^4)(4x^6 y^2)$$

$$= 64x^8 y^6$$

b. $(-5x^{-2})^2(3xy^2)^4$

SOLUTION

$$(-5x^{-2})^2(3xy^2)^4$$

$$= (-5^2 x^{-4})(3^4 x^4 y^8)$$

$$= (25x^{-4})(81x^4 y^8)$$

$$= 2025x^0 y^8$$

$$= 2025y^8$$

Lesson Practice

Simplify each expression.

a. $(5^2)^2$
(Ex 1)

b. $(b^4)^7$
(Ex 1)

c. $(-3n^4)^2$
(Ex 2)

d. $(9ab^{-2})^2(2a^2b^4)$
(Ex 5)

e. $\left(\dfrac{3y^4}{4}\right)^3$
(Ex 4)

f. $\left(\dfrac{-x}{7y^5}\right)^2$
(Ex 4)

g. A shipping container is in the shape of a cube with a side length of
(Ex 3) $3x$ inches. What is the volume of the container?

Solve each proportion.

1. $\dfrac{3}{12} = \dfrac{-24}{m}$
(31)

2. $\dfrac{-4}{0.8} = \dfrac{2}{x-1}$
(31)

3. $\dfrac{5}{12} = \dfrac{1.25}{k}$
(31)

4. True or False: All whole numbers are integers. If false, give a counterexample.
(1)

*5. Simplify $\left(4^4\right)^5$ using exponents.
(40)

*6. Multiple Choice Which expression simplifies to $-24x^4y^3$?
(40)

   A $(-2x^2y)^2(6y)$ **B** $-2(x^2y)^2(6y)$

   C $-(2x^2y)^2(6y)$ **D** $(-2xy)^3(3)$

7. Simplify $\dfrac{e^3}{r^5}\left(\dfrac{e^2}{4r} + \dfrac{r^9}{k}\right)$.
(39)

*8. (Cooking) Use the formula $A = \pi r^2$ for the area of a circle. A 6-inch pizza covers
(40) an area of $\pi(6)^2 = 36\pi$ square inches. What happens to the area of the pizza if you double the radius and make a 12-inch pizza?

*9. Verify Is the statement $(a + b)^n = a^n + b^n$ true? Verify your answer with a numeric
(40) example.

*10. Generalize When do you know to add exponents and when to multiply exponents?
(40)

11. (Painting) A rectangular top on a bench is to be painted.
(39) Its area is $\dfrac{wd^{-3}}{c}\left(\dfrac{d}{w^{-4}} + \dfrac{c^{-2}}{wd}\right)$. Simplify.

12. Simplify $\dfrac{a^2}{d^2}\left(\dfrac{a^{-2}x}{d^{-1}} - \dfrac{2x}{d^{-3}}\right)$ where d and $a \neq 0$.
(39)

*13. Geometry The equation of an ellipse is $\dfrac{wx^2}{g^2} + \dfrac{gy^2}{w^2} = 1$. To enlarge the ellipse, the
(39) left side is multiplied by $\dfrac{g^5}{w^{-2}}$. This expression is $\dfrac{g^5}{w^{-2}}\left(\dfrac{wx^2}{g^2} + \dfrac{gy^2}{w^2}\right)$. Simplify.

14. The trim around a window has a total length of $\dfrac{rt}{w^3}\left(\dfrac{rty}{w} + 2ty - \dfrac{8}{w^2}\right)$.
(39) **a.** Simplify the expression.

   b. Identify the variables that cannot equal zero.

*15. Find the GCF of $4xy^2z^4 - 2x^2y^3z^2 + 6x^3y^4z$.
(38)

16. Error Analysis Two students are simplifying the fraction $\dfrac{3x-6}{9}$ as shown below.
(38) Which student is correct? Explain the error.

Student A	Student B
$\dfrac{3x-6}{9} = \dfrac{\cancel{3}(x-2)}{\cancel{9}_{3}} = \dfrac{x-2}{3}$	$\dfrac{\cancel{3}x-6}{\cancel{9}_{3}} = \dfrac{x-\cancel{6}^{2}}{\cancel{3}} = x-2$

*17. (38) (Shipping) A shipping container is in the shape of a rectangular box that has a length of $10x + 15$ units, a width of $5x$ units, and a height of 2 units.

a. Write an expression that can be used to find the volume of the box.

b. Factor the expression completely.

18. (24) 0.78 of 250 is what number?

19. (25) Give the domain and range of $\{(4, 9); (4, 7); (2, 4); (5, 12); (9, 4)\}$.

20. (27) The heights of 8 trees were 250, 190, 225, 205, 180, 240, 210, and 220 feet. How could a misleading graph make you think the trees are all very similar in size?

a. Make a bar graph of the data using a broken axis.

b. Make a bar graph of the data using large increments.

c. Compare the two graphs.

21. (37) **Justify** Without changing the number to standard form, explain how you can tell that $-10 < 1 \times 10^{-4}$.

*22. (37) **Multiple Choice** What is $\dfrac{1.6 \times 10^7}{6.4 \times 10^2}$ in scientific notation?

A 2.5×10^4 **B** 0.25×10^5 **C** 2.5×10^6 **D** 4×10^5

23. (37) (Astronomy) The diameter of the moon is approximately 3,480,000 meters. Write this distance in scientific notation.

24. (36) The rectangles below are similar. Find the missing length.

*25. (35) (Drama) The cost of presenting a play was $110. Each ticket was sold for $5.50. The equation $11x - 2y = 110$ shows how much money was made after ticket sales. Graph this equation using the intercepts.

26. (34) **Justify** Is the sequence 0.2, 2, 20, 200, … an arithmetic sequence? Justify your answer.

27. (33) There are 2 yellow stickers and 4 purple stickers. Make a tree diagram showing all possible outcomes of drawing two stickers. How many possible ways are there to draw a purple sticker, keep it, and then draw another purple sticker?

28. (22) In a stem-and-leaf plot, which digit of the number 65 would be a leaf?

29. (31) **Measurement** How many inches are there in 18 yards?

30. (32) **Analyze** The rule for negative exponents states that for every nonzero number x, $x^{-n} = \dfrac{1}{x^n}$. Explain why the base, x, cannot be zero.

Using Deductive and Inductive Reasoning

Math Language

A **premise** is the foundation for an argument. It is used as evidence for the conclusion. A **conclusion** is an opinion or decision that logically follows the premise.

There are two basic kinds of reasoning: deductive and inductive. **Deductive reasoning** bases a conclusion on laws or rules. **Inductive reasoning** bases a conclusion on an observed pattern. Both types of reasoning can be used to support or justify conclusions.

All fruit have seeds. An apple is a fruit.

The two statements form an argument. The first statement is the premise, and the second statement is the conclusion. In deductive reasoning, if the argument is solid, the conclusion is guaranteed. In inductive reasoning, if the argument is solid, the conclusion is supported but not guaranteed. Consider the following examples:

Daryl	Aliya
According to Newton's First Law, every object will remain in uniform motion in a straight line unless compelled to change its state by the action of an external force. So, if I kick a ball, it will travel forward at a constant speed until it hits the wall.	In the past, I've noticed that every time I kick a soccer ball, it travels forward at a constant speed until it hits the wall. The next time I kick a ball, it will keep going until it hits the wall.

Daryl's reasoning is deductive because it is based on his knowledge of Newton's First Law of Motion. Aliya reasons inductively, basing her conclusions on her observations.

Identify the type of reasoning used. Explain your answer.

1. Premise: A student has earned a score of 100 on the last five math tests.
   Conclusion: The student will earn a score of 100 on the next math test.

2. Premise: The measures of three angles of a rectangle are all 90°.
   Conclusion: The measure of the fourth angle is 90°.

3. Premise: A number pattern begins with 3, 5, 7, 9, 11, ….
   Conclusion: The next number in the pattern will be 13.

Each premise and conclusion above can be written as one sentence. For instance, the second set could be restated as, "If the measures of three angles of a rectangle are all 90°, then the measure of the fourth angle is 90°." This is called a conditional statement. A **conditional statement** is a logical statement that can be written in "if-then" form.

A conditional statement is made up of two parts: a hypothesis and a conclusion. The **hypothesis** is the condition. It follows the word "if." The **conclusion** is the judgment. It follows the word "then." A conditional statement can either be true or false.

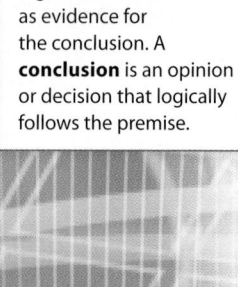

Online Connection
www.SaxonMathResources.com

Hint

If a conditional statement is true and you apply it to a situation in which the hypothesis is true, then you can state that the conclusion is true by deductive reasoning.